POLITICS, PARTNERSHIPS, AND POWER

POLITICS, PARTNERSHIPS, AND POWER

THE LIVES OF RALPH E. AND MARGUERITE STITT CHURCH

JAY PRIDMORE & CHRISTINE WOLF

MASTER WINGS PUBLISHING
CHICAGO, ILLINOIS

Master Wings Publishing
104 S. Michigan Avenue, Suite 1000
Chicago, Illinois 60603
312-374-9455
www.masterwingspublishing.com

ISBN: 979-8985788655

Cover design by Richard Ljoenes Design LLC
Cover image courtesy Evanston History Center. Photo first appeared in Chicago Daily News, March 30, 1940, and was later used as the basis for an illustration by John Jarvis. Box 5, Collection 321 "Papers of Marguerite Stitt Church". Evanston History Center. Evanston, Illinois.
Back cover photograph: Michael Cola / Shutterstock

Sonya Sindberg, Associate Publisher, Master Wings Publishing

Library of Congress Cataloging-in-Publication Data
Names: Pridmore, Jay, 1952- author. | Wolf, Christine, 1968- author.
Title: Politics, Partnerships, and Power : The Lives of Ralph E. and Marguerite Stitt Church / Jay Pridmore and Christine Wolf.
Description: Chicago, Illinois ; Master Wings Publishing, [2023] | Includes bibliographical references. | Summary: "This is the very first biography of a twentieth century powerhouse couple who, with prescient and persistent methodologies and hearts, gave four decades of legislative service and established much of Illinois' dedicated political tradition. Spanning everything from the awkward dance of prohibition in Evanston to Marguerite Stitt Church's involvement in the creation of the Peace Corps — with a particular focus on her remarkable legacy as a pioneer for women in government — this historical nonfiction is both a resource and a gripping delight." Provided by publisher.
Subjects: LCSH: Church, Ralph Edwin, 1883-1950. | Church, Marguerite Stitt, 1892-1990. | Illinois. General Assembly. House of Representatives—Biography. | United States. Congress. House—Biography. | Legislators—United States—Biography. | Legislators—Illinois—Biography. | Women legislators—United States—Biography. | Politicians' spouses—United States—Biography. | United States—Politics and government—20th century.

CONTENTS

CHAPTER ONE

SUDDEN DEATH

"DEATH, BY GRIM PARADOX, HAS put new life into the Republican lower house primary in the 13th congressional district," reported the *Chicago Tribune* on March 26, 1950. With its customary delicacy alloyed with barbed nuance, the *Tribune* described the new political reality occasioned when Representative Ralph E. Church died suddenly and unexpectedly five days earlier.[1]

If not a full-blown paradox, the sudden loss of Congressman Church on March 21 represented a definite problem for the local Republican party. Church had represented his district, centered in his hometown of Evanston, Illinois, for most of two decades. As a staunch Republican in a conservative district, his support was solid and discouraged rivals from either party for his seat. In the upcoming GOP primary to be held April 11, his was the only name on the party's ballot, already printed and legally impossible to change when he died.

Thus not only was the script—that Church would be nominated and breeze to victory in November—scuttled, there was now no time for a tidy rewrite. Instead there was speculation, some plausible and some wild, as to what would happen and who would emerge victorious. The vacancy brought out more than a dozen names of potential candidates from a pool of hopefuls fired with pent-up ambition.

Party elders were flummoxed. Things had gone well for years in a district which had been largely immune from infighting. Republicans in northern Cook and Lake Counties had flown above the storms that divided the party elsewhere: conservatives versus progressives, isolationists versus internationalists. Illinois Republicans didn't have quite the lock on the state that they enjoyed only a decade before. But in the northern suburbs, they could take satisfaction that the congressional seat representing their genteel constituency was secure.

But now, the rock-like, if sometimes quirky, presence of Ralph Church was gone. With news of his death, which occurred while he was speaking before colleagues in a committee meeting on Capitol Hill, party leaders were frantically on the phone, attempting to devise a course of action that would keep Church's seat in friendly hands. They wanted to make sure they weren't saddled with a Republican who was unknown or unloved by party regulars and to avoid a gross miscalculation that could let the election fall to a Democrat.

Two possible courses of action emerged. One was to conduct a write-in campaign, always difficult and especially in Illinois, where standard ballots lacked space for voters to easily write in a name. The other was to hope that the deceased Church would outpoll any write-in rival on the April primary ballot. It would then fall to the political hierarchy to install a new nominee well before the general election in November. If not unprecedented to elect a dead candidate, it all represented an uncommon way to choose a congressman.

In its reporting, the *Tribune* said that there were adherents to the write-in approach, because leaving it to party leaders might look too much like a backroom deal. This could be undesirable; it was a particular vulnerability to the GOP ever since the Republicans nominated Warren Harding for president in 1920 essentially in a "smoke-filled room." But then again, who would emerge from a write-in free-for-all?

The press mentioned a number of likely candidates at the outset, and one of them was Marguerite Stitt Church, Ralph Church's widow. She was known as a woman of intelligence and character, and was sometimes referred to as the "political and legislative teammate of her husband," as the *Tribune* knowingly reported, "having traveled extensively in Europe, twice engaged in country-wide speaking tours in Republican campaigns, and has been active in civic affairs."[2] Alongside her professional work as a consulting psychologist, Marguerite also participated in numerous volunteer efforts, perhaps most prominently as a member—and for one term the president—of the Congressional Club, a group of political wives in DC which organized non-partisan events. She was the first woman from Illinois to hold that position.[3] She was long active in the affairs of her alma mater, Wellesley College—including serving as president of its national alumnae association—and she took the organization of these powerful alumnae very seriously. A main mover in the civic life of Evanston, she had become her husband's indispensable political strategist.

That Marguerite Church would be, if elected, one of the few women in Congress was not seen as an impediment. Neither was the inference made that she was exploiting an unfortunate situation. Her history in Washington and in Illinois made it hard to brand her with any sharp liabilities. "I was not one of those congressional wives who served in the office or hovered around the office," she later said.[4] Most analyses of her candidacy in the local newspapers concluded that she was probably as qualified as any of her opponents, intellectually speaking. And it would be hard to interpret her seeming passivity, her claim that she would serve only if called, as anything but a political virtue.

Of course, others wanted the seat too, including, unbeknownst to many, the couple's eldest son, Ralph Jr. The opening also brought out Waukegan mayor Robert Coulson, who announced his intention to run with the support of the Lake County Young Republicans. Coulson, a former assistant state's attorney, had earned praise as the prosecutor in charge of juvenile justice cases.

Businessman Robert Kendler also threw his hat in; Kendler was a builder largely responsible for the growth of Skokie. Park Ridge Mayor Alfred T. Haake announced he was interested, as did Lee R. Fleming, a businessman and activist in Zion. These candidates had largely local expertise, which may not have been an advantage at a moment in which America was engaged in a cold war that had politics worldwide on edge.[5]

Then there was William McGovern, a professor of political science at Northwestern University. McGovern was a plausible candidate for a number of reasons, largely because of his knowledge of foreign policy and his conservative views. But McGovern was an unpredictable figure, known for "red-baiting" in the press and making bluntly sexist remarks in his classes.[6] Party "regulars" were not called regulars for nothing. The professor was a wild card, one willing to upset not only those who disagreed with him but also the local Republican establishment. GOP committeemen wanted regularity and stability, and the worst way to achieve that, it seemed, was to elect William McGovern.[7]

It became increasingly obvious that Marguerite Stitt Church was the Republicans' best and least disruptive choice. And the party leadership reasoned that a push from precinct workers could get her elected in a write-in election. But others weren't so sure. Some came from the rural townships west of Evanston where electing a woman, any woman, was out of bounds for many voters. What's more, McGovern had strong support in Evanston and especially at Northwestern, where a student-fueled campaign could rival the party's organization in the district, long untested by real competition. There was also the complication of Ralph Church's name remaining on the ballot.

To help mediate all this, William Busse, the county commissioner and party committeeman from Mount Prospect, rushed back from Florida where he was wintering. Busse, in his nineties and considered a dean of the party, met with other committeemen from the district. They discussed the situation and deduced that electing the late Mr. Church and then deciding what to do was their best option. This did not prevent the *Tribune*, a staunch Republican paper, to sardonically note that it was the first time in memory that any party in the area had endorsed a dead candidate.[8]

Political reporter Harold Smith explained the GOP leaders' reasoning in the April 9, 1950 *Chicago Tribune*. They found the whole write-in scheme too unwieldy and worried that it risked spoiling ballots altogether in the party's other primary contests. "Three prospective successors to Church have called a halt to write-in efforts in their behalf," wrote Smith. "One is the congressman's widow, Mrs. Marguerite Stitt Church, whom women's organizations in the district are backing."[9]

THE MODEST FRONTRUNNER

Marguerite, when asked, went with the party line. "I am asking that there be no write-in of my name on the primary ballot," she said, repeating the party's logic that too many write-ins might lead to excessive ballot spoilage, foiling the will of the people. She asserted the right of elected committeemen from the district to choose a replacement candidate. They might or might not choose her, she said. "Although making no active attempt to seek this nomination, I would accept it proudly," she continued. "It would be a responsibility and a privilege to continue the service of Ralph E. Church to this district and to intensify his fight for the American principals for which we have so staunchly believed. If chosen in my own right, I would serve to the fullest capacity."[10]

The dead candidate won the primary that April by a landslide. Certainly, many GOP voters were following the lead of the party leadership. Others, just as certainly, did not know that Ralph E. Church, the sole name printed on the primary ballot, had been deceased for less than a month. In any case, of the 61,103 votes cast, Church won the primary by a large margin, with 30,681 (50.2%); Republican McGovern took 11,143 (18.2%) write-ins; another 7,545 write-ins were split between Republicans Coulson, Murphy and Kendler (12.3%); and Marguerite Stitt Church, who had not sought write-in votes, garnered 375.[11] The decision now fell to the two dozen committeemen, all male, who would assemble in Waukegan in June.[12]

As the GOP hierarchy prepared to vote their choice, a kind of debate ensued among the write-in candidates and others who placed themselves in the running. Hopefuls parsed their virtually identical positions. All appeared to share opposition if not outright hatred of the Truman administration. As for the Marshall Plan, something of a conservative litmus test, most called it a mistake. Mrs. Church campaigned that it should be slashed and then "ended as soon as possible." She called it "a global give-away program.[13] Candidate George F. Spaulding from Glencoe, an ex-Rhodes Scholar, a banker, and head of a securities industry watchdog group, tried to go to the right of Mrs. Church, calling the Marshall Plan "disastrous." A state representative for Lake County, Richard J. Lyons, did the same, calling it an "international bribery plan." Mayor Haake was for moderating the Marshall Plan, he said, and making sure that US money did not finance socialism abroad.[14]

The consensus appeared that nuanced views of the Marshall Plan were largely unwelcome in the conservative Thirteenth. Candidate John Nuveen, an investment banker who had worked in Europe on distributing Marshall Plan funds, could only express that he was "disappointed in [the plan's] administration."[15] Then there was McGovern, running on a record and reputation of unnuanced anti-communism. He had originally supported the Marshall Plan as a bulwark against Soviet aggression but then saw the position as a losing one and called to end the program.[16] He castigated the Democrats and their so-called "China hands," US diplomats who were supposed to be representing American interests in Asia but, he charged, delivered China to the Communists. McGovern was a supporter of Joseph McCarthy, an endorsement that played to a mixed response on the conservative but outwardly polite North Shore. When Committeeman Busse was asked about McGovern, he acknowledged that he was "a professor, but no doubt a bright fellow."[17] Whether the "but" by the nonagenarian Busse was an accident or an intentional knock, it suggested that McGovern's positions, including the

Marshall Plan business, were too complex for a comfortably Republican congressional district.

While addressing the issues in her calm and steady way, Marguerite revealed little in the way of personal ambition in the campaign. She said she would serve her country if called and in order to honor her late husband. Was this deference to Ralph's memory and the party true, or an expedient? What is certain is that Marguerite on the campaign trail was often warmed by people who remembered her husband as someone who breakfasted with them, attended their community meetings, and invited them to sit with him on his porch in Evanston. His wife admired this quality and shared it.[18] Years later, after her twelve years of service in Congress, Marguerite said that both she and her husband "felt the most important part of the job was taking care of the people." In doing so she enjoyed "the support of a very great, large, and loyal group of people who believed in the Ralph Churches, so to speak." She concluded, "We loved people and they recognized that."[19]

At the committeemen's meeting in Waukegan on June 10, 1950, there was some initial suspense, but it evaporated quickly. With each committeeman entitled to as many votes as April votes cast in his township or ward, Marguerite polled 22,366 to 16,796 for McGovern on the first ballot. Richard Lyons got 8,211. Five others got scattered votes. By the second ballot, Lyons threw his support to Marguerite, and she had her required majority.[20]

The day after her nomination, Marguerite sat in her living room with a *Tribune* reporter, who described the GOP's newest nominee as "gray haired and slight," and "just as interested in her daughter's forthcoming graduation as the results of last night's convention in Waukegan." Marguerite told the reporter, "Of course I will be tremendously gratified if chosen." She continued, "It would be a great privilege to be able to carry thru [sic] any service to meet the needs of the 13th district." Still, according to the reporter, Marguerite's sadness was clear when she said, "Thrilling as it would be to become a member of Congress, please believe me when I say it's something I never wanted for myself. I would much rather have been just the wife of the representative of the district for the rest of my life."[21]

A NATURAL REPUBLICAN

While there was little doubt about her winning the general election in November, Marguerite campaigned as hard as her husband always did.

Among her early campaign talking points was unremitting opposition to Democrat Truman. While partisan, it seemed like a thoughtful touch when she said, "Since 1932 the country has placed too much emphasis on standards of living and not enough on moral conduct, both national and individual."[22]

This and many future calls on Americans' better angels were made more credible than the cant of average legislators by her apparent modesty and perhaps also her gender.

In the general election, Marguerite continued to address her gender and admitted that it was rare for a woman to seek political office as lofty as a seat in Congress. In the fall, she acknowledged that it was her gender and not her positions that had most people talking—and talk they did, in a most positive vein.

Evanston, after all, had a staunchly feminist past. It had been home to Frances E. Willard's Women's Christian Temperance Union, which empowered women politically long before they had the right to vote. By the turn of the twentieth century, Evanstonian Elizabeth Boynton Harbert was a leading suffrage figure, and a little later Mary Barthelme, also of Evanston, was the first female to assume a judgeship in Cook County.[23]

Women with power were hardly unfamiliar in Evanston, and that they deserved political equality was no longer debated by any reasonable resident.

Nor was it debated that women could, if organized, make a decisive contribution to the Republican cause. Marguerite's candidacy had support from a newly organized and very active Women's Republican Club of the Thirteenth Congressional District.

Late in 1950, the club held a rally of well-dressed and conservative women at the Edgewater Beach Hotel. They produced a chorus of boos whenever a Democrat's name was mentioned, boos that, the *Tribune* wrote, "were soprano." One woman high up in the party declared, "Our purpose is to put this country back in the hands of the men and women who love America and what it stands for."[24]

Marguerite held a master's degree in political science from Columbia University and was therefore likely hardly surprised that women could talk and act on political issues. But she remained largely quiet at that rally, certainly more reserved than her elevated status as heir presumptive might have entitled. While she knew that excitement was key in politics, and that the Democrats and their wastefulness were so-called "red meat" for Republicans, it was not her style to shout, and she did not. Personally, she was running in a deep-dyed Republican district. She could practice politics without going out of character, which in her case was relatively quiet and dignified.[25]

In her first congressional campaign, Marguerite made nearly twenty campaign appearances a week, which was about what her husband Ralph would have done. Yet it seemed hardly necessary. "Observers are agreed," the *Chicago Sunday Tribune's* Harold Smith wrote on election eve, "that nothing short of a miracle can turn the tide that is running in favor of the district's first woman Republican candidate."[26] Because she had campaigned on behalf of her husband for decades, she was probably not surprised that she won 74% of the November vote over Democrat Thomas F. Dolan, an Evanston attorney.[27] The exact count was 140,750 to Dolan's 49,187.[28]

The night she won, Marguerite said, "We must continue the fight for which we campaigned. We must work for peace without appeasement, but first we must set our house in order at home."[29]

Mr. Church's great political skill was in keeping his eye on his district and cultivating a vast array of friends and supporters. He also rarely revealed a prominent ego or personal ambition. For these characteristics, he was admired, if not loved, through his district.[30]

Against this backdrop and with these lessons of her husband's far more conventional career, we will see that humility and courage made Marguerite powerful well beyond the boundaries of the wealthy North Shore, or what many thought possible for the gentlewoman from Illinois. Together, the Churches' careers provide a snapshot of the American political climate across half the twentieth century, and Marguerite's successes in particular illustrate timeless lessons in public service and character.

CHAPTER TWO

THE CHURCHES' ORIGINS

IN 1848, THE YEAR THAT Ralph Church's grandfather, George William Frederick Church, immigrated to America and specifically to Vermilion County, Illinois, Zachary Taylor was elected president of the United States, and the Chicago Board of Trade was founded. Taylor's election went almost entirely unnoticed by George Church and others who were part of a steady influx of English immigrants to the area at the time. The Board of Trade, too, was a matter of remote interest to the Churches, who had purchased good land and hoped for good yields in the future. For now, however, they were subsistence farmers.[31]

More important to members of this English "colony" in Vermilion County, of which the Churches were a part, was a new rail line that came along near their farms around 1850. A new station was conveniently established near their settlement, called Butler's Point, and out of appreciation for having a stop on the line, the English farmers renamed the town that would grow up around it Catlin after the president of the railroad. Biographical sketches of Ralph Church, written when he was a state legislator and later a congressman, recorded his birthplace as Catlin, or often as "a farm near Catlin." Church's origins were entirely rural, distant indeed from the seats of government where he would serve. Catlin was remote and still is, and the Church farm even more so.

But Catlin had a lot going for it, especially in the mid-1800s, when Illinois was something of an arcadia for Europeans attracted by fertile soil and available land in the broad basin of the Mississippi River. This was not to mention the political and religious freedoms that America promised. It was a time when "American fever" took hold in many countries in northern Europe, with plenty of promoters saying that America was the antidote for everything that ailed the Old World.

MIGRATION TO ILLINOIS

Illinois was targeted by many English because a succession of writers praised the area for its many advantages. Among them was the well-known Morris Birkbeck who started a vaguely utopian settlement in the new state, where he believed that innovative farming and free democracy would flourish. "The land is rich natural meadow, bounded by timbered land, within reach of two navigable rivers, and may be rendered immediately productive at a small expense," wrote Birkbeck in *Letters From Illinois*, published in 1818. Later visitors wrote glowingly of Grand Prairie, as the great swath of Illinois was called. It included Vermilion County, longtime home of the Churches and many families related to them.

George Church, whose father was a prosperous banker in London, had farming on his mind as well. After considerable thought, he arranged passage on the sailing ship *Devonshire*, an American vessel, and he was described on the ship's manifest as a "Gentleman."[32] The voyage was about three weeks from Portsmouth to New York. George was a "cabin" passenger, which provided more comforts than for those in steerage, though the caste system on ocean voyages was rendered meaningless when the seas were roiling. Another passenger on the *Devonshire* wrote that "sea-sickness is a great leveler; it makes a man feel his humanity, purging him of vanity & conceit."[33] Under any circumstances, of course, passage to America was difficult and reflected a commitment to a new life.

Grand Prairie, an informal name for the area below Chicago and south to the towns around Decatur, became known in the eastern states and England as spacious, with government land for sale and fertile soil. It represented the opportunity to own significant farms that were unavailable to most folk.

Geologically, Grand Prairie was an ancient lakebed and extraordinarily flat, a feature that emphasized its vastness and, to some, its romance. Vermilion County, in the middle of the region, had special features: fertile soil and salt. For this reason, Native Americans had settled the area before the influx of white pioneers, and by the early 1700s they lived in relative peace with the French explorers who named the river the Vermilion and loosely organized the surrounding area beginning in the late 1600s. After the French and Indian War, English-speakers established a proper European settlement at Salt Springs, on a branch of the Vermilion River. Salt was necessary at the time as a means to preserve food, and that resource in particular represented a business opportunity and excellent reason to settle the area.

A slow trickle of settlers followed, and in 1820 a pioneer named Butler took up at a place where forest turned to prairie not far from Salt Spring, establishing Butler's Point, later renamed Catlin. For several decades, settlement of the Vermilion basin accelerated, as it did elsewhere through the vast "Northwest," due to the federal government's policy of selling land for as low as two dollars an acre at first. While it was initially a wilderness that could strike fear in many, this was overcome by courage and ambition, qualities of many families who would become important landowners in Vermilion County, which was organized and named in 1831.

While most of the early settlers came from other states, the influx from abroad was significant and began around the 1830s, when Abraham Mann from Bedfordshire, England, came with his family. Mann's father, a salesman of paints and oils, traveled the Mississippi Valley and eventually returned to England, but he enchanted friends and family with stories, particularly of Illinois. And when son Abraham decided to emigrate, he settled in the northern part of Vermilion County. He was shortly joined by other English and their families around Rossville, north of Danville. These included Reverend William Cork. Within a few years, as many as seventeen English-born households were clustered on approximately that many farms.[34]

It was not hard for another family of landowners in the county to get to know these English and to admire their "undying tenacity" in making their farms successful. These were the Sanduskys, whose original forebears arrived decades before from Russia. Tired of living under the rapacious czars, a pioneer named Sadowsky used the homestead laws and became a landowner beyond his dreams. In time, the Sanduskys, as they renamed themselves, were also land dealers. And in search of new settlers, Isaac Sandusky traveled to London in the 1840s to lecture, or sponsor lectures, extolling the great opportunities that Grand Prairie offered.[35]

It was through the Sanduskys that the extended family that included the Churches, according to family lore, learned of the area that was being "marketed" as Grand Prairie. The first to make the trip was Richard Puzey, a member of an old Berkshire family. English census records have Richard listed as a draper, and he also served as postmaster in the rural district where he lived. He was an early widower, which appears to have made him restless, or rootless, enough to contemplate emigration. This he did in 1847, perhaps after having heard a Sandusky lecture.[36] In short order he had a farm, and it wasn't much longer before he had a wife, the daughter of Rev. William Cork.

George W. F. Church's long-term intention was to join his uncle Henry Church, the first of the family in Vermilion County, probably in 1848. George arrived by ship in New York Harbor, also in 1848, but then detoured to upstate New York for a couple of years, where he could learn farming, or at least the basics, with another uncle. But George Church did get to what would become Catlin, and he was one of a long chain of immigrants from London and its environs, many known to each other. Within just a few years Puzeys, Joneses, Bentleys, and Clipsons settled near the Churches, intermarried with them, and began extended family lines that would do well in farming and other professions for many decades to come. Occasionally, of course, the families sent heirs out to success in the larger world. Among the latter category was Ralph E. Church, George's grandson, who went off to college in Michigan. Ralph never returned to live in the old Grand Prairie, but a part of Catlin never left him.

Records have George Church's uncle Henry Church registered as a draper by profession, like Puzey and several of Puzey's brothers.[37] This may have been how Henry, who lived in London, met his wife, Sophia Puzey, sister of Richard Puzey. Henry and Sophia were the first Churches to make the trip, the reasons for which are not entirely clear, as the Churches were well educated and prosperous in London. Henry's brother (George's father) was a banker. Their wanderlust may have been inspired by another brother, Thomas, who joined the East India Company, a trading enterprise that had brought him significant wealth.[38]

Author Karen Cord Taylor, who wrote about the Vermilion County English, asserts that there was some doubt that Henry was as ambitious as his brothers. He had a grocery in Butler's Point, though it was said that whatever success he had in that trade was due to his wife, Sophia. In any case, Henry was followed by several nephews, including George, who arrived in 1850 after his sojourn in upstate New York. By the following year, he had married London-born Sarah Elizabeth Jones and she had their first child.[39] In 1854, their second child, Henry George Church, was born. He would become father to the future congressman, Ralph Edwin Church.

FINDING A LARGER STAGE

It appears that these early English ignored politics, even if they did not disparage the activity outright. This is interesting in view of Ralph's eventual career. Taylor asserts that there's no indication that they took any interest at all in one of the central political events of their first decade in Illinois. That was the Lincoln-Douglas debates and the 1858 race for the US Senate. While the Puzeys, Churches, and most others from England abhorred slavery—and would not have immigrated to a slave state, according to Taylor—they took little interest in the debates, which addressed the "peculiar institution," as it was mildly termed. None of the Churches could even vote until one of George's brothers, Adolphus, took citizenship papers in 1860.

When the Civil War came, English enlistment from the county was not too robust. Records are that Catlin Township contributed eleven recruits to regiments that went on to war. One appears to have been another brother of George and Adolphus. The English attitude about fighting in the war was certainly highlighted by the suicide of Will Clipson, a member of the English colony, which appeared to have been triggered when he believed that two of his sons might have been lost in it.[40] (They weren't.) As for elective politics, a Church family member was elected township clerk in 1861, though there's no record of what he accomplished in that office. In any case, it is fair to say that whatever political impulses, not to say patriotic ones, that drove Ralph E. Church to public service were either latent in the family or were developed later after he left Grand Prairie.

Ralph Edwin Church was born May 5, 1883, on the family farm near Catlin and attended rural schools in his early years.[41] Whether it was for achievement or ambition, he made one his first moves to leave the place in which he was otherwise settled when he, with his family's consent, decided that he would enroll at Danville High School, which was about eight miles away from home. He made the trip daily in a horse cart. Ralph did well at Danville, not only academically but also on the football field. There's no indication that he enjoyed celebrity or social success in high school, despite his undeniable intelligence and physical strength on the farm and the gridiron. One key lesson incised by high school and repeated throughout his career was that his ambitions would be realized by earnestness and repetitive hard work.

Upon graduation from Danville High School in 1903, Ralph resolved to follow his pattern of moving on to a larger environment. That was the University of Michigan, a sign of significant ambition, since he might have chosen the University of Illinois, just an hour's drive or so from home, and Ann Arbor was a day's train. But Michigan had taken its place among the distinguished institutions of the nation. Its longtime president at the time, James Burrill Angell, a graduate of Brown University, had resolved along with his faculty to grow the school and model its programs after the research universities of Europe.[42]

THE MICHIGAN DREAM

For Ralph, enrolling as a member of Michigan's Class of 1907 was a sacrifice for his family and for him personally, as he certainly worked his way through. Beyond working odd jobs, he also stayed busy as a prolific joiner of campus organizations. Years later after he had achieved prominence, he was remembered by an alumni notice for "the habit of holding office when a collegian while he served as Treasurer of the University of Michigan Athletic Association, Treasurer of his Class, Chairman of its Prom Committee and Captain of [the intramural] Football Team, to name but a handful."[43] It appears Church was both a loner and a joiner, but not prominent in the latter category; he never ascended to the highest positions of leadership in college, though he tried.

He had talents. He was good with numbers, and as treasurer of the athletic association, which promoted college sports on campus and boosted attendance, Ralph did the good work of helping put the organization on a more stable and solvent footing. He did some of the same work for other campus activities such as banquets and fairs when they were organized. Yet despite this work, positions of acclaim adulation on campus and offices of exalted leadership eluded him.

In his senior year, he was also on the finance committee of the annual minstrel show, a blockbuster every year.[44] Minstrel shows were an old form of entertainment in which white men painted their faces black and performed satires that mocked Black music and diction. In 1907, this was hardly controversial at Michigan, though it would certainly (and rightfully) later become so. It is interesting that an article in the *Michigan Daily* promoting the annual show shared a front page with an announcement of a campus lecture by Booker T. Washington.[45] This juxtaposition of minstrels and Dr. Washington, founder of the Tuskegee Institute and a pioneer in Black education, is striking to the modern viewer. In fact, Washington was lauded in the campus paper for not pressing politics in efforts to improve Black lives.

Something was burning in Ralph, or at least smoldering, when he made a move in 1906 to be senior class president. Ralph believed that his participation in extracurricular activities might get him over the top. Instead it got him to second place, and that was all. The presidency went to Robert H. Clancy, a classmate whose profile was high on campus as a leader of several organizations and sports editor of the *Michigan Daily*.[46] He became the unanimous choice for the Class of '07's president after Ralph withdrew from the race.[47]

Clancy went on to make quick work of a political career when he served for several terms in Congress beginning in 1923. His first election victory was as a Democrat from a city district in Detroit. In the following cycle, he lost to Republican John B. Sosnowski, then switched parties and defeated Sosnowski in the 1928 GOP primary. Clancy was noted as an anti-prohibition candidate, a position popular among his largely immigrant constituency. This stance was highlighted when he was arrested, along with Detroit's mayor and Wayne County's sheriff, for the federal transgression of drinking alcohol. His arrest took place in the Deutsches Haus, a center of German-American life in the city. Whether the arrest helped or hurt him at the polls, Clancy could not prevail in the 1932 election after redistricting. Clancy and Church, former campus rivals, did not cross paths directly as members of the House of Representatives. There can be no doubt, however, that Clancy's political risk taking—specifically as a "wet" who practiced what he preached—provided a warning to Ralph, who would be a "dry" (though not abstemious) as he crafted his own careful political career.

CONTRACT WITH THE LAW

After graduation, Ralph decided to continue at Michigan, enrolling in the university's law school, a national leader in the field. He enjoyed some extracurricular success that first year when elected as president of the Taft Republican Club, a campus political group so called because William Howard Taft was the party's standard bearer for US president in 1908. Republicans were well organized on campuses around the nation at the time, and with the Taft Club, Ralph Church finally rose to the top of an organization. This club was overtly political, and it was interesting how even young Republicans reflected some of the fractiousness that was just beneath the surface of the GOP on the national stage. For example, when the *Detroit Free Press* announced Ralph's election to head the Taft Club, it noted that another member's appointment as the state's representative to the National Republican College League was "not entirely satisfactory to all members of the [Ann Arbor] club . . . However the club officers and members are mum on the subject, declaring there is perfect harmony on the club and they refuse to discuss the matter at all." Whether this contretemps was personal or political can't be known. Certainly, President Church achieved what he intended, which was for any rivalry or discord to disappear as much as possible.[48]

Despite personal recognition with the Taft Club and the opportunity of leadership, Ralph made what seemed for him like a rash decision the following year: to leave Michigan Law and move to Northwestern University. Northwestern had a good law school too, nearly at Michigan's level, and it had the advantage of being in the larger arena of Chicago. If any pattern emerged or was affirmed by this move, it was that the future congressman, even as a student, frequently sought an ever larger stage. Chicago would provide such a setting, which was important for him once graduation was nigh and the practice of law beckoned.

That he planned to be a serious lawyer was evident in his classwork at Northwestern, and particularly in his thesis, which was a comprehensive and remarkably erudite examination of contract law. He had chosen as a thesis advisor a young professor of promise, Charles Cheney Hyde, who would go on to become an authority on international law and a professor at Harvard—this before a high position in the Department of Justice and then a lucrative practice in Washington, DC. Church's thesis, entitled "What is the Place of a Contract—Where it is in Fact Made, or Where it is Performed?" showed many things, not just of the subject at hand but of the author's intellect and character. It indicated that Ralph Church did not shy away from complexity but instead appeared to comprehend it, and verbalize it articulately.

The thesis project demonstrated initiative on the part of the student—it was an ambitious work of research by any standard. It showed that the author possessed honed analytical skills. The subject was hardly trivial. It examined the issue of what jurisdiction should adjudicate a contract if that contract was created in one place and the terms of the contract performed in another. "[B]ecause of the long period in which this question has been in litigation, it is impracticable, if not impossible, to discuss or even mention by citation every case found in the French, English, American and other reports," Church wrote, in something of a disclaimer. "It has, however been the aim of the writer not only to give his own views on the subject, but also to cite, observe or criticize, as he deems fit."[49]

Perhaps tortuously, Church's exegesis gives precedence to the place where a contract was made, though his recitation of case law on the subject indicates that this general doctrine was hardly universal, especially in practice. "At this point, the great mass of decisions go astray," he wrote.[50] At the same time, while the writer appears eager to discover absolutes in the law, he's willing to admit that there was legitimate ambiguity in many cases. One which is resonant a hundred years later was his mention of some states that prohibited marriage between different races. The question arises: would a marriage made in a state where the union was legal have legal standing in states where it is not? "[I]f to give that marriage effect would be against the policy of law, or contrary to good morals, the marriage will often be given no effect," Church states factually and in a way that appears to accept the prejudiced doctrine.[51]

For someone who would have a hand in public policy in years to come, his intolerance for any inconsistency in the law is interesting. So is his cogency in arguing his subject, and not least, his obvious hard work. The thesis sheds light on his early choice of profession, moving into politics shortly after his graduation from law school. One can conclude that he was partly motivated to become a lawmaker to correct discrepancies—in a law, in a position, or even in a political statement. And as a member of the political minority for most of his legislative career, he became well known among his colleagues, if not his constituents, for attacking any inconsistency, especially when they came from his usually more powerful political opponents.

Also interesting and revealing of character is the tone and erudition of the 146-page thesis. Notable is the fact that he quotes in Latin passages of European law for as many as two pages. He found no need to translate the citation beyond a few key phrases. Along with the rest of the thesis, it illustrated what most people acquainted with Ralph Church knew: he was intelligent and well read, and did nothing to hide that fact in personal relations or the written word.

CHAPTER THREE

RALPH CHURCH'S POLITICAL DEBUT

IN MAY OF 1916, FORMER President Teddy Roosevelt visited Chicago on a tour of the Midwest to promote and gauge his chances for another run at the White House. It was eight years since he had left office, and four since he had engaged in a bitter battle with his former friend William H. Taft at the Republican convention. Roosevelt lost the 1912 nomination to Taft, then the incumbent, but the rupture in their party enabled the otherwise unlikely election of Woodrow Wilson. It also kept Roosevelt's ambitions alive.

Roosevelt arrived at LaSalle Street Station in a downpour, though the weather did not stop a throng of newspapermen on the platform from seeking some piquant quote from the man who was never at a loss for words. As Teddy stepped from his Pullman car, he faced the reporters and quite a few Republican well-wishers with his usual smile. Then he pushed his way toward the front of the train to do what he customarily did, which was to thank the engineer and fireman who got him to Chicago.

He then made toward the station exit, still smiling and greeting familiar faces. "Hello. Hello! I'm very glad to see you again," he said several times as he moved slowly through the station. Out on the street, he climbed in the waiting automobile of Evanstonian Harold Ickes, lawyer, reform activist, and Roosevelt's friend. The car started for the next stop, the LaSalle Hotel, but it rolled slowly as fans continued to wave and even climb on the running board. The *Chicago Tribune* said the ex-president loved every minute of it.[52]

Roosevelt arrived at the hotel where he was scheduled for a series of meetings with party stalwarts and supporters. But there were still reporters and more jostling. One of them called out and asked how the ex-president was feeling. "That I'm in first class condition goes without saying when you recall that I negotiated that crowd [at the station] and survived," he said. Some order was restored by the Secret Service, whereupon Roosevelt answered a few more questions. About the war in Europe, Roosevelt distanced himself quite fully from President Wilson, who was promising that America would stay out. "I have but one thing to say, and that is in reply to some of our good pacifist friends who are saying that preparedness means war." He paused, and became serious: "You might as well argue that we shouldn't permit our sons to learn how to write in school lest they become forgers."[53]

Foreign policy was much on Roosevelt's mind as he proceeded to a series of meetings, one with an editor from a German-language newspaper, who wanted an explanation of all the war talk, as it naturally alienated the German-American population. Another meeting was with party leaders supportive of Roosevelt's "progressivism" and his positions in favor of programs that addressed poverty and health, these not being conventional Republican stands. There was another in which Roosevelt explained his trust-busting efforts against corporations that monopolized markets, a delicate issue for the party of business. Meetings like that could be difficult. But the next one was a pleasure. It was with a committee of "citizen soldiers," men who had taken time off civilian jobs to prepare for military service by enlisting in the Citizens' Military Training Camp as part of an overall preparedness campaign. This committee included lawyer Ralph Church.[54]

"You are setting an example to which the whole country should come," Roosevelt said to the dozen or so men representing the hundreds who were taking part in the training program. The ex-president showed his ability to relate to the broad swath of voters when he said, "I want to put it in the power of every young fellow, of the mechanic's son and the laborer's son, as well as you bankers' sons, to secure this training." The camps were conducted at several Midwest sites including Fort Sheridan to the north of Chicago and Fort Benjamin Harrison in Indiana. Roosevelt congratulated the group, saying, "The middle west has been our bulwark. It was Illinois that gave to the nation Grant and Sherman and Sheridan . . ." and so on, as politicians, especially the most ebullient of them all, were wont to do.[55]

Ralph Church was happy to shake hands with the ex-president. Not yet a politician, Church's positions lined up neatly behind those of Roosevelt, and while the young man was not four-square behind every position espoused by the Hero of San Juan Hill, Roosevelt remained a model for anyone who had a career of elective office in mind. Roosevelt, then fifty-two, remained energetic, popular, and usually able to make even controversial stands look conciliatory. Ralph, who was already in his first campaign for elective office, would have certainly noted how Teddy glossed over what ailed the Republican Party. As the young man was eyeing a political career himself, he was paying attention to Roosevelt's knack for staying on the right side of most issues and sliding across others.

THE CITIZEN SOLDIER

Church had done well by enlisting in the Citizens' Military Training Camp. It squared with the young man's patriotism, always a stamp of approval for incipient candidates. It also lined him up with most if not all of the rest of his party, which had staked its claim against Wilson's and the Democrats' repeated (and ultimately futile) assertion that America would avoid war. Of course, the training exercises up at Fort Sheridan were nonpartisan—the camps were the creation of the US Army with the cooperation of private companies who encouraged employees to sign up. And it could hardly be disputed that the military had previously been coasting at so-called "peace strength," which was about half of what was regarded as "war strength," as the preparedness lobby called it. Prudence called for some bulking up.[56]

Church signed up for training for the first time in the summer of 1915, going up to Fort Sheridan, less than an hour north of Evanston, for a month. The "rookies," as they were called, slept in tents, marched every day, and took target practice. They received instruction in "the science of modern warfare," which largely meant communications and involved the laying of cable and operating handset radios that were becoming standard issue. A certain esprit de corps was evident at Fort Sheridan among the businessmen who chanted patriotic slogans at meals and during drill. "Remember Bull Run," they'd cry in unison, recalling one of the Civil War's first battles, a Union defeat that history chalked up to lack of preparation.[57]

The citizen training program positioned Church, then thirty-three, for his future. In the short-term that meant service in the army or some branch of the service if America went to war. And in another way, it established him on a political front, aligning him, if not with Roosevelt, then against isolationists in both parties. It also brought him into contact with well-connected people, notably Congressman Martin B. Madden of the Illinois delegation in the US House of Representatives. Madden and Church were both low ranking privates in the training corps. For Madden's part, he decamped at least once that month for a downtown Chicago hotel, where he got a good bath and decent bed. When asked, he said he was in Chicago "to scout for rations" (this with a straight face) and to pick up "some things for the colonel" (here cracking a slight smile).[58]

Church, for his part, took no leave of absence from his month at camp at Fort Sheridan, or at least there was no report of his having done so. Happily, he did get publicity when he won the high score in his company on the rifle range, as the *Tribune* reported. Toward the end of the month he also sought appointment to the committee that would help keep track of everyone in the program and encourage them to further training. Among those chosen for the committee from Company D were Ralph Church and Judge Charles A. McDonald. It was as a member of this committee that Ralph was chosen to meet with Roosevelt, the patron saint of preparedness.[59]

Church's eagerness to serve was obvious to anyone who knew about him or his resumé. He also became a member of the executive committee of the Training Camp Association, and he traveled to Washington to request for all men in military training a stipend of $100 a month ($2,817 in 2023), which was granted. Then in 1916 he was elected to the Illinois House of Representatives, but he still volunteered for active duty and entered officers' training at Fort Sheridan. His training was almost complete when a series of medical conditions disqualified him from service in the army.[60]

According to the April 5, 1918, *Evanston News-Index*, Ralph officially gave up his dream of military service due to "faulty eyesight" eliminating his eligibility. "Church has had more than his share of ill luck," the paper said. "When the first Fort Sheridan officer's training camp opened, he left Springfield to enter the school. He suffered a severe case of acute indigestion and while in the hospital came down with the mumps. This left his eyes in a weakened condition and he was given an honorable discharge."[61] The column added that Ralph had also "made trips to several cities in the interest of preparedness, urging the formation of training camps all over the country. He recommended twenty-five men to these camps, all of whom were given commissions."[62]

THE COMPLICATED GOP

There was a time, back in the era of McKinley, when being a Republican was a simple matter. You favored the gold standard, you supported tariffs, and you were suspicious of labor unions. While these were also the default positions of young Ralph, crystallized in his conservative thinking even as he came up from Catlin and certainly as he left Ann Arbor, things were changing. Most white Republicans favored business interests, and that wouldn't change, but to one side there were the progressives, and they were not shy about running a buzz saw through the party when it suited their purpose. They had even seceded from the GOP in 1912 as the Bull Moose Party. As that led to electoral disaster, progressives were, by the time of Ralph Church's political christening, largely back in the Republican fold. But Republican politics remained fragile despite Roosevelt's ability to talk as if everything would be fine, just fine.

In Illinois, the situation was even more confused. The state party had its conservatives and progressives. But it also had Chicago, where the Republicans had a political machine that fussed very little over ideology. This faction had been organized more than two decades before by Billy "The Blond Boss" Lorimer, who came from the working class neighborhoods of Chicago's West Side. Lorimer was hardly a classic Republican. He was an immigrant from England who took an interest in politics while still struggling to support his widowed mother and family. He shined shoes, carried coal, worked in the stockyards, and did other hard work. He noticed that many of the people whose shoes he shined worked in politics. He also noticed that while the Democrats had an organization in his neighborhood, the Republicans had none. He filled the vacuum, and within a few years he had a ward organization which grew to encompass most of Illinois' Second Congressional District. In 1894 those voters elected him to the US House of Representatives.

Lorimer was never known for legislative initiatives, but he was a sharp irritant to the establishment. In William McKinley's 1896 campaign for president, the Blond Boss would have been expected to line up with the party and support the clear favorite from Ohio. But Lorimer, never one to miss a chance to flex political muscles, decided that it suited his purpose and that of another Republican who was aiming for the Illinois Governor's Mansion to hold back.[63] They wanted the powerful to come to them. Lorimer's intransigence did not affect the outcome of the convention that year, nor the election that made McKinley the president. It did, however, set the stage for years of fractious Republicans in the state.

Like many politicians, especially at that time and in Chicago, Lorimer was not too concerned about the moral rectitude of the people who joined the Republican machine. First among these—first in stature and near the front in terms of moral amnesia—was William Thompson, who would become mayor of Chicago. Thompson was a wealthy sportsman with a family fortune from a real estate business that did not require much of the young man's time or effort. He was handsome and well-liked, which led to his being cajoled, largely by Lorimer, to enter politics in Chicago's Second Ward. This included a portion of the Levee vice district, and that turned out to be a natural environment for the ethically relaxed future mayor.

Thompson became a reliable tabloid figure in the first decade of the century, in part for being a star on the nationally ranked Chicago Athletic Association water polo team, and because he was a high-class sailor and perennial contender in the famous 333-mile Chicago Yacht Club race to Mackinac Island. Thompson's persona turned a little darker when he was inveigled to testify for a wealthy friend of his, William Pike, who was being sued by a woman who claimed to be his common-law wife. In court, Thompson said that the charge was ridiculous, that the woman was a prostitute, that Thompson was with Willie the night they met her at a bordello. It was embarrassing but did not unrecommend him to Boss Lorimer, who saw Thompson as a politician whose looks and simple good cheer made him eminently electable in Chicago.

For his part, Church was still in college when these Republican antics developed, though they defined the Chicago GOP for another decade or two. In 1904, the "Lorimerites" lost the governorship to a so-called reform Republican, Charles Deneen, but Lorimer and several cronies retained their seats in Congress. Two years later, Lorimer, who pined for higher office, placed himself before the Illinois General Assembly as candidate for the United States Senate—Senators were elected by state legislatures in those days. It took more than a dozen ballots in Springfield, but Lorimer finally got a majority and was ready to take his place in the upper house in Washington.

Billy Lorimer didn't stay in the Senate long. Just a few months after being sworn in, news came from Springfield that a member of the state House, a Democrat no less, admitted to having been bribed $1,000 ($32,318 in 2023) to vote for Lorimer. While there was little outcry initially about this, the *Chicago Tribune* became vocal when it discovered that an alleged $100,000 "slush fund" ($3.2 million in 2023) was liberally distributed to get the Lorimer in "the world's greatest deliberative body." With remarkable speed by US Senatorial standards, members voted to expel the Illinoisan.

It was a bad pass for Lorimer, but it wasn't the end of his machine. To the chagrin of regular Republicans like Ralph Church, Lorimer's and Thompson's popularity locally hardly waned. Thompson had his own problems, such as the arrest for gambling of many of his drinking buddies, which got plenty of ink too, with the Tribune leading the charge against Thompson.[64] But the Cook County Republicans were not chastened. When Lorimer returned from his defeat in Washington, the would-be senator and his wife were met at the station by a welcoming party and a brass band. Someone unfurled an American flag, and they marched through the city to honor Lorimer as a "martyr."[65]

Thompson continued to lead the chorus, excoriating "the trust press," which of course meant Robert McCormick's Tribune. The Thompson-Lorimer line even got the blessing of the pastor of Saint Mary's Church, on the South Side near the vice district, and one of the largest Catholic parishes in the city. "We know that powerful interests have poisoned public sentiment against him," he said of Lorimer. "We know that the *Chicago Tribune* is the greatest criminal in Illinois, a moral leper, unfit for association with decent people."[66] In this eminently ironic view, the press, even the Republican press, was nothing but corrupt.

UNITY IN EVANSTON

Church could be pleased that the town that he chose to live in, Evanston, tacked hard against the Chicago GOP. The state party, clearly divided, would have its ups and downs, especially as Thompson's Teflon-like image drew him into collusion with the rise of organized crime. When the Eighteenth Amendment was ratified in 1919, ushering in the Prohibition era, Thompson railed against it, assuring the support of working class and immigrant voters, while also doing everything he could to help the bootleggers and criminals who benefitted richly from the amendment. Thompson gave a whole new meaning to the political label "wet."

But Evanston was able to step aside of this maelstrom. Suburban Republicans could have their disagreements, as there were progressives who sometimes supported Prohibition. Perhaps on the theory that drinkers on the North Shore were going to have access to alcohol anyway, these voters had their eye elsewhere. Nationally in the 1916 election cycle, Roosevelt dropped out of the presidential race and the staunchly Republican *News-Index* was enthusiastic about the eventual nominee, Charles Evans Hughes.[67] Hughes was conservative and pro-business but progressive enough for most Bull Moosers. Given the corruption in Chicago, Evans was fine for the likes of the *Tribune*, not to mention Ralph Church, who was getting ready to run for the state legislature.

The Illinois House of Representatives was a large body with fifty-one districts and three members from each district. Happily for Church, the Sixth District, mostly in Evanston, had open seats due to recent redistricting. A portion of the district was in Chicago with a more heterogeneous electorate, but as long as Church cleaved to the conventional conservative positions, especially those of the Women's Christian Temperance Union, he had a good chance.

It was no shoo-in for the young lawyer, of course. There were ten candidates running in the party primary. But if he could win one of the two slots in the primary, three of the four candidates in the general would make it in. It required self-confidence to run against a large field. Best known in the GOP field was Allan J. Carter, also of Evanston, a former assistant US attorney whose progressive credentials could be checked against the antitrust cases that he prosecuted in recent years. At first, Church did not look too different from the rest of the field.

Nor did Church stick his neck out in his earliest campaign flyers. There was a certain progressive streak in his rhetoric. He claimed to be in favor of "good government," code for anti-waste and anti-corruption. In one of his first campaign ads in the *Evanston News-Index* he declared that he would stand his ground. "After a few [people reputedly interested in] CLEAN POLITICS had pledged their support for my candidacy, I was [later] urged to obligate certain persons to me by withdrawing from the field," he wrote. This oblique phrasing appears to claim that wolves in sheep's clothing wanted him out of the running.[68] Of course, he did not surrender.

In later ads he staked out other positions. He was for the free use of the lakefront by all people. He was for lowering taxes and "eliminating graft and extravagance in public office." And there was one position that he declared more emphatically than all the rest and in capital letters. "MR. CHURCH IS A DRY CANDIDATE," his ad for the primary proclaimed.[69] It was the propitious, if obvious, stand to take in Evanston, where the WCTU was never shy about flexing its political muscle. In 1916, of course, the Eighteenth Amendment was not yet a reality. But even then, "local option" votes were being promoted to outlaw alcohol from precincts and townships by popular referendum.[70] In fact, Evanston had no need for a local option vote. Way back in 1850, Northwestern's charter eliminated intoxicating beverages within seven miles of the campus. Evanston, or "Heavenston," as it was sometimes called for its piety, was incorporated only subsequently and had done nothing to remove this strictly-enforced ordinance.[71]

So Church's favoring the local option was not controversial to a large portion of the constituency that he sought to represent. The candidate knew his district. The "drys," as pro-temperance forces were known, were hardcore in Evanston, where "wets" were more or less anathema. Truth be told, "blind pigs," or unlicensed purveyors, operated near the western edge of town. But blind pigs were effectively curtailed by 1915 when the *News-Index* took delight in naming not just the proprietors but customers present whenever a sheriff's raid shut one down.[72] Prominent Evanstonians were sometimes included in these roll calls, and maybe Ralph Church, who was not a teetotaler, felt lucky not to be among them. In any case, Evanston's dry position was strong well before 1919's Volstead Act, the measure enacted to carry out the spirit of the Eighteenth Amendment.

GOOD SIGNS FOR A POLITICAL NEWCOMER

Church's coverage was lighter than that of the better-known Carter for most of the campaign. But as front-runners they looked like running mates in the sense that three candidates would be elected to the state House from a pool of two Republicans and two Democrats. Church had some nice endorsements of his own to set him apart. The local chapters of the Anti-Saloon League of America gave Church their seal of approval. The Swedish Temperance Church Federation did likewise.[73] Ultimately, the *News-Index*, in their endorsement, treated Carter and Church as a single ticket: "In Mr. Church and Mr. Carter, the voters of Evanston have two candidates whom they really know and whose fitness they are assured." In fact, Church had chosen the right office to run for; as an Evanstonian in a district heavily weighted toward the town, his election seemed assured.[74]

Whether it benefitted Church or not, his legislative race was hardly a priority in the minds of most voters that November. What overshadowed everything else, and particularly to the editorial writers of the *News-Index*, was the presidential election. An animus against the incumbent Wilson raged among almost all Republicans that year. A *News-Index* article frankly entitled "Republican Catechism" listed a long litany of points on which Wilson was disqualified. "No credit whatever," the "catechist" wrote, "is due to President Wilson for keeping us out of war, as he claims, while the utmost discredit must attach to his weak and wabbling [*sic*] policy."[75] It was a matter of urgency throughout Evanston that Hughes be elected.

If there was any drama in the way Evanston would vote, it was related to women, who through Illinois state law in 1913 had been enfranchised to vote in some, though not all, state elections. The *News-Index* was encouraging women to get out and vote, and of course for the GOP. While women would hardly prove to be a monolithic Republican voting bloc in Illinois or elsewhere, temperate women in "Heavenston" were, the paper rightly believed, reliably Republican.[76]

One of the biggest of a series of Republican rallies in the fall of 1916 featured Marion Drake, a progressive woman who had previously taken her fight for government reform to the lion's maw, having run a year or so before for Chicago alderman against the corrupt "Bathhouse" John Coughlin, who represented the notorious Levee. Drake explained that from her point of view, the Republican ticket was a progressive one. She pointed out that she had been a Roosevelt supporter but easily moved to support Hughes, who was more conservative but, according to her, a reformer at heart.[77]

The *News-Index* admitted that Drake was no spellbinder. But her message was clear, and with few more rallies like this, the paper declared, Evanston "is liable to cast its largest [ever] Republican vote on Nov. 7." As the editorialist continued, "The particular surroundings which distinguish Evanston, the city of homes, an educational center, a community in a class by itself, mean that its residents are thinkers who reason for themselves. They want peace, prosperity and the good of humanity the world over."[78]

In the general election, Ralph Church could campaign with the confidence that schisms suffered by the party elsewhere hardly echoed in the Sixth Legislative District. Unity was the watchword. That was the GOP's message as transmitted by the *News-Index*: "Republicans Vote Straight and Save Time," the paper advised in a banner headline. "Just mark a cross in the circle at the head of the ticket and you will help the cause," was its advice.[79] Ralph ran in a tight political kinship with the popular Allan Carter, and when they woke up on November 8, they learned that they had prevailed, along with many other regular Republicans.

Nationally, results were not as happy for the party. Wilson was reelected, but not because of Illinois, which went for Hughes. The state also elected Republican Frank Lowden as governor, and many other party stalwarts were successful for state and city offices. From various perspectives, it looked like the world was safe for the likes of Ralph Church as long as he navigated his way through the drys, the progressives, the conservatives, the suffragists, and the others that had a home in Evanston and in the Republican Party. Church would enter the legislature in early 1917. If he played the very favorable hand that he was dealt with even moderate intelligence, he was destined to enjoy a successful, if unspectacular, political career.

CHAPTER FOUR

STRIKING THE AMERICAN DREAM

BY OUTWARD APPEARANCES, RALPH CHURCH'S union with Marguerite Stitt was a case of a man "marrying up." Ralph came from the humble roots of a family farm on the Illinois prairie. Marguerite came from New York, Manhattan, the Upper West Side, a large apartment on West 79th Street.

While the Churches of Catlin, Illinois, were involved in the cycles of the agricultural life, the Stitts moved in arguably more exciting circles, such as the polo crowd on Long Island and the social set that embarked on ocean liners for long vacations in Europe.[80] William Stitt, a husband and the father of two daughters, had found success as an industrialist, a glove manufacturer, which enabled the family to live a life of ease and occasional splendor.[81]

As their lives had such rarefied touches, one might have wondered if the Stitts were blue-blooded Americans, descended of a long line of oligarchs. In fact, Ralph Church soon learned that his future wife's background was not so far removed from his own. At least some of Marguerite's grandparents were immigrants from Ireland and Scotland, arriving in New York, likely poor and beleaguered by famine. Just as Ralph Church's family had established themselves in Illinois and became prosperous farmers, the Stitts settled in New York and rose from humble beginnings as well. Marguerite, like Ralph, remained mindful of this legacy—of family, humility, and the American dream—for her entire life.

Marguerite's paternal grandfather, James Samuel Stitt, was born in Belfast in 1824 or 1825 and was a young man when the Great Famine hit Ireland in 1845.[82] This disaster, responsible for one of America's great migrations, was caused by a persistent fungus in Ireland, *Phytophthora infestans*, which for at least five years wiped out the potato crop, the country's primary food source. Compounding the famine was the 1847 typhus epidemic, followed by cholera one year later. The situation was dire in all of Ireland, but in the northern city of Belfast, conditions were particularly appalling. Filthy streets and overcrowded houses conspired with Belfast's woefully polluted river, the Lagan, to make poor Belfasters, of which there were many, some of the most vulnerable people in the British Isles.

Belfast was not always desperate. At times it rivaled Dublin in size and in importance, with a centuries-old agricultural economy that sent exports of salted meats, butter, hides, and wool among other commodities to far-flung markets. In the mid-1700s, the population swelled with the arrival of French Protestants and the consequent introduction of linen weaving, which created a new and primary economic sector. In 1773, Belfast exported seventeen million yards of linen, much of it woven by hand in the homes of citizens and villagers, and the city took its place as an industrial center and major port city. Shipbuilding, not incidentally, became important as well. By 1800, Belfast's population reached 20,000.[83]

While the Stitts likely enjoyed some success when Belfast was prosperous, they undoubtedly endured the horrors of the Great Famine when it came. Marguerite's grandfather James Stitt joined the exodus of Irish from their homeland, a movement of people that numbered two million—one quarter of Ireland's population—between 1845 and 1855. Most went to America, leaving behind a million who succumbed to disease and starvation. Immigration records show that twenty-six-year-old James arrived in New York in 1850, where the Irish made up 43 percent of the foreign-born population. Census reports have James Stitt's professions as "porter" in 1860, "clerk" in 1870, and by the year 1900 he was listed as "capitalist," or what might today be considered an investor, receiving his income, or at least most of his money, from stocks, bonds, and other securities, or from funds loaned at interest.[84]

In 1854, James Stitt married Sophia Hardy, seven years his junior. It remains unclear when the two met, or whether she was born in New York or Ireland (both have been reported). Her immigration records were likely lost in an Ellis Island fire in 1897. What is certain is that James and Sophia Stitt married in New York, raised five children there, and that their eldest, William James Stitt, Marguerite's father, was born in 1856.[85] Life was hard in these early years, with the family living in a crowded tenement on Dutch Street, downtown and not far from South Street Seaport. As life had been intolerable in Ireland, it was rough going in America as well. Beyond the poverty, there were troubles such as those of Sophia's brother, Charles Hardy, who was implicated in a murder in 1860. News of the "Twelfth Street Murder," as it was called in headlines, was enthusiastically shared via telegraph with papers around the country after Sarah Schanks, a fifty-year-old widow, was brutally murdered in broad daylight in her embroidery shop in New York.[86] Sophia herself could not escape talking to someone from the *New York Times*, to whom she described her fugitive brother as "a small-sized man, dark complexioned, with large dark moustache and whiskers," and a "peddler of dry goods and embroideries."[87] She said that "he came to my house [after the murder] and said he wanted to see my baby; he told me that he intended to leave the City that evening, but he did not tell me where he was going . . . I have not seen him since."[88]

Ultimately, Sophia's brother was cleared when another man was arrested and convicted. That person, described as "unemployed" and "half idiotic," was sentenced to The Tombs, the city jail, and later committed to the State Lunatic Asylum at Utica.[89] That Charles Hardy escaped what may have been a false conviction cannot but have left the family with another sign that life is fragile, with tragedy only a step away, and that this was especially true for the poor.

On Marguerite's maternal side, her great-grandparents, John and Margaret Forsythe, were born in Ireland in 1800 and 1803, respectively, then immigrated to New York with their four children in 1837.[90] In 1850, the same year Marguerite's paternal grandfather, James Stitt, arrived in the United States, John and Margaret Forsythe's sixteen-year-old son Joseph reported his profession as a "weaver," perhaps a carpet weaver, just like his father.[91] Joseph—who married Mary, also an Irish immigrant whose parents were born in Scotland—would eventually become an oyster dealer.[92] The sixth of Joseph and Mary Forsythe's ten children, Adelaide (Marguerite's mother and namesake), was born in New York on January 3, 1859.[93] By 1870, Adelaide's mother, Mary, was a forty-two-year-old widow with ten children—the first six of whom were girls.[94]

EDUCATION AND MODERN FAMILIES

These families were hard-working and, by all evidence, ambitious to get ahead. This made them not too different from millions of immigrants in New York in this period. There was one element that augured well for this family, and that was the value placed on education—specifically the education of women. This latter impulse went well against the grain in the mid-nineteenth century, as women were rarely encouraged to pursue the then few and unusual paths available toward higher education.

In the 1830s and 1840s there was significant debate around women attending institutions of higher learning. Conservatives then, scholar Patsy Parker writes, believed higher education would "destroy the role of women in the household as homemakers, wives, and mothers," whereas liberals, she says, claimed higher education would only improve those roles.[95] In any case, higher education for women was normally conducted in strict separation from men. And when women did further their education, it was often to train as teachers.[96] Adelaide Forsythe chose this path, and in 1876 she graduated from the Normal College of the City of New York (now Hunter College), which prepared women for the teaching profession.[97]

To be sure, this was hardly college as we think of it today; rather, Adelaide earned the equivalent of a high school diploma, a point that activist Catherine Beecher spoke to in 1851: "Those female institutions in our land which are assuming the ambitious name of colleges, have, not one of them, as yet, secured the real features which constitute the chief advantage of such institutions."[98] Others echoed the view that women's colleges were "ornamental," perpetuating an intellectual gap between men and women.[99] Nevertheless, seventeen-year-old Adelaide Forsythe was more fortunate than most of her female peers and, upon graduation, was certified to teach—something most women with an education ended up doing. Eight years after her graduation, she met twenty-eight-year old William Stitt, and the two were married on February 7, 1884.[100]

Few, if any, public details exist about Adelaide's employment. It is unclear if she was ever employed as a teacher: US Census reports between 1900 and 1925 list her occupation as either blank, "none," or "housewife."[101] Her *New York Times* obituary describes Adelaide serving from 1926 to 1933 as president of the Methodist Church Home for the Aged, a position for which she did not receive compensation but to which, according to the organization, "she had given unstinting service, and the great accomplishments of her regime are a tribute to her administrative ability and vision."[102]

The Methodist Church Home for the Aged first opened in 1850 following an exceptionally harsh New York winter, during which members of the Methodist Episcopal Church noted women of age, illness, or lacking friends and family that were in need of a place to go for support. The twenty-three Methodist Episcopal churches of New York at the time issued a bulletin of concern for these indigent or elderly women in need, who would otherwise be institutionalized in "godless poorhouses" and receive a "pauper's grave."[103]

In March of 1850, a century before Ralph Church's death, a committee of seven women were appointed to draft a constitution for an organization to guide this effort, which was approved and passed the next month. In May, an initial board of managers was created: thirty-six men and thirty-three women. Two months later, in July of 1850, seventy board managers—all women—were elected, and the men were remanded to advisory positions. Naming themselves The Ladies Union Aid Society, "their first order of business was to find a location, a nice home where these women could gather under one roof and enjoy the rest of their days under the fostering care of the Church." In November of 1850, the group opened its Horatio Street home to twenty-five elderly, Methodist women and spent $52 per year (equivalent to around $2,000 per year in 2023) to care for each one.

As New York's population and social problems grew, so, too, did its need to support women who struggled, including widows and the unemployed. It is noteworthy that by 1870, Adelaide's mother, Mary Forsythe, was one of those women: forty-two-years-old, widowed, mother of ten. Thanks to the determination of these pioneering women, the organization not only thrived, expanded, and evolved through the decades, but also served as an anchor for service by Marguerite's extended family. It cannot have escaped the family's notice that Adelaide Stitt's generosity and goodwill was helping to sustain a charity that was indispensable to her family only a generation before.

Under Adelaide's leadership as president during the Great Depression, the organization raised funds and moved eight miles north—from Amsterdam Avenue between 92nd and 93rd Street, a two minute walk from the Stitts' home—to its current, significantly larger and more bucolic setting in Riverdale, the Bronx. In November of 1929, one month after the stock market crashed, Adelaide stood at the entrance on opening day of the newly renamed Methodist Home For the Aged, welcoming residents to their new accommodations.[104] Adelaide and William Stitt were among the organization's most loyal and generous supporters, helping to convert the home from gas to electricity, bequeathing rooms and creating endowments in perpetuity in honor of their parents.[105] Adelaide's sense of service to society, seemingly born of her own family's privation early in her life, certainly influenced the same in her daughter, Marguerite.

When Marguerite's parents first met, William Stitt had been working for glove manufacturer Jacob Adler & Co. for ten years, a company in whose industry Adelaide's brother, Joseph, also worked. Joseph eventually became treasurer of Howell-Hinchman and Johnson Leather Companies.[106]

William Stitt described his own appearance on his 1889 passport application as being 5'7" with a "broad forehead", "dark gray" eyes, "medium" nose, "large" mouth, "round" chin, "dark brown" hair, "fair" complexion, and "oval" face.[107] He had already shown himself to be smart, having made it from his immigrant-family origins to the College of the City of New York before beginning in earnest his career in business.

After they married in 1884, young Adelaide and William Stitt settled at 230 W. 104th Street, between Broadway and Amsterdam Avenue. This marriage, by many public accounts, modeled a rare-for-the-time partnership approach; William not only supported Adelaide's pursuits outside the home, but he also played an active role in them.

They welcomed Edna Walmsley Stitt on Christmas Eve that same year (she would eventually serve, like her mother, as president of the Methodist Church Home for the Aged, from 1946 to 1964).[108] William was quickly moving up the ladder at the Adler firm, becoming a partner in 1892.[109] He turned thirty-six that year, the same year that his daughter Adelaide Marguerite Stitt was born on September 13.[110] By this time, the family's position was such that they appeared on occasion in the society pages, which reported that Marguerite was born ten days after her family had returned from summer vacation at the Fenimore Hotel in New Jersey's Asbury Park. The Fenimore, an upscale place within a block of the popular beachfront, provided a welcome respite to the Stitt family, not to mention close proximity to the pleasures of the

Jersey Shore, including vaudeville shows, fireworks, and relaxing times in the summer sands. This remained a favorite destination for the Stitts in years to come.[111]

Marguerite was born at the beginning of the so-called Progressive Era, a period of political activism and political reform centered in New York that began roughly around 1890. At this time, several groups in America were prohibited from voting, including Asian Americans, Native Americans, and women of any race.[112] This was the era of the women's rights movement, leading to women's suffrage in America in 1920 and to a growing interest in the power of social science as a way of addressing social ills, many of them wrought by the industrial revolution.[113] While the Stitts benefited from the organization of industrial society, they also raised and educated their daughters surrounded by the impact of the Progressive Era. Is this what motivated them to send their daughters to a school which, among other things, was dedicated to preparing girls for a college education?

While ambivalence about educated women remained in most quarters, it found a strong counterweight in schools such as St. Agatha Day School for Girls, not far from the Stitt home in Manhattan's Upper West Side. As timing would have it, St. Agatha opened in 1898, the same year Marguerite began her formal schooling.[114]

At St. Agatha's, Marguerite received a grounding in science, mathematics, and language even as a young girl. She attended while headmistress Miss Emma Sebring, a Smith graduate, almost single-handedly organized St. Agatha's as an adjunct to the all-male Trinity School, whose trustees had elected Sebring and described her as "eminently fitted to take charge of the organization and conduct of the school as Principal."[115] Given just two months' time to prepare and open the new school, Sebring later wrote, "When I accepted the leadership of St. Agatha, I was terrified at my audacity, for I was young, green, and if you will believe it, timid."[116] She was breaking new ground for girls, whom she believed deserved the same intellectual stimulation and advantages as boys, casting an indelible impression on Marguerite from an early age.[117]

Marguerite described herself as a timid child, but she excelled in her coursework, often earning straight A's and test results higher than most of her peers, particularly in English, mathematics, French and Latin.[118] Her father's glove company was a frequent advertising sponsor of the school's bi-monthly school newspaper, the *Forum*, a publication introduced during Marguerite's senior year of high school and for which she served as general manager.[119]

Marguerite's schooling took place during a time that was seeing a shift in the importance of education for women. By 1912, the number of women in American high schools, colleges and universities combined would outnumber men by 50,000, and while the majority of those women were in secondary education, the numbers pointed to a sea change.[120] Each female enrollment increased every woman's voice, giving rise for opportunities to affect social change.

The luxuries that the Stitt family enjoyed—and there were many—were afforded by the fine career of William Stitt. The trade magazine the *Glover's Review* recounted that "diligence and ability made his rise rapid, and his diligence only increased as his responsibilities grew."[121] Known as a tireless member of his industry, he traveled widely, almost weekly from the Adler office in Brooklyn to the factory in Gloversville, near Albany. He also made trips around the country to promote Adler's high-end glove lines for men and women. As the nation grew in this period, primarily to the west, William's travel increased proportionately.

Wife and daughters sometimes accompanied William on his travels, often to Europe on business trips, where the family naturally took time to see sights and absorb the culture. The Stitts also became familiar with the capitals of Europe. In 1910, the magazine *Notions and Fancy Goods* reported that William was sailing on the steamer *George Washington*, which would make landfall at

Southampton. He was "accompanied by Mrs. Stitt and his daughters . . . to look over the raw skins market of Europe and make the customary purchases of skins for the business of 1911."[122] In moments of leisure, and when they accompanied their father to a business-related events, wife and daughters were always well dressed. Fashions of the period favored linen duck skirts, gowns with Cluny lace, bright-green panne velvets, foulards, shepherd's plaids, printed and embroidered chiffons, mousselines de sole, black and white hairpiece ribbons, and long, dark, narrow tulle bows. What gloves ought to complete such ensembles? The Stitts would know.

William's income also afforded the family a summer retreat in Sound Beach, Connecticut, now known as Old Greenwich, thirty-two miles from their New York City residence.[123] But this was just one of the fashionable resorts they frequented, not because they had entered the ranks of the idle rich, but because of business. Specifically, William found himself in the polo business. The sport of polo had just taken off in the United States—introduced in 1876 by the publisher of the *New York Herald*—and it called for specialized gloves, a line proudly manufactured by Jacob Adler & Co.[124] Consequently, William traveled often—be it to polo matches to promote his products or to various spots throughout the world to obtain the finest materials and inspect the competition.

Through her father, Marguerite witnessed the full range of an industrial activity. When William went to the factory at Gloversville, he was sometimes accompanied by his family. The facilities in Gloversville housed curing tanks and machines for treating raw hides, a process that washed, shaved, buffed and finished the tanned leather, as well as cutting equipment and commercial sewing machines.[125] William was well versed in every aspect of his industry. To his card-playing friends in New York, he may have appeared to be a man of leisure, but his family knew he was a man who managed a large operation and understood every piece of it.

William was also responsible for contracts that governed the partnership, and he oversaw those who managed the sales force, factory operations, and quite naturally, relations with the labor unions. William had been an exceptionally gifted writer with a strong sense for business management and political acumen, skills his younger daughter, Marguerite, may have been witness to from an early age. Though many assumed Marguerite's political readiness stemmed from her marriage to a legislator, it may have been her father's tactful engagement in the legislative process—writing to and appearing before members of Congress on matters of tariffs—that formed the bedrock of her legislative style.[126]

A PROGRESSIVE AND DELICATE SOCIETY

Another element of business that the family understood was that prosperity came with risk. Gloves had become a fashionable accessory, and as demand increased Adler became a leading maker. But with explosive growth came epic disasters, catastrophic blazes that disabled the business just as the firm thrived and inventories bulged warehouses. The demand for gloves had never been higher, requiring substantial inventory and consequently storage, but this was a time when fireproof buildings were not yet the norm. In 1882, a fire began in a basement and destroyed the five-story loft building at 471 Broadway, where the Adler Company occupied the second floor. The company lost about $50,000 ($1.5 million in 2023) in merchandise, due entirely to smoke damage.[127]

Two decades later, on December 11, 1913, another fire destroyed a building that the firm owned along with the merchandise inside, a disaster ultimately valued at $750,000 ($23.2 million in 2023).[128] Before all the losses had been tallied, the *New York Times*, on December 12, described the blaze with the headline "$600,000 Fire Gives Broadway A Scare," printed amidst other scintillating news items such as "Mr. Taft On Diet, Loses 70 Pounds" and "President Wilson Ill Again: His Cold Returns, with Some Fever, and He Is in Bed."[129] The resulting loss to Jacob Adler & Co. was estimated between $250,000 and $300,000 ($7.7–9.3 million in 2023).

Losses were covered by insurance, fortunately, but recovery only made the firm, and the family of the firm's owner, increasingly mindful that no one was immune from setbacks, and some more than others. So accustomed to fires was William Stitt during his career with Jacob Adler & Co. that he would eventually hold positions on boards of trustees for Guarantee Fire, a fire and casualty company he helped to incorporate in 1919.[130]

As the company was vulnerable, so were the workers on whom it depended. The hard lives of people not so privileged as they were was a fact the Stitt family could neither ignore nor properly assuage. By 1913, the glove business was running into a number of structural problems. One difficulty was with tariffs, and William did his best to convince his representatives in Washington that protections were needed to save his industry. He pleaded in a letter to a US senator that a reasonable duty on foreign luxury goods could have three basic outcomes, all desirable. One, he said, was an increase in government revenue. The second was a moderating influence on consumer prices, and the third was a more stable domestic glove industry.[131] But nothing satisfactory was passed by the next year, and the most conspicuous victims were workers, whose wages had not increased for more than twenty years. By 1914, cutters, the leather workers who did the upfront heavy work cutting the blanks from the finished leather, only earned $2.26 ($69.39 in 2023) for six days' labor, and, except for small adjustments, their wages were still held at 1890 rates.[132] Labor unrest was already a perennial part of the working life of cutters when their union called a strike in August of 1914.[133]

The cutters went out, demanding better working conditions and a raise of twenty-five or thirty cents per each dozen pair of gloves cut. A fifteen-cent raise was offered by manufacturers after the strike was a month old, and when the cutters turned it down, tensions rose until violence broke out in the streets of Gloversville. The state government got involved, and William Stitt testified before the New York State Board of Mediation and Arbitration on behalf of the manufacturers. "The fact that in this industry we have not been able to make any serious advance in wages has been because we are up against a strong foreign competition where labor is so much cheaper than here," he said. Even with the war in Europe, French gloves were being made and shipped to America. "Just after the War was declared there was a feeling that foreign gloves would be more or less shut out but that does not prove to be the case," he concluded.[134]

It got worse in Gloversville before it got better. While some cutters with families survived as wives took on additional work by cutting leather and sewing gloves at home, it was hardly enough for the workers' families or for the industry. Violence continued with the horror of glove factories being burned, and then there was the stabbing of Isaac Moses, secretary treasurer of the Elite Glove Company of Gloversville. Herbert M. Engel, in *Shtetl in the Adirondacks: The Story of Gloversville and Its Jews*, writes, "It became a matter of not working and starving, or abandoning the union and eating."[135] After five months, settlement was finally reached in January 1915, engineered by the mediation board.[136] It provided cutters with a flat increase of fifteen cents a dozen. The manufacturers came out ahead in this agreement, as even the state admitted, not only because of the exiguous raise but because the industry secured higher tariffs from the federal government, lower rates on raw materials, and even reduced restrictions on immigration—all at about the same time.[137]

As these developments and the turmoil touched the Stitt family in this period, Marguerite was certainly attuned to the details. She was always curious and well-informed, and it was natural based on her family experience that she would go on to concentrate on—among other subjects—economics in college. She understood that the Gloversville situation involved public policy, not least of which were tariffs, which were a constant political football between Republicans (who favored them) and Democrats (who did not). She also knew that harsh fluctuations in raw materials were affected by the war in Europe. Nor did it escape Marguerite's notice that moral ambiguity abounded: another glove factory owner, Lucius Littauer, was a former Republican congressman who in 1914 was convicted of the felony of smuggling jewels without paying duties.

The labor department concluded in its post-strike analysis that the workers lost this strike because they were "unwilling to permit their wives and children to suffer (any) longer for lack of the necessities of life." The glove companies returned to profitability, and while cutters were back to work, their lives were hardly improved. The muckraking press had no trouble finding stories like that of worker Otto Rannen, whose hard life ended when he drank a bottle of carbonic acid. It is hardly a stretch to conclude that the strike against her family's business struck Marguerite deeply. She was a future Republican who was able to see the world through the entrepreneurs' eyes, but the awfulness of the cutters' strike and the fragile lives that the workers lived likely made her view a compassionate one—as would be evidenced by her college career.

EYES OPEN IN MORNINGSIDE HEIGHTS

Initially, Marguerite did not travel far to start her higher education. In 1910, she enrolled at Barnard College, the women's college at Columbia University which oversaw multiple undergraduate and graduate colleges and programs. Just twenty-seven years earlier, all but one member of the all-male Columbia College's Board of Trustees had voted against coeducation. The single dissenting vote came from President Frederick A. P. Barnard.

Nevertheless, in July of 1883, the college established the Collegiate Course for Women. Once admitted, female students could enroll in Columbia University courses, though they were banned from lectures and required to sit for exams off-campus, presumably away from their male classmates. The program lasted six years, enrolled ninety-nine women, and granted undergraduate degrees to six.[138] One student, Annie Nathan Meyer, lasted only one year. Later, her 1888 letter to the *Nation* sparked a movement that led her and other advocates to create a women's college—an annex similar to Harvard's women's annex (later known as Radcliffe College). On April 1,

1889, Barnard College was approved, with the stipulation that courses be taught by Columbia faculty.

In a very short period, Barnard established itself as an excellent school, a worthy partner to Columbia. Barnard was, if anything, a practical choice for Marguerite when she finished at St. Agatha's. Her sister Edna was already a Barnard graduate.[139] Plus, it was close to home—just a thirty-minute walk to Barnard's Morningside Heights campus from the Stitts' Upper West Side apartment.

Marguerite's courses freshman year constituted a well-rounded core curriculum: English composition, solid geometry, trigonometry, Latin, French, English literature, musical theory and piano.[140] She would eventually graduate from college with a major in psychology and minors in economics and sociology, suggesting her interest and aptitude for the social sciences. It seems, however, that she and Barnard were not meant for each other. And it was, perhaps, not her course load that distressed her that first year of college, but rather other circumstances that would motivate her to seek a change in venue.

During Marguerite's freshman year, from 1910 to 1911, Barnard was hardly seen as a paradise of women's rights. In 1906, Dean Laura Drake Gill had forced the resignation of Barnard physics tutor Harriet Brooks when Brooks became engaged to a physicist at Columbia. Marguerite must have wondered if there was something ominous in that three-year-old story, about which Gill had written, "The good of the College and the dignity of the woman's place in the home demand that your marriage shall be a resignation."[141]

Brooks left Barnard, broke off her engagement, and went to the Curie Institute, the Paris-based laboratory of Marie Curie.[142] In her resignation letter, Brooks was as defiant as a woman in polite society could normally be. "I think it is a duty I owe to my profession and to my sex to show that a woman has a right to the practice of her profession and cannot be condemned to abandon it merely because she marries," she wrote. "I cannot conceive how women's colleges, inviting and encouraging women to enter professions, can be justly founded or maintained denying such a principle."[143] For Marguerite, a young woman who would later demonstrate her belief in gender equality, knowledge of the Brooks affair must have had a nagging, even prophetic, meaning.

Campus life at Barnard also left Marguerite adrift as she witnessed discrimination and social barriers built up among peers. She may have been dismayed to learn that some of Barnard's eight sororities, which were central to social life on campus, excluded Jewish girls from membership. (Marguerite was a lifelong Methodist.) It was around this time that debate on this subject heated up the Barnard campus, ending with the abolition of sororities (then called "fraternities") which "fostered snobbishness, established race lines, created 'artificial barriers against natural intercourse,' caused emotional distress to those not invited to rush, and distracted members from academic achievement," according to vocal dissenters.[144]

The student paper *The Barnard Bulletin* also conveyed other grievances on a regular basis. In one case, undergraduates complained that they couldn't attend a student-run theater production because the seats they thought had been reserved for them were sold off. "We are too commercial here as it is; there should be fun for fun's sake at times," the paper opined.[145] Rancor of a different kind was triggered by a fire that broke out during a faculty tea. The *Bulletin* scolded a group of seniors for doing nothing except standing helplessly to the side and watching. "Where were the members of the Suffrage Club? Why did they miss so glorious a chance to show what emergencies the feminine mind is equal?" wrote the paper.[146] This event, in particular, would prove a harbinger of tragedy that would overshadow Marguerite's senior year and impact the course of her life.

Then there was an anonymous letter to the editor. The writer, a first-year student in Marguerite's class, analyzed in some detail the social life on campus which was, according to the author, distinctly unsatisfactory:

> *Perhaps the greatest, the most lasting benefit that college can give us, is a certain tolerance and big-heartedness—the idea that every one of us has something to give, and something to receive from every one else . . . So my plea is for a broader social life, and by this I mean the daily attempt of the part of each one of us to know all her neighbors better, for only thus can we have true class and college spirit—only thus can we realize our highest college ideal.*
>
> *A Freshman.*[147]

It is impossible to know whether Marguerite wrote—or even read—this plea for a more harmonious Barnard existence, but what is certain is that she left Barnard after her freshman year. She never claimed to be a feminist, as the term itself had an entirely different meaning in 1910. What seems reasonable is that she may have then embraced what today is known as intersectional feminism. Marguerite, may have observed myriad issues at Barnard—including overlapping inequity regarding matters of education, race, class, culture, ethnicity and gender—and decided the student body's approach to these matters was not to her liking.[148]

As for Barnard, the 1970s ushered renewed debate about admitting women to Columbia College, but by then, many of Barnard's students and administration stood in opposition. A century after the experimental Collegiate Course for Women was established, Columbia began admitting women. Columbia's first coed class graduated in 1987 with a female valedictorian and salutatorian. Columbia's ultimate reason to go coed, however, was not for the benefit of women's education, but rather "motivated by the college's need to raise application numbers and improve the quality of life for its students."[149]

After her freshman year at Barnard, Marguerite decided to enroll at another Seven Sisters college—Wellesley—and began as a sophomore. For Marguerite, a decision to "walk away" from anything unfinished seems antithetical to her steadfast character, as she would exhibit in years to come. The act of leaving was something she would do only a few, necessary times in her life. But she was also an idealist. Wellesley would be a very different environment, in a rural setting and a close-knit community.

Marguerite's decision to leave New York, the home she'd always known, to attend college some 200 miles away may have at first seemed uncharacteristically impractical, but using her voice at a tender young age allowed her to remain steadfast to her principles—principles upon which Wellesley had also been built. In reality, she was not walking away, but rather walking toward something better.

CHAPTER FIVE

BECOMING A WOMAN OF CONSEQUENCE

SOCIAL EQUALITY FOR WOMEN WAS much discussed in 1911, but it must have seemed a long way off to those watching the progress of American women at the time. Full voting rights were nearly a decade away, and most professions did their best to bar women from entering them. Gloria Steinem, in her 1988 commencement address at Wellesley College, noted the prevailing opinion of the education of women in the early twentieth century—that women's "natural calling of marriage and childbearing would prevent them from using that education."[150]

Thankfully, Wellesley had already assumed a special role to prepare women for positions of consequence regardless of gender. Its curriculum was designed not only to prepare women to be teachers—as most institutions of higher education did for women then—but also to provide degrees equal to those of elite male institutions.[151] Wellesley also had a community spirit and sense of solidarity that anchored women with the knowledge that they mattered in society. It was the college that Marguerite chose for herself.

Wellesley College was founded as Wellesley Female Seminary in 1870 by Henry and Pauline Durant, who considered themselves blessed by wealth and bidden to use it to accomplish something of note. Their reason for opening this women's college was actually born from heartache. The Durants' dreams of raising a beautiful family disintegrated on July 3, 1863, when their eight-year-old son Harry died of diphtheria, six years after the loss of their infant daughter, also named Pauline.[152] The Durants were bereft after having lost both of their children. Henry Durant, unable to reconcile his professional life with his shattered family and shaken sense of faith, became an evangelical Christian. To honor their beloved children, the Durants devoted the land they'd bought—originally intended for a summer residence for their expanding family—to the only work Henry, a lawyer and philanthropist, now felt capable of doing: the work of God. For a time, the couple considered building an orphanage, but Henry, a trustee at Mount Holyoke College, and Pauline, who'd helped found the library there, "both believed strongly in the education of women and began dreaming of another great college dedicated to that purpose."[153]

On March 17, 1870, the Durants' original vision for their land took an entirely new and clear focus when they formally incorporated The Wellesley Female Seminary. With remarkable leadership—and sparing no expense—the Durants created an exceptional learning environment amidst unparalleled aesthetics, using the motto: *Non ministrari sed ministrare*—Not to be ministered unto, but to minister. The Durants were determined to provide higher education for women built upon the highest standards in the most pleasing of surroundings. The finest furniture was placed in the dormitories. Wedgwood china was set out on the dining room tables. There were frescoed walls, stained glass windows, and expansive gardens for outdoor enjoyment. Yet it was always the school's progressive curriculum that defined the institution. Wellesley would be one of the first higher education institutions to offer courses in all the major sciences to women. The school would eventually grow an unparalleled alumnae organization some would call "the most powerful women's network in the world."[154]

Wellesley was modeled as an education "equivalent to those usually provided in colleges for young men."[155] The Durants wanted a women's college as much as possible like Henry's alma mater, Harvard University. Wellesley's course catalogue was not as voluminous, but it was progressive in a way that even other women's colleges were not. Wellesley did not shy away from the sciences, and by 1891 it was one of the first colleges anywhere to have a psychology laboratory.[156] The Durants encouraged physical exercise for women—an unconventional notion in that era—and clearly believed that they could prepare their students for productive lives in professions traditionally reserved for men.[157]

The Durants were evangelical Christians and infused religious training in their otherwise secular courses. "You mistake altogether the significance of the movement of which you are a part if you think this is simply a question of a college education for girls," Henry said to the students and faculty in 1875, the year Wellesley opened its doors to students. "I believe that God's hand is in it; that it is one of the greatest ocean currents of Christian civilization; that He is calling to womanhood to come up higher, to prepare herself for great conflicts, for vast reforms in social life, for noblest usefulness. The higher education is but putting on God's armor for the contest."[158]

Henry Durant understood that the mission of women's education went against the grain.[159] "We revolt against the slavery in which women are held by the customs of society," he wrote, "the broken health, the aimless lives, the subordinate position, the helpless dependence, the dishonesties and shams of so-called education. The Higher Education of Women . . . is the cry of the oppressed slave.'"[160] It is most likely that Marguerite was made aware of and sympathetic to these unconventional sentiments during her three years as a student at Wellesley. In 1941, nearly three decades after her graduation, Marguerite completed a Wellesley Alumnae Association card describing her time at the school. Listing herself as a "Republican," she described herself as having been a socialist in college, with general activities and interests including "Peace" and "International Relations."[161]

Throughout her college years, it must have been impossible to ignore how quickly things were changing in the United States. By 1910, the Women's Political Union held a suffrage parade in New York City, the first of its kind on such a grand scale. And as women continued to earn the right to vote, the

Socialist Party also gained momentum. By 1912, nearly 1,200 members of the Socialist Party held public office. "Many socialists were involved in the struggle for women's rights, and vice versa," explains Peter Dreier, an E. P. Clapp Distinguished Professor of Politics at Occidental College.

The Wellesley board included the president of Yale and dean of Harvard's theological school, reflecting the Durants' values and support. They were also mindful that the college must cater to students beyond the upper stratum of wealthy Easterners, so they made a point of enrolling students from all over the United States and from foreign countries. They also sought students from different economic circumstances. In Wellesley's argot at the time, wealthy "velvet girls" were mixed with less-well-off "calico girls."[162]

Marguerite was a velvet girl, certainly, but she never lost sight of the fact that her parents grew up more modestly. Minimizing the distinction between velvets and calicos was idealistic, perhaps, but it guided many of her life choices, and it reflected Marguerite's later career when she crossed easily between economic divisions in her large congressional district.

Women's rights were an undercurrent at Wellesley, but neither Marguerite nor many of her friends were militant.[163] In her 1974 reflection for the Wellesley College Club of Los Angeles, Marguerite wrote of a reporter inquiring about why she'd attended Wellesley. "'To be near Harvard,' I truthfully answered." The reporter, according to Marguerite, then replied, "'And I suppose that you married the chap and lived happily ever after!'" Marguerite then quickly responded: "'Oh no! But I had a superb education!'"[164]

It must be noted the isolation and exclusivity that Marguerite necessarily experienced with this education. Later in life, an eighty-two-year-old Marguerite wrote that, while at Wellesley, "We had little contact with problems outside our sphere," clarifying that "what we did have were high principles, stamina, goodwill, and an incredible submission to Victorian concepts and restrictions."

What is clear is that she never regretted attending Wellesley. The school left her with the "conviction that one can never learn enough, do enough or live fully enough, no matter how long life lasts."[165] There was something empowering about Wellesley from the time it was conceived by the Durants, and its effect on students continued from the time one matriculated and never ended for thousands of loyal alumnae who sensed its solidarity and force.

SOCIAL STUDIES: PSYCHOLOGY AND ECONOMICS

After completing her first year of higher education at Barnard, Marguerite entered Wellesley as a sophomore, one of eight new students that year in a class of 343.[166] She took French, Latin, geology, hygiene, and English composition. She also had a class on biblical history that year; it was a standard offering in a college where religion was easily woven into the rigors of world history. The next year she expanded her personal interests, especially in psychology, which was part of the philosophy department due to psychology's largely speculative nature at the time. She took "Introduction to Experimental Psychology," which examined the application of statistical methods, as well as the mechanics of memory. The course also acknowledged the limits of psychology, as it included philosophical discussions of perceptual relativism.

Marguerite's overall preferences verged to what we would now call the social sciences. Her interest in psychology continued into her senior year with a course in psychological research.[167] Of that, the catalogue described that the "methods are wider than the problems and are adapted to training students in the fundamental demands of research."[168]

Training in politics, her eventual milieu, was covered largely by the economics department, in which she took four rigorous courses. "The Economics of Consumption" got into potentially political subjects, such as Thorsten Veblen's theories of conspicuous consumption. It ranged from the vagaries of the macroeconomics of nations to the "function of women in directing household expenditure," a subject on which she lectured extensively later in life, both during and after her career in politics. As a senior she took a new economics course offered that year, "Social and Industrial Legislation."[169] Marguerite's school papers and her teachers' comments and grades are unavailable for analysis; Wellesley's College Hall Fire in March of 1914, during Marguerite's senior year, destroyed most personal items and school records.

What she did not take in the Wellesley years were artistic courses. Though she did study musical theory and piano at Barnard, it seems the time she spent at Wellesley focused on practical knowledge. It would also seem Marguerite wanted something other than the offerings mentioned in job postings appearing in the Wellesley College News, including the following that appeared during her junior year: "Manager for School Lunch in New York; Inspector of Food and Cooking Teacher in large Orphanage; Trained Young Women's Christian Association General Secretary for association near Boston; College graduate with knowledge of stenography for secretarial position in New York which requires ability in organizing and directing office work."[170]

While it remains unconfirmed whether Marguerite was an official member of Wellesley's Club for the Study of Socialism, formed on February 10, 1913, during her junior year, chances are high that she was aware of the group, since it sometimes carried out collaborative programming efforts with many other organizations at the school, including the Women's Suffrage League.[171] Marguerite, already then president of the Debating Club, had plenty to do.

It would come as no surprise that Marguerite was a debater *par excellence* at Wellesley. In fact, Wellesley's Debating Club had suffered from disinterest for some years before Marguerite filled the void and spearheaded its revival. "The first meeting of the Debating Club was held on Monday evening, a great many more members being present than at the opening meeting a year ago," reported the *Wellesley College News* in the fall of 1913. "Marguerite Stitt, whose efficiency the society recognized by re-electing her to the presidency, presided over the meeting."[172]

Under Marguerite, the Debating Club organized intercollegiate events, something that hadn't happened for at least a decade.[173] It became a matter of some consequence that the first intercollegiate debate between Wellesley and Mount Holyoke took place in South Hadley on March 14, 1914.[174] The question: "Resolved, that the legislation of all states apply the minimum wage principle to all occupations, industries and trades of the United States." The Wellesley team, represented by the school's three best debaters, which included Marguerite, took the negative side of the argument and won.[175] It can hardly be ignored that the future conservative Republican would endeavor to eviscerate the minimum wage. In any case, she came to the evening's contest debate with sufficient passion, not to say superior information, to prevail.

It was perhaps characteristic of Wellesley that the school at large expressed pride in the victories earned by fellow students, but a victory as momentous as this, the first intercollegiate debate against Mount Holyoke, was something particularly special.[176] In the fall of that year, five months prior, The Debate Club's announcement in the October 2, 1913 *Wellesley College News* encouraged the school's support of their efforts. "Any inter-collegiate activity requires careful work supported by unlimited enthusiasm," the paper read. "The Debating Club has grown from a small handful of girls to an organization of real importance in our intellectual life."[177]

On the morning of March 16, 1914, a school-wide celebration was held in the massive atrium of College Hall. Center, as it was called, was indeed the heart of the main school building, in which most of Wellesley's classes, dormitories and administrative offices were found. As the Debate Club stood on the curved, wooden stairway, they looked up to see the entire student body leaning over bannisters in the five-story, glass-roofed atrium, cheering for the victorious debate team. It was a proud moment, not just for the girls who'd won the debate, but for everyone who witnessed the solidarity of the college and the goodwill and mutual support that infused the student body.[178] It was certainly the kind of thing that Marguerite had sought at Wellesley when she transferred here from Barnard—a sense of unity and female empowerment.

Wellesley President Ellen Fitz Pendleton offered a prescient remark to the celebrants—all of whom, with her, would face one of the school's worst crisis within hours: "It is a fine thing to be enthusiastic over victory, it is better to learn from defeat." The young women had no way of knowing they'd gather only once more in this space—that less than twenty-four hours from now they would be surrounded by flames.[179]

THE FIRE

By the time Marguerite Stitt began her senior year in the fall of 1913, Wellesley's student body, faculty, staff, and campus had expanded. College Hall, no longer the only building at Wellesley, was now one of twenty-three buildings, including nineteen other residence halls, two refectories, and one hospital. The founding class of 1875 had 314 students; by 1913, there were 1,480—843 of whom lived on campus, and 198 of them living in College Hall. Seventy-eight of those women—like Marguerite Stitt—were seniors. There were also 225 members of the staff, 72 of whom lived on campus—eighteen of them in College Hall.[180]

At 475 feet in length and five stories tall, College Hall was made of brick and Nova Scotia freestone; the Renaissance design, with its towers and pointed spires, was somewhat reminiscent of Bryn Mawr.[181] Its layout—a double cross—was intentional, a nod to Wellesley's emphasis on Christian education, designed by architect Hammatt Billings, whose original drawings appeared in *Uncle Tom's Cabin*.[182] The building also incorporated Gothic elements, including finials, arches, pinnacles and towers, all thought to add touches of delicacy and femininity.[183] Through the Main Entrance on College Hall's north side, twelve commanding exterior pillars preceded the doors to 'Center,' in which a five-story, glass roofed atrium—one hundred seventy feet long and sixty feet wide—made a spectacular first impression.

The thought of fire was not absent from the minds of students and faculty, as structural fires were a common and often deadly occurrence in those days. In 1903, a fire at Tennessee's Walden University, known as "the first institution organized for the education of colored people in the South," killed twelve women and injured fourteen more. There was no fire escape.[184] Then, in 1906 at Cornell University, a swift-moving fire fueled by "a terrific gale" raced through the stairwells of the Chi Psi fraternity house, cutting off all means of escape. The fire claimed the lives of four students and three firemen, leaving several severely—if not fatally—injured.[185]

News of these fires made an impression on the women of Wellesley, who, as a result, mobilized their own safety precautions. According to the April 6, 1914, *Wellesley College News*, "Fires were already prohibited in College Hall, and the strictest precautions were taken to avoid the danger of fire."[186] A small fire and gas leak in the chemical lab years earlier led to the lab being moved out of College Hall entirely, to the foot of Norumbega Hill.[187]

On May 10, 1912, the *Evansville Press* in Evansville, Indiana, ran a ten-line blurb, buried on page five, with the simple headline, "Wellesley Fire Drill," stating, "If there should ever be a real fire at Wellesley College the girls will be able to save themselves, as they are said to have a fire drill so perfect that the buildings can be emptied in two minutes. The grill [*sic*] is called at unexpected times so that they would not be alarmed if it was necessity that called them out."[188] And in 1913, the Wellesley student fire brigade insisted on mandatory, unannounced nighttime fire drills. Facing resistance from Wellesley's resident physician, Dr. Katharine Piatt Raymond, who suggested the drills risked panic and girls' jumping out windows, the students found an ally in Olive Davis, director of residence halls. Regular drills were led by Fire Brigade Captain Muriel Arthur of Detroit, class of 1915. The faculty and staff were exempt from these drills.[189]

The blaze in College Hall began at approximately five o'clock on the morning of March 17, 1914. The girls congregated in their assigned spaces in the Center for a formal roll call as student fire lieutenants counted off their squads, twenty girls each. Everyone observed the rule not to speak the word "fire."[190] One faculty member who lived in College Hall later told the *Wellesley College News*: "I heard no outcry; in fact, I heard no human voice about the hurrying feet, no lamentation, no questioning, nothing but the automatic quick march of people down the stairs, in the order in which they had been told to go."[191]

Tracy L'Engle, a Wellesley student at the time of the fire, writes, "As the girls came running down the steps, they were amazed (thinking this was a usual fire drill) to see great pieces of burning wood coming from the roof, falling into the center of the rotunda, crashing through the glass dome. . . . I remember, too, there was dead quiet—no hysteria as each girl took her place by one of the posts, her assigned place in former fire drills. Then I recall so vividly two girls bringing Miss Case down the last flight of stairs in her wheelchair."[192]

It was a credit to the discipline of more than 300 resolute women that they all made their way down the stairs and to the atrium in a few minutes. Only then did everyone realize that there was a ferocious fire, which started on the third floor and was about to consume the whole building. In the very few moments left, many girls calmly collected books and works of art before leaving College Hall for the last time.

Martha Hale Shackford, then an associate professor of English literature, recalled that the whole building:

> *"seemed to catch fire at once, and the blaze rushed downward and upward, leaping in the dull gray atmosphere of a foggy morning. With a terrific crash the roof fell in, and soon every window in the front of College Hall was filled with roaring flames, surging toward the east, framed in the dark red brick wall which served to accentuate the lurid glow that had seized and held a building almost one eighth of a mile long. The roar of devastating fury, the crackle of brands, the smell of burning wood and melting iron, filled the air, but almost no sound came from the human beings who saw the irrepressible blaze consume everything but the brick walls . . . Seen from the campus below, the burning east end of the building loomed up magnificent even in the havoc and desolation it was suffering."*[193]

Fire brigades from several towns came to fight the fire. Also on hand was a coterie of reporters who were only too happy to provide an added dose of sensation to the conflagration. Headlines in newspapers claimed that many of the girls panicked, and that they were running about in nightshirts. "Students saved by volunteers," cried one newspaper.[194] "Many girls hysterical," blared another.[195] A reporter exaggerated, "The girls were hurried or assisted out of the buildings by squads of rescuers, who ran through the halls, smashing in doors and awakening students." Readers were encouraged to imagine a scene of frantic, under-dressed females in a screaming, "wild scramble" to escape.[196]

"We had been thoroughly drilled for fires," one student recounted. "A Boston paper said there was a great deal of excitement, but this was not true. Everything occurred in such a calm, matter-of-fact way as we marched down the brightly-lighted halls and stairways. And as the roll was called . . . no one thought of getting excited."[197]

At 7 o'clock that morning, College Hall was still burning. As some girls scribbled telegrams and letters home, others sat upon couches and chairs they helped to save, watching the final stages of the destruction. One letter reads, "The woodwork in the College Hall Library was still burning when I got there, but the building was already as far removed from today as any ruin of Rome . . . majestic, hoary, infinitely dignified and touching."[198]

Firefighters attempted to pump water from Lake Waban directly into College Hall, rushing from caved-in lecture halls to rooms filled with rows of typewriters aflame. Their efforts seemed no match for the raging fire. Although the blaze would continue to smolder for days, the gravity of the situation had yet to hit the campus, nor could a full tally of the loss be reached for weeks. Soon enough, however, the sum would appear of all that College Hall gave up to the flames, including administrative offices and records, archives, academic departments, the cashier's office, telephone and telegraph facilities, the school post office, twenty-eight lecture rooms and classrooms, laboratories, study halls, and residence rooms for more than 200 students and members of the faculty. College records were considered, by many, the greatest loss. While the dean's papers were saved, many others, including grades, conduct of work, research materials, and records of historic significance were destroyed.

In the morning, Marguerite likely walked with her fellow students toward the campus chapel, joining the faculty and staff in silence, stunned and exhausted.[199] "The service," one alumna later wrote, "was perhaps the most impressive ever held at Wellesley."[200] Members of the choir—some having just survived the fire—walked up the center aisle singing "O God Our Help In Ages Past," followed by an address by President Pendleton to her student body. Perfectly composed, chin held high, Pendleton wore robes and an expression of undeniable calm while reading from the Bible and never once shedding a tear. Students "were crowded into the chapel, feeling the power of Wellesley more than ever before. The night's disaster, like the electric spark in a chemical experiment, had changed us from a mere mixture of diverse elements into one indivisible body."[201]

Summing up her feelings about the tragedy she and her Wellesley sisters survived, Marguerite wrote, "That fire destroyed the major physical and academic center of the college—but not its heart and courage."[202]

It goes, perhaps, without argument that Wellesley's catastrophic fire ignited in its student body the very sense of lifelong unity Marguerite sought but could not find at Barnard. The class of 1914's bond was unlike any other, a sisterhood seared for life into the hearts of young women who'd faced their fears and stepped into their futures—together as survivors.

One member of the faculty wrote: "I saw expressions on faces that day which will go with me to my grave, of pure human comradeliness [*sic*], of an almost divine compassionateness and oneness of everybody with everybody else. We stood in that gray light of early morning as if we were disembodied spirits, head and heart at their highest and purest. The burning of College Hall will always bear supreme witness to the worth of college discipline and college unity."[203] This was the Wellesley way.

Education at Wellesley, Marguerite said, "went far beyond the academic; we learned to live with our fellows, with our teachers, with ourselves. The outlook was broad, the vision high, as our sights were raised to help us become useful citizens in an unfolding world.[204]

"Finally," she wrote, as "a government official said: 'Wellesley? In every crisis I look for a Wellesley girl. They are the only ones I know who so combine a sense of personal responsibility with an indomitable faith that miracles can still be wrought!' "[205]

STEPPING INTO A MORE CROWDED WORLD

Commencement came later that spring. It was an understandably emotional one for everyone under the circumstances, and in the days leading up to it, sentiments were deepened by Wellesley leaders who declaimed on the expectations of the graduates. Specifically, they were encouraged to anticipate bright and useful futures because of the lessons they learned from Wellesley. They were also reminded of their "inevitable element of detachment from the church" which they'd presumably experienced during college life—and were urged to embrace the church after graduation because, as the *Wellesley College News* reported one educator to proclaim, "Membership in the church is a universal obligation which cannot be shirked without shame."[206]

There was also, at that time, a contrary view of life after Wellesley. It was outlined in an essay submitted to the *Wellesley College News* by its former editor-in-chief and a recent graduate, published a few days before commencement that year. Entitled "Of Misfits, Informally Observed," its author Kate Parsons, class of 1911, did not intend to discourage. But neither did she mind providing a touch of realism for those about to go out in the world.

"The majority, the big, ignorant, unthinking public," Parsons wrote, "does not like the college girl." Her premise was that graduates hoping to find any position other than that of a teacher would find the going very rough indeed.[207]

Parsons wrote, "The public does not concern itself over much with the college girl who marries, except to fancy, quite wrongly, that she doesn't. It is concerning those girls, fifty per cent of them each year in the output of the eastern colleges, who enter any of the professions or who go into business, that the public has a vast number of uncomplimentary remarks to make." And she spoke of the 25 percent of Wellesley graduates who enter occupations beyond teaching. "Get the story of some persistent soul who has been hammering away at the stone wall which confronts the girl who refuses to slip through the chink of pedagogy. She will tell you in very plain terms how much the public wants the college graduate." Perhaps the most damning of her words were these: "Go, for instance, to the Intercollegiate Bureau of Occupations here in New York City, which places college graduates in occupations other than the pedagogical ones. Raw from college—and raw is the word—there is practically no hope of a position for you."[208]

The tone of the essay could not have encouraged Marguerite, even though her record was superlative. She was a Durant Scholar, the highest honor afforded Wellesley women, as well as a Phi Beta Kappa, president of the Debate Club, and a member of the Zeta Alpha society house. She must have known without reading Parsons' piece that finding a place outside the confines of the college might be tough. In fact, she was able to put off leaving Wellesley for at least a year when she was offered a position as a lecturer in biblical history at the college.[209] She would be surrounded by supportive Wellesleyans, teaching a familiar subject she loved.

That summer, before she began teaching at Wellesley, Marguerite traveled to Europe with her family. This had always been enjoyable for her, but the atmosphere this time was different and heavier with the Great War in its doleful first stages. Their passage home from Liverpool took nine days on the SS *Celtic* (no doubt traveling in first class, as they regularly did), arriving in New York on August 15, 1914—just in time for Marguerite to return to Wellesley to prepare materials for her students.[210] Especially after the fire and especially after Europe, the safety of the campus likely consoled her. She would be with friends whom she valued and who valued her. Among the pupils in her biblical history class was a sophomore, Mayling Soong, daughter of a wealthy Chinese merchant. Mayling was elegant and intelligent and she and Marguerite struck up a lifelong friendship. The friendship would continue over the years, partly because of their mutual affinity, largely because they both fell into public careers. Mayling became Madame Chiang Kai-Shek, the First Lady of the Republic of China.

In the summer of 1915 Marguerite served as her father's emissary during the Panama-Pacific International Exposition, the San Francisco world's fair. The fair was largely an opportunity to show the world that San Francisco had recovered from the earthquake of 1906; it was also to celebrate the opening of the Panama Canal, and more broadly the closer relations that the American West might have with the East moving forward. The New England Shoe and Leather Association, of which William Stitt was a powerful member, had an exhibit at the fair, and one demonstration was of long-distance telephone. It was reported under a subtitle, "Greetings Exchanged Over the Telephone by Leading Shoe and Leather Men," that Marguerite was one of several people who spoke to association members in Boston, 3,500 miles away, on a first-of-its kind line installed by the New England and American Telephone Company for the event—and that her exchange with a twenty-two-month-old drew the historic event's greatest applause.[211] The world was changing, and Marguerite was an active participant.

Marguerite's next move was back to Morningside Heights in New York City, which she had left when she transferred from Barnard to Wellesley. She was now enrolled in Columbia University's Faculty of Political Science, Philosophy, and Pure Science (currently known as the Graduate School of Arts and Sciences). Officially, Marguerite was a student of the Faculty of Political Science, but also a student in the Department of Economics and Social Science. At the time, "political science" was a catch-all for social science and included studies in economics, history, mathematical statistics, public law and government, and sociology. Marguerite focused her coursework in sociology and economics in her efforts toward a master's degree in "political economy." The title of her thesis, "The Social Function of Certain Metropolitan Journals," indicated that her interests were broad and worldly, and that she was determined to exercise her own impact on the public.[212] During this time, Marguerite also served as Wellesley's corresponding secretary and alumnae councilor for the New York Wellesley Club, the first of many alumnae positions she would hold.[213]

With a master's degree in hand, Marguerite's first position in 1917 might not have been the employment opportunity she was looking for, but she was needed to administer psychological testing to individuals about to enter the military. As was common in times of war, women held positions that otherwise might not have been open to them.[214] That job ended after what was probably a few months, at which point she landed with the State Charities Aid Association of New York. It had her giving psychological examinations to children who were under the supervision of the Child Placing Agency, which would have included orphans.[215]

She seemed a promising young psychologist, as evidenced by having worked with Dr. William Healy, a pioneer in child psychology and at this time named head of the Juvenile Psychopathic Institute in Chicago, the country's first child guidance clinic.[216] Healy's work included Progressive Era efforts connected with reforms in juvenile justice, with Jane Addams's Hull House, and with the social work movement at large. His 1915 book *The Individual Delinquent*, considered a seminal work in the fields of psychology and criminal justice, is described by the Illinois Council of Child and Adolescent Psychiatry as "a compendium of social and environmental, psychological, and medical characteristics found in the youths he evaluated."[217] Healy lectured far and wide in this period, so it was natural for Marguerite to fall into his orbit. In 1912, Healy returned to Harvard, his alma mater, to lead a two-week seminar. The sessions were well attended, and if Marguerite, then at Wellesley, did not attend the Cambridge sessions, it is reliably certain that she was influenced by Healy.

Certainly, Healy and his multidimensional perspective were on Marguerite's mind before she left Wellesley in 1914. It is likely that Marguerite visited Healy's institute in Chicago, where the young Wellesley alumna had many friends. At any rate, it was in Chicago where she had an even more fateful meeting, that with her future husband.

CHICAGO AND MARRIAGE

Marguerite's sister had been married in an elaborate church wedding in New York in 1914.[218] By now, Marguerite's classmates were being seriously courted, which must have tended to break down her ambivalence on the subject of marriage and what it would do to her career plans. But the ambivalence was there as Wellesley women were well aware of the dangers of "femininity," of which marriage was a convention. An essayist in the *Wellesley College News* wrote around this time, "We college women are condescendingly amused or bored by [femininity] when we read about it, and then, straight away, go and show how much of it we possess."[219] The writer insisted that "the mind so largely occupied with essentially feminine activities is a narrow mind."[220]

There is no evidence that Marguerite seriously dated men while in college or graduate school. But then, probably in 1916, she met Ralph Church, lawyer and candidate for political office. As indicated in an article in the *Chicago Examiner*, the pair met at the home of Chicago alderman Oliver L. Watson, a real estate man who had gotten into politics. Like Ralph, Watson was from Vermilion County, Illinois, and they were both Republicans, so Ralph's acquaintanceship with him is perhaps no surprise. Posterity has not given credit to whomever brought Marguerite to the Watsons', though there were plenty of contacts who might have introduced them. "I was interested immediately," Marguerite later said. "He was such an earnest young man."[221] And even later, speaking of Ralph fondly in 1978, Marguerite described him as "a very just man."[222]

While it's clear she devoted her life to her husband and her family, navigating her own career as a consulting psychologist to act as her husband's political partner, Marguerite's family friend and eventual congressional secretary, Una Corley Groves, would say this of the union between the posh, New York socialite and the downstate Illinoisan: "Women have very funny attractions. She knew that she could run him with her money and his position in life . . . that was her ride to wherever she could go."[223]

While Groves' recollection may stand in sharp contrast to others, her years spent working in the Churches' homes in Evanston and Washington, DC, gave her, perhaps, a deeper perspective on a marriage many seemed to see as ideal. Marguerite, known as an independent thinker, was, as one reporter wrote, "outwardly calm, cool and collected" and had "the inner fire of zealot in her convictions."[224] While supporting her husband's political dreams, was Marguerite simultaneously carving her own path? While the couple built an unquestionably successful political partnership, it's not unreasonable to wonder about their personal dynamics.

In 1917, Marguerite finished her graduate studies, the same year Ralph entered the Illinois legislature and the same year Jeannette Rankin of Montana became the first woman elected to the US House of Representatives. Marguerite drew upon her undergraduate studies in psychology and took employment with the State Charities Aid Association in New York, administering psychological evaluations and exams to children.[225] It would be thirty-three years until Marguerite followed in the pioneering footsteps of Rankin – who had at one time been a social worker herself—to Washington as Representative Marguerite Stitt Church. Also in 1917, in New York, Marguerite and her parents prepared to move into the twelve-story, brick, stone, and terra cotta Renaissance Revival her parents now owned, called The Kelmscott, at 316 W. 79th Street. By contrast, Ralph now lived in a small, humble apartment at 1411 Chicago Avenue, in Evanston.

For as much as their two busy schedules would allow—Ralph's as an attorney and newly elected legislator, Marguerite's as a graduate student and alumni counselor—they seem to have enjoyed a two-year, long-distance courtship. Between January and March of 1918 alone, Ralph visited Marguerite in New

York on four separate occasions, coordinating his visits with side trips to Washington, DC, in his ongoing (but futile) attempts to enter the military.[226]

If the courtship seemed long, it was characteristic of Marguerite's deliberative and independent nature. It squared with Ralph Church as well. He was deliberative too, and one could even say indecisive. The latter quality was expressed in his political life whenever he had a big move to make, from the state legislature to Congress, for example. If he was truly hesitant on the subject of marriage, it might have inspired the planting of a mysterious article in the Chicago Tribune, which falsely reported in November 1916 that he had secretly traveled to upstate New York to marry a fictitious ingénue.[227] Friends who may have pranked him with this piece must have wondered how long it would take for a real fiancée to materialize. Ralph, then a legislator-elect, insisted that the elopement story was a sham, and that as a newly elected state representative he was married to the State of Illinois for the time being.[228] That was hardly romantic of him, but not an exaggeration. Marguerite was silent on this matter. Whether or not Marguerite Stitt and Ralph Church knew each other at the end of 1916, or had been engaged in 1917, they kept their friends in suspense until 1918.

The wedding announcement, featured in the *Wellesley College News* on April 11, 1918, also appeared in papers across the country and described Marguerite's active involvement in "club movements" such as the New York Wellesley Club and the Women's University Club. In the *Chicago Examiner*, the *Washington Post*, the *Chicago Tribune*, and even the *Dispatch* of Moline, Illinois, her socialite credentials were listed, but no mention was made of her professional accomplishments.[229]

Why wasn't her employment included in the announcements? While professional women existed, they were still outliers; it was hardly uncommon for a woman to downplay her own career in deference to their husband's, and Marguerite walked a fine line between established and progressive beliefs about a woman's role in society. For Una Corley Groves, who served as Marguerite's congressional secretary, this sentiment held true almost seven decades after she'd worked for the representative: "Men don't like strong women," Groves, in her mid-90s, said in 2018. "They're threatening."[230]

Twenty-six-year-old Marguerite and thirty-five-year-old Ralph were married in a simple ceremony at her parents' New York apartment on December 21, 1918. Press reports, while not breathless, were workmanlike in reporting the marriage of an Upper West Side girl to a young politico from Illinois. Marguerite's brother-in-law, a prominent minister, co-officiated at the wedding. The attendants included Ralph's best man, Anderson Pace of Chicago and New York, as well as Marguerite's five bridesmaids: matron of honor and sister Edna Stitt Robinson; cousin Elsie Leal Stitt; and three of Marguerite's sisters from the Zeta Alpha society house—Miriam Gladys Dowley, Gertrude Folger, and Lydia-Belle Kuehnle – the last of whom had been, with Marguerite, a member of Wellesley's Debating Club.[231] Gladys and Lydia had, with Marguerite, escaped the College Hall fire of 1914.[232]

A small reception followed the wedding. The *New York Times* wedding announcement said that the couple would honeymoon for two weeks in the south, but a later report suggested that any trip south was a short one and secondary to a more pressing honeymoon that the newlyweds had in Boston.[233] Ralph, ever the eager public official, used their honeymoon to talk to Massachusetts officials who had been involved in the recent rewriting of their state constitution. Illinois was contemplating something along the same lines. This was Ralph's idea of pleasure and, it seems, Marguerite's as well—talking to political types on Beacon Hill. Perhaps this was less romantic than Marguerite's friends might have expected. But if anyone complained, it was not registered by either Mr. or Mrs. Church, both of whom became consummate politicians in the decades to come.

There is not a lot of public comment from Ralph or Marguerite on each other, but it is clear that the two cared for each other deeply. Many years in the future, Marguerite would make a public plea that she "would give anything to get back a ship's clock which was stolen from her home," as it belonged to Ralph and was "the only possession he highly prized that she had to remember him by."[234]

Considering Marguerite's upbringing, it is perhaps surprising to hear Groves look back today and say, "They were not a glamorous family." As Groves recalls, "They were gracious and wonderful, but they were not fancy."[235] Speaking of Ralph in particular, Groves says, "He was a very common man type. Not 'highfallutin,' and Marguerite kept him even."[236] Though Ralph, born and bred in the Midwest, had arguably married "up," his wife downplayed chatter of her own privileged background and described the couple as simple, thrifty, hardworking, scrupulous savers.[237] Still, the Churches eventually bought a home in Evanston that overlooked Lake Michigan, and travelled internationally with their children, signaling a life—if not glamorous, then—a far cry from middle class.

CHAPTER SIX

RALPH CHURCH IN SPRINGFIELD

EVANSTON SENT RALPH CHURCH TO Springfield in 1917, and if he went with marching orders, at the top of the list was to get laws passed that would prevent the sale of alcohol. Evanston, founded by strict Methodists, was the longtime epicenter of the sobriety cause as the national headquarters of the Women's Christian Temperance Union. Founded in 1874, the WCTU was still a very active voice against alcohol. By the time Church was elected, the Anti-Saloon League was also a political force and had solid support in Evanston, where nary a drop of alcohol had ever been legally sold. There was little room for dissent on this subject in most of Church's Sixth District.

The new representative executed his mandate quickly. Within a month of taking his seat in the House, Church proposed a so-called "residence district" bill, which would grant areas as small as voting precincts the option of banning the sale of alcohol. The bill did not make it through, but it marked Church as a temperance vote, and a proactive one at that.[238]

Young Church was on a political bandwagon. In 1917, full-blown Prohibition was more than two years away. But the politics that led to the Eighteenth Amendment and the Volstead Act seemed already inevitable. The Illinois legislature was turning out half-measures—outlawing liquor sales on Sundays, for example, or preventing consumption on trains and near state universities. Ralph Church's residence district bill was buried by

Thompsonite Republicans, mostly from Chicago, who had little patience for the drys in their own party or any other. But the Prohibition cause was on the upswing, as were the political prospects of those elected on its platform.

Later that year, an outright ban on alcohol in Illinois came before the legislature. It got through the Senate but not the House—a temporary setback, as it turned out, but one that showed how complicated the politics were. The temperance issue did not line up as Democrat versus Republican. Some saw it as urban (wet) against rural (dry), and others as immigrant (wet) against American-born (dry). It was enough to flummox all but the most steadfast politician, or one blessed with a steadfast constituency like Evanston which, happily for Church, was home to mostly native-born Protestants who, if they wished to imbibe, were discreet enough to do it at home.

CHURCH PUMPS PROHIBITION

Ralph and Marguerite were quickly settled in two homes as newlyweds. In Evanston they held an apartment in an eighteen-unit, three-story brick building, sunny enough with a single projecting bay, in a new complex on Judson.[239] And in Springfield they rented a place within walking distance of the Capitol.

In 1920, Ralph and Marguerite responded to the questions of a US Census worker, who listed Ralph as an "Attorney" and Marguerite a "Psychologist" under *Trade/Profession/Particular Kind of Work*. Under the column heading *Industry, Establishment or Business In Which At Work*, Marguerite responded "At Home," whereas Ralph responded "Practicing Law." As for *Employer, Salary, Wage Worker or Working On Own Account*, Marguerite and Ralph both indicated they were self-employed.[240]

Ralph dove into his work at the beginning of the legislative session while Marguerite began setting up the homes, writing thank you notes after the wedding, and in one detail sent off a postcard to Wellesley. It indicated that she had a married name, Mrs. Ralph E. Church, and a new address, which she listed as 1006 S. Second Street, Springfield, Illinois. Between the two homes she settled in, slowly phasing out her career as a psychologist and beginning a new one—a career which she, at least while Ralph was alive, said she cherished: that of partner to her husband, the legislator. And yet, though outward appearances may suggest she abandoned her own interests for her husband's, history has proven this was anything but the case. Marguerite, ever strategic and forward thinking, followed her heart—and her long-established interests in politics, economics and sociology—thereby preparing herself for the congressional role she would ultimately hold.

As for Ralph, it was a momentous year in the legislature. On January 14, 1919, the Illinois legislature ratified the Eighteenth Amendment, which banned the manufacture and sale of liquor in the United States. Nebraska did the same two days later and became the thirty-sixth state to ratify, making Prohibition the law of the land. That wasn't the end, however, as state legislatures everywhere remained busy with enabling bills, enforcement measures, and other questions that required votes. Prohibition remained a gnarly issue for many politicians on both sides of the aisle. But for Ralph Church it was not complicated at all, and he did what he could to become a leader of the drys in his legislature and his state.

Church's political standing in Evanston was hardly threatened by Chicago Republicans such as Mayor Thompson and his allies, who remained as wet as wet could be. They were for lax enforcement of alcohol laws, and in time they would be in almost overt collusion with the bootleggers of organized crime. They sympathized with immigrants whose consumption of beer and spirits was outlawed. Some legislators sided with Thompson and company; others temporized in districts where Prohibition was unpopular. But not Church, who was always eager to identify himself as drier than dry. It happened frequently as state laws were passed to uphold the new amendment. And it happened emphatically in 1921 when the new governor, Len Small, a Thompson protégé if not puppet, attempted to cut the appropriation of Attorney General Edward J. Brundage. Because Brundage was the state official directly responsible for alcohol enforcement, Small's move, which benefited the underground liquor business which was a Thompson client, forced many in Springfield to take a stand.

First on his feet was Church, who jumped at the chance to support Brundage's challenge to the governor. "Church," said the *Chicago Tribune*, "cancelled a month's vacation at Bayshore, L.I. and will arrive in Chicago on Wednesday to offer his services free to Mr. Brundage." Like many controversies in state government, this one began rancorously and ended without commensurate climax. Brundage's office continued largely as before. But it marked Church, by now in his third term, as a representative unafraid of taking a stand against "big dogs," even if Governor Len Small usually lived up to his name.[241]

Church was similarly enthusiastic when it came to supporting women's suffrage. The Nineteenth Amendment, granting women the right to vote in all elections and in all jurisdictions, came before the Illinois legislature in June of 1919. Just days prior, Congress passed what was informally called the Anthony Amendment (for suffrage pioneer Susan B. Anthony) and called on the states to ratify it in their legislatures. Illinois made quick work of this, passing it through both houses within a week. Church's vote was an enthusiastic aye. Suffrage was a key position of the Women's Christian Temperance Union, and also of the Evanston Woman's Club, which Marguerite would join in 1922.[242]

It remains unclear if Marguerite was in Chicago for any part of the fifty-first convention of the American National Suffrage association—February 12-18, 1920—as she was newly expecting the couple's first child, Ralph Jr. However, she surely read about the group's president, Carrie Chapman Catt, telling the *Chicago Daily Tribune*, "I hope this will be our last convention. It may be, for the dreams of woman suffrage are about to be realized. I think it will be only a short time until an amendment will be added to the national constitution giving the right of suffrage to all women. For fifty years we have been fighting for the rewards we are now reaping and our full reward is in sight."[243] In August of that year, when Tennessee became the thirty-sixth state to ratify, the Nineteenth Amendment became law.[244]

WORKING THE DISTRICT

Church's overall conservative credentials were happily matched to his district, but he was not a complacent politician. He knew there would always be others who would covet his seat, so the representative was assiduous in knowing what was going on in his district. This meant all of the district, which extended into Chicago and the Rogers Park community, where in the early '20s a tenants' movement was brewing. Rogers Park was predominantly if not entirely white and distinctly middle class, where the three- and six-flats that lined many of its streets were occupied by white collar workers. These renters were generally well-off, but they were feeling the pinch of the post-World War I economy of inflation and high prices. While blue-collar workers had successful unions and the wealthy had their securities, there was a quiet movement, a "middle-class union" as some called it, to protest against high prices for food and clothing and to represent tenants' grievances—rent gouging and less than pristine living conditions—against landlords.[245]

Just south of Evanston, across the Chicago border, it was not that rents in Rogers Park were necessarily higher than elsewhere, but the combination of tough landlords and persistent community organizers gave rise to the Rogers Park Tenants' Protective Association, which pushed new state laws to protect their interests. The leaders of the organization knew who their legislative representatives were and they got them to come to meetings. It was a potentially controversial issue, as landlords were voters too, but in the end the tenants outnumbered them. They were, moreover, convincing upholders of conservative values. "They feel that they are fighting for the preservation of the home, for a wholesome community, in which to bring up their children," the association's president said of his members. Church helped pass a law against "rent profiteering" the following year, and won a loyal voter base in Rogers Park, more diverse demographically than Evanston, that supported him for years to come.[246]

So, too, did the Black population of Church's district encounter hardship. Though Black residents were "once scattered in clusters throughout town, [they] were systematically forced west. Drawn up by developers or neighborhood associations and defined as a network of agreements between neighbors, covenants prohibited them from buying or renting in white neighborhoods."[247]

In July of 1919, as the Churches settled into their first year in the city by the lake, many Black Chicagoans—already facing unconscionable discrimination, a tight labor market, and high unemployment—were pushed to the brink during a national uprising, known as Red Summer, which broke out on Sunday, July 27, 1919, after a white Chicagoan killed a young Black swimmer who accidentally drifted across a rope set by police into a section of Lake Michigan water designated for whites only. Over a period of ten months, more than 250 Black citizens were killed in at least twenty-five outbreaks of racially motivated violence throughout the US.

Black Chicagoans fled to the safety of the suburbs—including Evanston. Evanston was largely segregated, with Black residents mostly on the west side of town, but they tended to vote with white Evanston, as they remained in this period traditionally Republican. Though segregation drew Ralph and Marguerite and Black constituents to different churches, hospitals, recreation centers, restaurants, and clubs, it seems the Churches and a large majority of Black Evanston came together in their loyalty to the party of Abraham Lincoln. The *Chicago Defender*, one of the strongest Black dailies in the nation, continued to praise the party's "sane, businesslike and humane domestic policy" and its "conservative progressivism," and stated that it "saved the Union, rid America of the blight of slavery, and gave to the Constitution the war amendments that made slaves citizens."[248]

While being a Republican could mean walking a political tightrope, Church could be thankful that his name was connected mostly with the humdrum of state government. He rarely found himself caught up in the dramas of shifting alliances, scandalous revelations, and occasional indictments that most people assumed was standard in Springfield, and not least among the GOP. He garnered some public notice beyond his own district with a bill that proposed special punishments for auto theft. Stealing cars was "a basic crime leading directly or indirectly to many others," as a local newspaper in Kinmundy, Illinois, explained Church's reasoning.[249] While neither the law nor Church attained widespread acclamation for this achievement, it moved the legislator into a slightly more prominent category. Another measure that he championed was a bill to appropriate $30,000 (equivalent to $514,569 in 2023) for a mechanical system of voting in the houses of the legislature. Efficiency was a trait that Ralph Church believed in deeply, and he hoped that it might distinguish him from his colleagues in the House. The electronic system, he said, might eliminate long roll calls and even shenanigans that could be committed in the process of voice votes. Alas, efficiency in governance did not find a following in Springfield. The United Press wrote that Church's system might work *too* fast, that a vote "would be over before many of the members found out what was being considered."[250] In any case, the measure got little traction among legislators, and even less among voters, and was unsuccessful. Voice votes continued in the Capitol.

It was something of a surprise when Church announced that he would run for speaker of the House of Representatives in 1923. This seemed like a long shot, as Gotthard Dahlberg of Chicago, a member of the Thompson Republican machine, was the current speaker and was running again. But now, it appeared Dahlberg's main supporters were weakened. Thompson had been accused in a variety of kickback schemes, long the mayor's stock-in-trade but only now uncovered. And Governor Small had been indicted for malfeasance when he was state treasurer. Enter Ralph Church with the reasonable pitch that he could make the legislature more efficient, if not substantially more honest. "The closing days of our last session were well-nigh disgraceful," he told the *Tribune*. He described bills rushed through at a rate that made careful consideration impossible, pointing out that this was misrule by any standard. "If elected speaker I should conduct that office in a way that adjournment in less than three months instead of six months would be possible."[251] If a shorter session sounded good to family men like Church, it sounded less good to old pols who enjoyed the boys' club that was Springfield in these years (and in years to come). Mr. Church from Heavenston was realistic enough to expect no more than a few votes by the time the voting began, which is what he got in the course of the five ballots necessary to elect a dripping wet David Shanahan of Bridgeport in Chicago.[252]

A POLITICAL HELPMATE

Throughout these legislative episodes, Marguerite may have been described as the period's perfect political wife. She kept her distance from reporters about the minutiae of lawmaking. Her views on political matters were not a matter of public record. But she spoke frequently and convincingly to groups large and small. She supported the family business, which was politics, and as a political wife, she also dealt in social graces. She became a well-regarded participant in events where community affairs overlapped with what from the outside would be regarded as high society. In a period when charity events were the work of the wives of prominent men, Marguerite was often present. The Illinois Children's Home and Aid Society was just one such important organization. Marguerite's name appeared as a committee member for its charity balls, and she worked to steer the group as a member of its Board of Directors. This was along with names such as Dawes, Burnham, Hines, and others that made Evanston one of Chicago's most powerful enclaves.[253]

Philanthropic ties were galvanized by relationships of other kinds. By February of 1919, the newlyweds had joined Evanston's eight-year old First United Methodist Church.[254] The church would be an easy eight-block walk from their apartment and, eventually, two blocks from the home they would buy in 1925.[255]

By 1929, it was called the First United Methodist Church of Evanston, and Marguerite's devotion to its future was clear, as reported in the June 2 *Chicago Tribune* that year. The question of resituating the church had come before the congregation, and Marguerite, one of several board members, had a decision to make. The building, at the corner of Hinman Avenue and Church Street, had significantly increased in value. A donor had offered $265,000.00 ($4.8

million in 2023) as incentive to move, though the cost to establish a new site was estimated at $1.3 million ($23.3 million in 2023). The paper, describing Marguerite as "Mrs. Ralph Church, wife of the Illinois state representative and the dissenting board member," didn't report what she actually said, though her sense of fiscal conservatism was no doubt on display, since the decision was made not to move the church, which remains today at the same location. However, it seems Marguerite paid a price—albeit in good fun—for speaking out. According to the paper, Marguerite "lost a $25 ($449 in 2023) bet with her husband when she told the assemblage why she had voted no." As noted by the *Tribune*, "She said before she left home that evening that she wouldn't talk." Therefore, the reporter quipped, "her ten minute speech cost her $2.50 ($45 in 2023) a minute."[256] As such a buttoned-up and formal couple, one can only imagine the lighthearted—even playful—discussion that led to this badinage.

The Churches' Evanston credentials were affirmed in 1925 when they purchased a prominent Victorian house on Sheridan Road, at the corner of Church Street. It was a significant step up from their apartment on Haven Street—a large Queen Anne designed by the not-insignificant architects Baumann and Cady in 1889 for a Mr. Brown.[257]

For the Churches, more room was going to be important, as their first son Ralph had been born in 1920, and second son William in 1924. A daughter, Marjory, would come in 1929. The house had improvements over the years, most importantly a garage in back, and a log cabin in the yard which came when the boys were old enough to play in it. Politically, it was a good house, as it had a veranda which might well have made Ralph think of William McKinley's "front porch campaign" for the presidency, when the voters and the press came to his Ohio home to hear the candidate speak from the porch. Not that Church had open pretensions to a career in high office, but in later years he spent as much time as possible on the front porch and invited constituents to sit down with him and discuss their concerns.

The Churches were house-proud to the extent that they contracted for some significant renovations shortly after moving in, not least to its exterior, which was transformed from an old-fashioned wood-frame design to a more stately Tudor profile with exposed timber beams and plaster work. This was a fashionable approach to renovating something from the nineteenth century into a more modern design. For example, another nearby Baumann and Cady Queen Anne, the home of Vice President Charles Dawes' brother Rufus, was converted radically into an English Tudor by the prominent architect Ernest A. Mayo. (The house is now the Evans Center of Northwestern University.)[258] The Church conversion was less elaborate and not signed by an architect, but their builder did a fine job with a light touch. Also at this time, the family had their address at the corner changed from 1640 Sheridan Road to 300 Church. This was hardly to fool the world into thinking the Church family reached farther back in Evanston than it did, though it allowed them to say they were the Churches of Church Street.

THE CHURCH IDENTITY

Marguerite's interest in public affairs came out in her signature, understated ways. During the 1920 Republican National Convention in Chicago, for example, she volunteered as a hostess at the hospitality suite for Governor Frank Orren Lowden, a leading candidate for the presidential nomination that year. Marguerite's association with Lowden that year marked her, if anything, as a woman of good taste, as Lowden was considered an elegant and principled candidate compared to the others. It also helped establish her, and more pointedly her husband, as antagonistic to the buffoonish Thompson, Lowden's nemesis who would do anything to derail the governor's chance for the White House.[259]

Beyond Marguerite's seemingly genteel foray with Governor Lowden, she was seen as slightly more forward that same year as a supporter in the Republican primary of David F. Matchett for state's attorney. Marguerite's support of Matchett came during a period of changing perceptions of gender roles, making way for new and evolving legislative opportunities for women.[260] A full-page advertisement taken out by the campaign to address the "Republican Women Voters of Cook County" explained that Matchett represented the "Harmony Republican Organization," and was running against Robert E. Crowe of the Thompson machine. The ad, to which "Mrs. Ralph E. Church, Evanston" signed her name, stressed Machett's virtues. It said nothing of Crowe's tolerance of, if not complicity with, crime bosses. Appropriately, it appealed to the voters' sense of "high civic morality" to put Matchett in office.[261] Nevertheless, Crowe, whose political-machine ties were well known, won. According to Matthew Wasniewski, historian of the US House of Representatives, this was a period of changing perceptions of gender roles making way for new and evolving legislative opportunities for women. Citing Irwin Gertzog's *Congressional Women: Their Recruitment, Integration, and Behavior*, Wasniewski writes of the first two generations of women in Congress (1917–1934 and 1935–1954) who "tried to integrate themselves as knowledgeable, 'professional' insiders." So, too, it seems, did Marguerite—albeit with a smaller, Midwest audience.[262]

For most of the period of Ralph's eight terms in the Illinois legislature, what was known about Marguerite did not go beyond the assumption that she, and presumably her husband, belonged to a stately upper middle class, and that they had a more than passing acquaintanceship with Chicago's aristocracy of meatpackers and lumber merchants made good. Like the Swifts, Armours, and Hineses, the Churches themselves, not just their organizations, became a subject of interest to the people who wrote and read the society pages. When the family summered in Europe in 1927, for example, the trip was duly noted, and mention was made that Rep. Church would be joining the family across the pond only when the legislative session was completed. This emphasized his dedication to duty, a frequent theme. It was also reported that Mr. and Mrs. James Condon would be renting the Church home in the family's absence that summer.[263] Mr. Condon was a Chicago lawyer with political connections, and Mrs. Condon received frequent mention in the society pages herself.

None of this social reportage would be of much interest except for the fact that the Churches understood that one's name in the paper—outside of scandal, at any rate—was almost always positive. Name recognition meant votes. This may have been at the front of their minds when the Church campaign alerted the *Tribune* that the representative had his lamb's wool overcoat stolen while he was riding on the Northwestern commuter train. "Watch your overcoat . . . thieves are busy," was their message.[264]

Along the same lines, when the couple made a winter visit to Florida earlier in 1927, the *Palm Beach Post* noted their arrival: "Senator Ralph E. Church, who is prominent in the Illinois legislature and has been active in Middle Western politics for many years, has arrived from Evanston, Ill, for a winter visit in Palm Beach with Mrs. Church and is a guest at the Everglades Inn."[265] One can imagine Marguerite or one of her friends having made contact with the newspaper to ensure a mention, no matter how small. One can equally imagine Ralph discussing Illinois politics with the local scribe at such length that the reporter surrendered to the assumption that the "Senator" was prominent among Illinois lawmakers.

In her 1967 address to the Evanston Historical Society, Marguerite shared a bemusing story illustrating not only her husband's efforts to keep his name "relevant" in political spheres—but also a behind-the-scenes look at some family dynamics. In August 1924, Marguerite had been visiting her mother on Long Island. "I received a very succinct telegram from my spouse saying, 'Please wire exact location of best lace tablecloths,'" she said. "I'm sure you can all wonder what a wife would think when wondering what her husband was going to do with her best lace tablecloths."

Marguerite continued, "And though we didn't telephone easily in those days, I telephoned home and Ralph said, 'Now dear, relax, you don't have to come home. You know they are having a big celebration. They are going to notify [Evanston's] Mr. [Charles] Dawes of his nomination [for US vice president], and I've sent a letter to every member of the Illinois Senate and House in Springfield, telling them to make our house their home.'"[266]

"Well," Marguerite told the crowd in 1967, "I came home, and some of you who are here, I know one person, helped bring in molded fruit salads, because every friend I had, had to pitch in and help. [Our Evanston] house had been closed for two months, but it was a great day . . ."[267]

AVOIDING POLITICAL MUD

By 1930, Ralph's position was perhaps not lofty, but he could be pleased that it was stable. The Great Depression was taking its toll on many people of every class, except of course legislators, who got their regular pay. Then something happened that appeared to change things: Marguerite's father, William Stitt, died of a heart attack on a train to North Carolina, where he and his wife were visiting friends. A prominent obituary in the *New York Times* remembered him as a glove manufacturer, director of insurance companies, and a leader in church and charity work.[268]

Recorded more discreetly was the fact that he left an estate valued at $1.4 million ($25.7 million in 2023), half inherited by his wife and a quarter by each daughter.[269] Between 1930 and 1932, Marguerite and her sister Edna each inherited property with a value of approximately $350,00.00, or $6.5 million in 2023.[270] Even if its cause was tragic, this was a welcomed bequest to the Churches, who, it turned out, were not the vastly wealthy power couple outsiders assumed them to be. According to a United States Tax Court document filed in 1948, Ralph's 1941 income reflected a considerable decrease as a result of his service in Congress, compounded by an unsuccessful Senate run in 1940.[271] Furthermore, in 1941, the couple's children, then aged twenty-one, seventeen, and twelve, were all enrolled in private schools. Also unfortunate was the plummet of the shares that comprised most of the inheritance. Within two years, the share prices were halved, and not too many years later, the three companies, including Stitt's Jacob Adler & Sons, were dissolved.[272] Marguerite was at least half-truthful when she pushed back at reporters who assumed Ralph Church was a wealthy politician.[273]

Throughout his career, it seemed that Ralph worked hard to maintain his reputation as a humble farmer's son from downstate Illinois—as did his upper-class and ever-supportive wife. A 1940 column in the *Chicago Tribune* reported allegations that "money [Marguerite] inherited has financed her husband's campaigns were denied by Mrs. Church."

The paper quoted her response:

> *"'That is silly, malicious, and untrue. Ralph Church is not that kind of a man. He is a successful lawyer. What we have he has earned by hard, unremitting work. In the early years of our married life we saved scrupulously one-half of his annual earning. Thrift is very part of my nature and training. We had a four room flat and I did my own housework. We have always lived simply. Never since I married have I received an allowance from my family. I have not inherited a fortune. We are a comfortably, soundly established middle class family, no more, and make no pretension of being anything else.'"*[274]

State politics could be hard work or no work at all, depending upon preference, and Ralph Church became known for the former. The Legislative Voter's League, a government organization, routinely supported Church's reelection, labeling him as conscientious.[275] It helped that Church supported measures preferred by the wealthy and largely conservative officers of the Legislative Voter's League but Church was certainly no slacker on a state payroll, taking the train downstate to attend each session, awaiting for recess to take the admittedly fancy vacations to Europe, the Adirondacks, or the wealthy playgrounds of Long Island where the Stitts had a country home.

Illinois politics were always complicated, and this period in particular made it difficult for Republicans to know who was allied with whom. Democrats were not exempt, but GOP loyalties shifted with frequency. Political lovefests often turned sharp corners and became bitter rivalries. One constant, however, was Ralph Church and his support of Prohibition.

The Saint Valentine's Day Massacre in 1929 was a shocking event that triggered a reaction against laws that had benefited a generation of gangsters. But Evanston, usually peaceful, remained firm on temperance, its political identity, and so did Church. By 1930, there was a series of referendums to measure dry sentiment. Illinoisans, like citizens of other states, would weigh in on laws that made booze illegal and the likes of Al Capone rich. Representative Church held on.[276]

It was nevertheless a period of political shifts, and Church had to have been attuned. The Anti-Saloon League was on the downswing. Its fiery leaders, at home in Evanston, still inveighed against repeal of Prohibition laws, but many politicians throughout the state were having second thoughts. In the Tenth Congressional District, which included Evanston, Congressman Carl R. Chindblom was rumored to have requested that the Anti-Saloon lobby not endorse him in the 1930 election, despite his being known as a longtime dry. Beyond that, the drys could find hardly any candidates to endorse for anything in Chicago, which always liked its beer. And downstate, an area once a Prohibition stronghold, the Anti-Saloon League had many blanks on their sample ballot.[277]

Ralph Church of Evanston was not vacillating; he was dry as ever, he said. While many drys openly worried that a big win for the wets in the referendum would be awkward, Church wasn't bothered. When the *Tribune*, which was largely anti-Prohibition editorially, asked Church for a comment on the subject, the Evanstonian was unapologetic. He confirmed that he was not just dry, he was parched, and he didn't view the referendum as binding anyway.[278]

The 1930 referendum went wet, as expected, after which the Anti-Saloon League went almost silent. At the same time, their anti-Prohibition rival, the Crusaders, were getting braver all over the country. Prohibition was still the law, but the Crusaders were encouraging legislatures to repeal search and seizure laws and otherwise weaken enforcement. Then in August of the following year, wet forces felt strong enough to approach Church again. Rumors were that Church was contemplating a run for Congress. In search of a likely coal-mine canary, the Crusaders publicly asked Church, "the recognized floor leader [in the legislature] for the Anti-Saloon League and the WCTU," if he had changed his view. Church did not answer immediately, likely partly because he would not be cowed by opponents, and also because he saw that the dry position was futile.[279]

By 1932, Church was running for Congress, and he discussed Prohibition as little as possible. He was probably fortunate that Chindblom, the incumbent, was getting most of the heat, from both sides no less, for having shifted to a "moist" position, which meant he was strongly non-committal. By now both political parties were talking about "modification," which would create laws to allow beer and "other alcoholic beverages," assuming that the Eighteenth Amendment would be repealed. If Church once basked politically in the temperance issue, he now wished it did not exist.[280] If Marguerite had an opinion on this matter, she did not make it public. As the 1932 Republican primary approached, the *Tribune* took some pleasure in reporting that two long time political drys, "Congressman Carl R. Chindblom and Ralph E. Church have embraced the wet side. Six or seven weeks before the primaries they have come out as modificationists."[281] It represented a shaky early step as the man representing the WCTU's hometown attempted to move up the political ladder. It tested Church's agility on positions which could be a moving target for the whole of his career. If the young office holder was not always graceful in shifting his stance, he was typically attentive to the necessity to do so.

CHAPTER SEVEN

CLIMBING TO WASHINGTON

WHEN RALPH CHURCH ANNOUNCED HIS desire to run for Congress, many constituents must have asked what took him so long. Ralph had been a legislator in Springfield for sixteen years, a long time for a man of even moderate ambition. His personal life was by all measures secure, and his family was supportive and capable. Certainly, Ralph was comfortable in the statehouse. He was winning reelections by margins that discouraged any possible opponent, and he was a prominent member of the minority party in the House. These were reasonable cues that it was beyond time to take the next step.

Ralph Church had even accumulated a spotless, if not stellar, record in Springfield. He was smart and honest (his wife's characterization of "earnest" suits him) in a milieu where petty corruption and second-rate intellects were rampant.[282] He had proved himself to the satisfaction of wealthy activists of the Legislative Voters League, to editorialists for newspapers, and especially to the voters in his district. This may have been, in fact, a reason why he stayed in place so long. He was enjoying mild success. He was not voracious for the emoluments that most politicians covet from elective office. He was comfortable.

Church also had his law practice in Chicago, and it was going along nicely. His offices on LaSalle Street saw a steady flow of business, in no small part due to Ralph's modest prominence. His partners Traxler and Kennedy appeared happy dividing the lucrative work between the two of them while dividing the earnings of the firm three ways. Church, Traxler, and Kennedy was not a white-shoe law firm, but they still attracted corporate work and good private clients. All three partners were getting from the firm what many lawyers hoped for from the time they ventured to law school: moderate prestige and above-average pay.

Marguerite continued managing the family's activities with the assistance of two live-in servants, according to the 1930 census.[283] Though she downplayed her family's wealth to help her husband project a more modest existence, the Churches nevertheless lived in privilege. Marguerite's movements typically flew under the radar compared to Ralph's, though the couple appeared together on September 13, 1931, in the *Chicago Tribune* as sponsors—and she, the colonel in charge—of the women's resident division of the Central Association of Evanston Charities. The group operated out of a space in the North Shore Hotel at 1611 Chicago Avenue in Evanston. Marguerite, in her role, managed a team of more than 600, who appealed to the public to raise $95,000 for the organization ($1.9 million in 2023).[284] It would seem she brought an indefatigable level of passion, precision and coordination to all she did, and she would continue to do so throughout her life.

In 1932, Marguerite spent the summer, as she often did, with her children at Bay Shore, Long Island, in the family's vacation home. The *Evanston News-Index* ran a picture of Marguerite and the kids—then eleven, eight, and three—out for a stroll upon their return.[285] It wasn't uncommon for candidates to keep their private lives private, as pointed out in an unattributed clipping at the Evanston History Center featuring that same photo—with text under the title "A Candidate's Family" which reads: "Little is being said in political campaigns about the home life of a candidate. However, it is expected this fall that the people will want to know their representatives a little more intimately. Mrs. Church is quite prominent in Evanston social circles and charitable work and the children are typical healthy American youngsters."[286]

In October of that year, the *Glencoe News* reported a tea held in honor of Marguerite, who was to meet with members of that town's committee supporting Ralph in his reelection campaign. The event was held by Mrs. Dunbar Lewis, Marguerite's best friend from Wellesley College.[287]

THREE-WAY RACE FOR CONGRESS

Getting elected to Washington might have helped his law practice take another step forward, though that was probably not too much on Ralph's mind when he announced in 1931 that he would be a candidate for the new Thirteenth Congressional District of Illinois. What he probably saw was a tactical opportunity. The Thirteenth would be part of the statewide redistricting based on the 1930 census, with the new seat centered in Church's beloved Evanston. It would extend west to suburban Cook County and north to the North Shore suburbs and all of Lake County.[288] As the population was conservative and largely dry, it appeared custom-made for Ralph Church, though the redistricting of this area was already in the courts and risked being thrown out because of imbalances in population.

It is not that there wasn't an incumbent involved. That was Carl Chindblom, a seven-term Republican from the old Tenth, which encompassed Evanston, North Shore, and quite a few Chicago wards to the south, where he lived. Chindblom, Republican and dry, was acceptable to the likes of Evanston. But he was a nervous conservative, since his working-class city voters were not as sold on Prohibition, nor on other conservative positions, as were voters in the tonier suburbs. Chindblom was not young, sixty-two in 1932, but he was eager to win an eighth term, and since his chances in the new district where he lived were nonexistent—it ran south from Chicago's north border into the city's wards populated by immigrants—he moved north to the new Thirteenth, to a hotel in Evanston.[289]

What complicated the situation in the Thirteenth was a third candidate from a powerful family with homes on the North Shore and rural Lake County. That was James Simpson Jr., the son of James Simpson Sr., formerly the head of Marshall Field's and at the time chairman of Commonwealth Edison. The senior Simpson was one of Chicago's most prominent business leaders. He had run Marshall Field's when it went public, built the Merchandise Mart, and was chairman of the Chicago Plan Commission as the city undertook great public works like Wacker Drive. Now he was restructuring the finances of Commonwealth Edison after the utility's catastrophic collapse. The twenty-four-year-old son, in addition to being a member of such a well-laden family, represented youth. He also discerned that the Volstead laws were on their last legs and labeled himself vehemently anti-Prohibition.[290]

With a fourth candidate, Stephen A. Day of Winnetka, declaring himself a "wet zealot," the *Tribune* anticipated a spirited primary. "This great congressional district . . . is being given an opportunity to inflict a smashing blow against bigoted reformers," Day said, referring to prohibitionists in general, and Church and Chindblom in particular.[291]

Ultimately, the race for the GOP nomination was overpopulated, and Day dropped out, preferring to compete for one of Illinois' two at-large seats in Congress, testing the relative wetness of the whole state. That left the two drys and a wet, still significant labels in the identity politics of the day. If that wasn't confusing enough, the new Thirteenth Congressional District, just a few months before the primary, was abolished; the Illinois Supreme Court ruled that the state's whole reapportionment scheme was grossly imbalanced, population-wise. The new Thirteenth reverted mostly to the old Tenth.

This might have seemed an advantage to Chindblom, who had lived in the city and had support there. That was Church's perception initially when he said he would drop out of the race after the court ruling. He claimed that his responsibilities in Springfield made the congressional campaign too burdensome, "that the regular session of 1933 at Springfield will require the unselfish service of experienced legislators."[292] But it wasn't long before he reversed himself, saying his responsibilities in Springfield were not so onerous after all. He also noticed that Evanston, still the epicenter of the district, wanted him and not Chindblom, who looked like a carpetbagger. It was a three-way race again.[293]

In a day when polling was not as scientific as it would later evolve to be, prevailing wisdom was that Church's indecision hadn't hurt him too much with his Evanston base or with the North Shore fold that he had been cultivating in the legislative district for years. The papers began to characterize a two-man primary, Church vs. Simpson, with Chindblom looking like yesterday's news. They were largely right.

On election night in April, the initial returns had Church as the winner. But it was close. Simpson's side called for a recount, and that put the young scion on top by a few hundred votes. A subsequent series of recounts had the totals going back and forth for several weeks until the election commission placed the primary in the state courts. This should have been a venue where Church, a lawyer, was comfortable, except that he found himself up against a legal team sent in by Simpson's father. Countering that kind of firepower would be difficult even under the best of circumstances. In Illinois, where politics and money stirred a corrupt potion at the bottom and at the top, Church was in trouble. A series of technicalities connected to the way election judges were installed at a few of the polls put Simpson in front in the end. Specifically, Simpson's lawyers had succeeded in disallowing 300 Church votes (more than Simpson's overall margin of victory). It was a legal outrage, Church and his supporters said.[294] It's unclear how Marguerite felt about this political blow.

As Ralph believed that he had rightly won the primary, he concluded wrongly that he could win the general election as an independent. He failed. Simpson defeated Church easily and squeaked past the Democratic candidate Charles H. Weber, a result which opened Church to accusations that he had done nothing but split the GOP vote.[295] And to be fair, it is conceivable that Church preferred a weak Democrat to win in the staunchly GOP district to make his path easier in '34.

In any case, Simpson went to Washington. Church went back to his law practice downtown, which was lucrative but outside the political realm that he loved. Both got ready for what looked like a one-on-one primary two years hence.

Ralph Church could only hope that the power of incumbency would not be strong enough to make Simpson unbeatable. He needn't have worried. Simpson did nothing to distinguish himself in the Seventy-Third Congress, uttering only a few words on the floor of the House in his first term. Simpson got involved in an effort to reopen Great Lakes Naval Base in North Chicago, but whatever political capital he earned doing that was squandered when he missed an important vote when the measure passed.[296]

Marguerite, it seems, was meanwhile building and nurturing a virtual army of female support—one that would only prove an asset in the years to come. After her 1931 venture spearheading the effort to raise funds for the Central Association of Evanston Charities, she addressed a gathering of women at a Zonta Club luncheon at the Georgian Hotel in Evanston on February 11, 1932, discussing "various phases of the present tax situation" according to the *Evanston Revue*.[297] This was perhaps one of her first public speaking engagements documented in the press. The Zonta Club, later renamed Zonta International, was founded in 1919 and became a global service and advocacy organization empowering women to this day.[298]

There was little public information available about Marguerite in 1933, when she became president of the Chicago Wellesley Club. One must picture her balancing that role with her other volunteer work, consulting psychology efforts, domestic responsibilities, and heavy involvement in her husband's political campaigns.

THE NEXT VICIOUS PRIMARY

The 1934 primary promised to be a fierce one. It would be Church, the aggrieved loser of '32, against Simpson, the wet-behind-the-ears socialite whose expertise was more in polo, yachting, and grouse hunting, his enemies said, than governing.[299] And on top of whatever else Simpson had to endure, there was Samuel Insull, founder of Commonwealth Edison and an ally of the Simpson family, who had fallen to scandal—the collapse of the utility empire was exposed as a house of cards which destroyed the savings of ten of thousands who had put their savings in Insull securities. In fact, a connection between the young congressman and the disgraced tycoon, who had been indicted and was a fugitive from justice, was a stretch. But Insull was in the papers every week, and the mere implication of a tie seemed powerful enough to harm Simpson's chances.

One could say that real issues hardly separated the two candidates. The positions of each were standard conservative Republican, and neither were very specific. Church's platform was for balancing the budget and for waging a battle against graft and high taxes. He portrayed himself in newspaper ads as "Able—Fearless—Experienced—Dependable," and claimed that he "belongs" in Congress.[300] Simpson, for his part, "has voted for all measures to decrease the tax burdens," according to his campaign ads.[301] Both paid lip service to the need for government to provide what would later be called a "safety net" for citizens economically beset by the Depression. But neither had a shred of patience for the New Deal that Roosevelt was cooking up.

The candidates invited the voters to consider other things. Church hardly missed an opportunity to claim that he had been the rightful winner of the previous primary, while Simpson replied that this was past history. Why should the voters care about that? In an open reply to an open letter of accusations from Church, Simpson said, "By your tactics, and to my mind, you have not only sacrificed your right to an honored position as an officer of the court"—reference that Church was himself a lawyer—"but you showed yourself to be a poor sport." That may have resonated. He also said, "you became a tool of the Democrats and stabbed the Republicans in the back by running as an alleged independent" in '32. Nor was Simpson shy about citing Church's past as bone-dry on Prohibition, a cause that by 1934 had gone the way of spats and knickers.[302]

Observers admitted that it was going to be a close one, and some unusual weaponry was brought out. For example, Winnetkan Harold Ickes got in the fray. Ickes had been a Teddy Roosevelt Republican earlier in the century, meaning socially progressive and unaligned with the hard-right Republicans (as which both Church and Simpson would qualify). In 1933 Ickes became Franklin Roosevelt's secretary of the interior. It wasn't that a New Dealer was apt to turn the tide in any GOP primary. But Ickes had a particular animus against Commonwealth Edison and Insull, and by association Simpson. He wrote a letter, widely circulated, that Simpson was little more than a dilettante who had the backing of a rich father and a corrupt utility cartel. He made a point that the young incumbent had accomplished little on his own beyond honing skills as a wealthy sportsman. Ickes did not specifically endorse Church, and given Roosevelt's unpopularity in Evanston and the North Shore, maybe that was best.

The ultimate tally in the primary was 34,848 for Church and 31,964 for Simpson. It was close, but decisive. And the general election was less close, despite the fact that a Democratic wave increased pro-Roosevelt majorities in Congress. Ralph's persistence once again paid off. He was going to Washington, and it looked like he would be there for a while.

RISING FEMININE INFLUENCE

By January 30, 1935, Ralph had been in Congress for less than a month when the *Washington Star* reported that the family had taken up residence at 2344 California Street NW in DC's Kalorama area.[303] This in itself was notable as the neighborhood was and is fashionable enough to have attracted six former or future presidents, including Barack Obama after his presidency. The place the Churches rented was a spacious colonial and was chosen, no doubt, for its suitability not just for the family but for the modest entertaining that was a part of the family's custom. For this and other reasons, the new congressman and his wife became a couple to watch in the social geography of Washington, DC.

The Church children—Ralph Jr., a high school freshman, along with Bill and Marjory—would attend school in Washington while Congress was in session. Ralph Jr. would start high school at St. Albans School; his younger brother William would enroll in the lower school at St. Albans and sister Marjory at the Potomac School, all private.[304]

It wasn't long before the *Star* had Marguerite's photograph front and center in on the society page with a caption stating that Mrs. Eugene A. Howard, who had been a member of her wedding party and was a the wife of a building products tycoon from Winnetka, was her guest in Washington. Also noted under Marguerite's picture was that she was getting ready to entertain the local Wellesley Club.[305] Wellesley was prestigious almost anywhere it was mentioned, but especially in Washington, where a highly transient population used schools as sure certification of social standing. It wasn't long before Mrs. Ralph E. Church was herself such a tag and established any affair that she attended as worthy of note.

But Marguerite was different from many of the traditional wives of Washington. In 1936, a *New York Times* article about an anonymous (or composite) congressional wife may well have described her. It certainly described an approach to Washington which was different from the stilted environment that evidently prevailed in the capital when the Churches arrived. The fictional wife, "Mrs. Blumpus," whose husband was from the equally fictional midwestern state of Paw Paw, said that the older generation of congressional wives "were practically keeping the Eighteen Nineties embalmed here in Washington." It continued that "when you went to a tea in those days, they either froze you with the stiff kind of dignity women used to put on . . . or they would break down in little confidential huddles and trade notes on what they did for their husbands' indigestion."

The author of the article provided insight beyond the atmosphere assessment to detail the subtle expected obligations of a successful political wife. A good wife may "remember names that her husband might forget" and "tells him when it would be best to stop talking." And overall, she should "consider herself a listening post—a kind of intelligence service."[306]

Marguerite listened, but also spoke. She shared her impressions of her new life in Washington during the Woman's Republican Club luncheon on November 25, 1935. According to the *Evanston News-Index*, Marguerite revealed: "I am thoroughly convinced that there is something wrong with the administration."[307] Elaborating, Marguerite explained, "There is no depression in Washington. There is animation and the exhileration [sic] of crowds of prosperous people who, with the exception of the 106 Republicans, think everything in the country is going well."[308]

Marguerite also described the protocol followed by new wives of congressmen, intended to help them acclimate—a system in which first-timers called upon more experienced wives for guidance and counsel. Mondays were with wives of Supreme Court members; Tuesdays with wives of the House of Representatives; Wednesdays were teas with cabinet wives; Thursdays with wives of the Senate; and Fridays with diplomats' wives.[309] According to *Evanston News-Index* columnist Neola Northam, Marguerite said, "One Tuesday when I called on the representatives' wives, I found 21 [of them unavailable]," then added with a laugh that she "returned home to find I had missed 11 callers [myself]."[310]

As Marguerite had been a stalwart committeewoman in Evanston—social chairman of the powerful Evanston Women's Club—and a presence among Wellesley alums, she continued to increase her own voice beyond these familiar confines.[311] The year that her husband started in Congress, she was invited to California to address the Institute of World Affairs on the subject of women's roles inside and outside the home. She participated in a round table where she was described as a graduate of Wellesley and a woman who had done "considerable work in social economy."[312] Her experiences in psychology, philanthropy, and politics were obviously of interest and generated invitations such as this one.

During the 1935 thirteenth session of the Institute of World Affairs, a forty-three-year-old Marguerite presented her piece titled "Feminine Force in a Changing World."[313] Director Charles E. Martin later wrote that the conference convened "with a definite sense of responsibility and a sincere conviction that much was wrong with the world."[314]

It was at this conference, during the talk at the Mission Inn in Riverside, California, on December 16, that Marguerite stepped up to the rostrum and began her speech with a bang, describing herself as one who stood without crossing at the precipice of a changing feminine ideology: "[I] ask that nothing that I may say be construed as either direct or indirect criticism of the efforts made by individuals or organizations in the last fifty years to increase the strength and sphere of feminine influence. Nor, on the other hand, do these comments come from a speaker who is avowedly a feminist."[315]

Marguerite then continued: "I belong to that old-fashioned group which still feels that the strongest way, and certainly the easiest, for a woman to exercise influence upon the outside world is to choose early the right material and then to work quietly and forcibly behind that good and brave man."[316]

She was intentional in her acknowledgement of spheres of influences, while nevertheless laying the groundwork for women to step up to the plate: "In other words," she said, a woman "must become part of an eager and active feminine force struggling to diffuse the principles of living as developed within the home into the larger field of education, of community problems, and, finally, of governmental activity."[317]

She explained that the most troubling part of her new life in Washington, DC, "has been the signal lack of appreciation and interest on the part of the average woman regarding national issues, even those issues directly affecting the welfare of the women involved." It was clear to Marguerite that "the need for an enlightened public opinion among women was never more vital."[318] Describing the nation as a "hungry and desperate population," one "refusing, perhaps rightly, to count present or future cost," Marguerite lamented America's "economic and social bankruptcy."[319]

In her appeal for women to rise up as "an aroused force which, if properly trained and mobilized, could extend an influence invincible," Marguerite outlined certain governmental problems in which a woman's "instinctive" talents were needed, namely balancing and curtailing the government budget and spending. "The American woman," she elaborated, "through long years of actual domestic spending does understand what it means when you tell her that the government is spending $2.15 for every dollar taken in, and that our national public debt has jumped to over thirty billion."[320]

It was perhaps her concluding remarks that most clearly revealed her earliest voice as an advocate of particular international women's empowerment:

> *"Beyond any estimate . . . would be the force that could be brought to bear, in the interest of peace and democracy. A citizenry of enlightened women, fired by civic consciousness, would be a potent and irresistible factor in the preservation and enforcement among all peoples of those ideals which alone can save the civilization of the world."*[321]

While Marguerite was careful not to label herself a feminist, and while she supported many traditions of the woman's role in the family and in society, she also advocated strongly, sometimes radically, for expanded female influence in politics.

CONSERVATIVE IN NEW DEAL DC

Most freshman congressmen, especially those in the minority, assume the role of backbencher and remain quiet, listening attentively, reluctant to speak. Ralph Church exercised reticence on the floor in his first term, but outside he exhibited political savvy, sometimes aggressiveness. He had legislative experience. He understood how to take a position. He also understood when not to, as he did, for example, a couple of weeks after his arrival in Washington. A reporter asked how the new representative would vote on an appropriation bill that included funding for Naval Station Great

Lakes. Church was not taken by surprise; rather, he sounded like he found the question impertinent. "I have nothing to say about the proposition, one way or the other," he said. To deconstruct: he was saying yes, the base was in his district. But the Appropriations Committee was chaired by Democrats, and Church was a fiscal hawk. No, he was not going to begin his first term in Congress with a promise to spend money placed on the table by his rivals.

Ralph Church did not betray the Great Lakes; he eventually voted for the funds. But on-the-run answers to a reporter this early in his term would not do. He had time. He was being proposed for the Naval Affairs Committee, where he could hold forth on this subject more completely, support preparedness (and the local economy) on one hand, and gesture to tighten the purse strings with the other.

The following October, reopening ceremonies at the naval base attracted 10,000 spectators, where sailors and commanding officers filled the dais along with dignitaries including Ralph Church. Speakers lauded the navy as an indispensable instrument of peace, "a standing threat against war-ambitious nations." Church himself did not speak from the podium on that occasion, but he didn't have to. For the rest of his political career, he claimed credit for the reopened base. Opponents attacked him for taking too much credit. But Ralph was used to balancing positions as a politician. While Naval Affairs was hardly a high-profile committee appointment, it enabled him to speak in support of both the military and fiscal responsibility on the same platform.[322]

Sometimes being against Roosevelt's spending was a simple matter for the congressman from suburban Chicago. Normally he preached what the choir wanted to hear, as he did before a meeting of the Wilmette Civic League and the League of Women Voters of Wilmette and Kenilworth. He said, "This administration has deliberately and willfully set out to enact measures bound to affect the morale, self-confidence and sense of security of every American citizen. It attempted to reduce and confiscate your savings . . ." and so on. At this meeting, held at Marshall Field's in Evanston, he went on to say that the Roosevelt administration was out "to kill all personal incentive to industry and thrift." Its policies represented "a dastardly attack on business recovery."[323]

Standing foursquare against tax-and-spend Democrats (as they would be called in a later generation) was essential in a district dominated by the families of affluent businessmen. Republicans were in the minority nationally, but not in the Tenth Congressional District of Illinois. Yet Ralph Church was not one to depend on demographics. He worked the district tirelessly, and not just in campaign seasons. He got to know local chambers of commerce and political groups—not to mention women's groups and charity organizations, thanks, most certainly, to his socially connected wife. He and his team wrote articles for local newspapers in the district. Everyone knew of his opposition to Roosevelt. And as a politician eager to greet and be greeted, he found solidarity on that front on the streets of Evanston and neighboring towns. In these manners, he was a retail politician *par excellence*.

Wholesale politics was a harder market to crack, but Church made it his business to work the levers of conservative power in Illinois. This operation occurred for the most part about ten miles south of his district. That was on Michigan Avenue, at Tribune Tower, where "Colonel" Robert R. McCormick, the redoubtable owner/publisher of the *Chicago Tribune*, led the charge against all things Roosevelt. McCormick was considered a political dinosaur by some; he was called "the greatest mind of the fourteenth century" for his autocratic ways.[324] But he was an extremely effective publisher. The *Tribune* may not have been "the world's greatest newspaper," as the masthead proclaimed, but it was without a doubt widely read.

Church wrote many letters in the early months of his service in Congress, as he did throughout his tenure. In an early letter to McCormick in 1935, he wrote, "Dear Colonel McCormick, It occurs to me that you would be interested in having at hand a copy of H.J. Res. 117, appropriating $4,880,000,000, ($109 billion in 2023) which passed the House last Thursday." If there was any doubt, Church wanted the publisher to know that he had voted against it. "Because of the large sum involved and the fundamental principles of government, you will doubtless be commenting on it editorially . . . Personally, I was prompted to voice my objections to it on the floor of the House, as you will probably note in the Record." He ended with "all good wishes and assurance of my desire to be of every possible service." It was the beginning of mostly fruitful relationship between Church and McCormick, conservative publisher and plutocrat.[325]

Near the end of 1935, the *Evanston Review* described Ralph Church slated to address an evening session of the convention at the Evanston Country Club. Among other speakers scheduled to appear was Henry Cabot Lodge III of Massachusetts, and it all was preceded by two parades originating in Waukegan and Chicago and including 350 cars. According to the paper's December 19 edition, Ralph's concluding speech said to more than 1,000 attendees that the Roosevelt administration had "deliberately forced thousands of bills through the two houses in such a way as to keep the country in confusion as to the real state of affairs in Washington."

Church took every opportunity to berate almost any Roosevelt program that came before the House. There was something called the Resettlement Administration, a New Deal program to move impoverished workers and their families into planned communities. Resettlement was chronicled in John Steinbeck's novel *The Grapes of Wrath*, about the lives of migrants from the Oklahoma dust bowl. The program ignited resentment because it appeared starkly socialistic to many, including Ralph Church, who was never shy about accusing the Democrats of anti-capitalistic tendencies. To a *Tribune* reporter, he lambasted Rexford Tugwell, the Columbia economics professor who led the program. "Tugwell is engaged in 'satellite towns,' 'dream villages,'" he said. Tugwell "represents the actual practitioner of the communistic theory of government."[326] Legislatively, of course, the Republicans were powerless to curtail the program. But under the weight of vilification launched by Church and others, the Resettlement Administration was disbanded in 1936.

A new year's message from Ralph in the *Evanston Review* was a "word of appreciation for the loyal support of the people of Evanston, both in personal contacts and correspondence with me in my effort to serve them." It was, he continued, his "highest ambition to stay on the job and continue to serve well my fellow townsmen and other people of the Tenth District." And stay on the job he did—though serving well would be up for debate.

CHAPTER EIGHT

MR. CONGENIALTY IS NOT IN

IN THE BEGINNING OF HIS second term, Church entered voluntarily into a controversy that would brand him, for better or worse, for the rest of his tenure. This was his attack on a fellow Illinois congressman, Adolph Sabath of Chicago, for actions that Church considered negligent and possibly corrupt. The Sabath story began in 1934 when a special House committee, chaired by Sabath, undertook an investigation of abuses connected to real estate bondholders' committees, of which there were many after the stock market crash of 1929. Sabath, a Democrat, had strong ties to the New Deal and came to the investigation as an unvarnished progressive. Previously he had characterized the Depression as an "orgy of high financing and manipulation," and now his special committee appeared focused on abuses concocted by the interests of the wealthy at the expense of small bondholders.[327]

Three years later, unfortunately, the Sabath committee had not made much progress, and by 1937 there were calls from Republicans to disband the committee that seemed to be going nowhere. Still in the minority, Republicans induced Ralph Church, in the beginning of his second term, to take the floor and discuss their point of view on the Sabath committee. As Church began to speak that day, he was met with the usual lack of attention from most House members present, but that changed as the accusations took form. Church stated, for instance, that Chicago Title and Trust had been an early target of the investigation, but then the Chicago law firm of Sabath,

Perlman, Goodman and Rein was hired to represent the Chicago Title and Trust in other matters. Suddenly the House was in an uproar. Many members tried to shout down Church, while others called for him to continue.

Continue he did with a series of other apparent irregularities, such as Sabath's friends and colleagues extracting substantial stipends from the courts for unspecified services to various bondholder's committees. Church specified other abuses that looked like corruption, if not benefiting Sabath directly, then benefiting Sabath's law firm. Before Church was finished, Sabath himself rushed Church and said, "By God, I want to answer these contemptible . . ." He did not finish, as the speaker gaveled an adjournment.[328]

Nor was Church finished, and in subsequent days it became clear that he was going for the jugular of a Democrat who appeared vulnerable. Yet, Church offered no firm proof that Sabath had profited personally; rather, he was reiterating what was already known about Sabath's poor administrative skills. But Sabath was well liked by most members of Congress, was at the time the body's longest-serving member, and was regarded as the "dean of the House." On other occasions he had been lauded for "unimpeachable integrity."[329]

So Church was on thin ice. Still, he forged ahead with accusations against various people, many of them lawyers, who had profited from their tie to Sabath and the investigation. Perhaps he went too far when he said, "All of us who are to the slightest extent acquainted with the reorganization procedure . . . know that the greatest curse to the speedy and economical adoption and completion of a plan of reorganization is the so-called shyster lawyer." Before he sat down, he used the word *shyster* again, undoubtedly calling up Sabath's being Jewish.[330] While such a slur would correctly not be tolerated today, it was not particularly noted, though Church's general treatment of a colleague was not endorsed by the majority of the House. For his part, Sabath spoke for many Democrats when he opined that Church was "spokesman for the large trust companies and other highbrow racketeers."

Very few members of the House were favorably impressed by Church's conduct of Sabath's investigation. But it was commonly believed that most of the Chicago congressman's foibles and missteps could be chalked up to his indifferent command of English, as Sabath was Czech-born. Even Everett Dirksen, then a Republican representative from downstate Illinois, was unhappy with the way Church had gone about the thing. While it seemed clear to everyone that Sabath's management skills were shoddy, Dirksen's hardest words were for Church who, he said, had disrupted the "good feeling" in the normally collegial chamber of Congress.[331]

Ralph Church was winning no congeniality prizes among his House colleagues. Whether by strategy or personal predisposition, Church replaced his lack of legislative muscle with well-developed vocal cords. He became a scold and did not mind making his colleagues groan somewhat when he got up to speak. Drew Pearson, syndicated columnist of "Washington Merry-Go-Round," suggested a number of times that Church was not well liked in the House. Pearson didn't mind calling him a "cocky socialite from Chicago's swanky North Shore" and reported that the Sabath affair accomplished nothing except that "Republicans and Democrats smothered Church with condemnation."[332]

He was labeled in other press reports as his chamber's "most unpopular member," in part for the Sabath affair, in part for his habit of blocking attempts to adjourn by calling "point of order" to demand consideration of a minority measure that would not pass anyway.[333] His most egregious—and most reviled—point of order came the day before Thanksgiving in 1937 when he was the sole member to object to recess for the holiday, a privilege granted any member by the rules. He was demanding that the House consider a tax cut to relieve the slumping economy, which it did not. The session lasted sixteen minutes after Speaker Sam Rayburn opened it, saying, "We are here by the grace of our friend from Illinois, Mr. Church."[334] When Church tried to reply and perhaps propose his measure, he was shouted down. Church might have been pleased that at least that the speaker referred to him by his state. Already, certain colleagues had taken to calling him "the gentleman from Evanston," an apparent swipe at his seemingly swanky provenance.[335]

WASHINGTON POLITICAL ASSET

If Ralph was winning no popularity contests, the opposite could be said for his wife Marguerite.

Certainly, Marguerite's social standing in Washington was dependent upon her husband's position, but there can be no doubt that she improved his as well. In 1938, for example, they were on the bipartisan guest list of an important gala military reception at the White House. The Churches attended in part because of Ralph's position on the Naval Affairs Committee, but the invitation went out knowing that Congressman Church had been harsh in his criticism of the host, President Roosevelt. The First Lady, Mrs. Roosevelt, no doubt took some solace in the fact that he would be accompanied by Marguerite, and the press covering the affair was pleased, too, noting, "Mrs. Church, gracious and smiling, had a becoming costume of white chiffon, the deep cape-like bertha forming sleeves to the elbows." A journalist noted that the Churches were "warmly greeted everywhere they went" that evening.[336] It can be reasonably assumed that the warmth was generated not by the congressman but rather his wife.

Reports of Marguerite's social success were mixed with organizational benchmarks, such as her election as president of the Wellesley College Alumnae Association in 1939, which would amplify the prestige of her alma mater. This would provide a stately platform from which she could express "hope that while the past prewar years had been given over to a betterment of our standard of living, the years ahead would be dedicated to improving our standards of conduct."[337] If this sounds as if it is verging on a political speech, she's not there quite yet. Marguerite was still cleaving to the notion that women of her social stratum might well have opinions, but if they expressed them they were best leavened by cultural niceties and elegant manners, and made through their husbands, a process in which Marguerite was talented.

Marguerite again called for the international empowerment of women in a piece she wrote for the October 1939 issue of Zonta International's magazine, the *Zontian*. Marguerite's piece, titled "Wanted: A Will For Peace," expressed the urgency for women to wake up. She wrote, "To keep out of war is today the biggest and the best task for the women of this nation." In specific, she believed that "woman's vast influence for peace must be immediately and continually directed toward detecting false propaganda and toward shaping a public opinion that will, whatever our sympathies, keep this country strictly neutral."[338]

She did more than describe her concerns, though. She offered concrete suggestions to address them: for instance, "revitalizing of our moral standards—in the home, in the school, and in every aspect of national and international life." She called for American women to "eradicate every sentiment and policy foreign to our own American system of thought and action. Throughout all our population we must seek a new unity through a true vision of what we proudly term 'The American Way.'"[339]

She went on to add, "The fate of the world today may well be resting in the hands of the average woman of this and other countries. A united band of peace-demanding women could not be withstood. Such women hold for brilliant use an indestructible and irresistible weapon—the force of public opinion."[340]

Marguerite, who had for so long seemed content working in the shadows of her husband's career, was now increasingly using her voice to encourage female empowerment—though for now, and at least publicly, for white, heterosexual, American women only. Years later, during her first term in Congress, she addressed Evanston's First Baptist Church to present a talk titled "The American Dream." Following the speech, a tea was held at the house of worship. Marguerite's talk was organized by three women-led committees of the congregation—the Christian Citizenship committee, the Christian Social Progress committee, and the Program Committee of the

Women's Society—and likely served as a way for her to learn more about her constituents.[341]

RELUCTANT ISOLATIONIST

Ralph Church, for his part, was a strong ideologue, though sometimes a clumsy one, who moved carefully through the political brush. On one hand, he was a member of the opposition in Congress, so his GOP colleagues, not to mention his conservative constituency, expected him to speak and vote against the Roosevelt program. This he usually did with ease. But there were other issues and other realities that sometimes complicated his position-taking. One such area was that of foreign policy. For example, Church had made a name for himself before World War I as a preparedness advocate. This combined with the large naval base in his district might have marked him, if not as an interventionist, as a voice in favor of security on an international basis. But Colonel Robert McCormick, Church's sometime patron, was an implacable isolationist, forcing the congressman, like Marguerite, to cast his political lot with the America First faction.

His ambivalence on the subject was sometimes hard to miss. Roosevelt was allowing arms sales to China in 1937. In an op-ed piece, Church challenged the administration to "stop the shipment of arms to either China and Japan," though the congressman admitted that this would have the practical effect of assisting the stronger Japan. Church toed the isolationist line while also acknowledging Japanese aggression and listing their atrocities. With some inconsistency, he concluded, "Whatever the explanation, the American people want peace. They do not want again to be involved in a foreign conflict."[342]

Church continued to thread the isolationist needle, complicated by his membership on the Naval Affairs Committee. No one could fault him, he no doubt hoped, for encouraging whatever appropriations were on the table for Great Lakes. He also pushed for the beginnings of what became Naval Air Station Glenview, also in his district.[343] At the same time, he did challenge the administration's eagerness to expand naval operations overseas. In early 1938, he was the committee's most active, if unheeded, voice to slow a bill that would provide a 20 percent (approximately $30 million, or $653 million in 2023) budget increase to build up the fleet. He was more successful when he spoke forcefully against the expansion of the American harbor at Guam, a position that he would later regret.[344]

Church had an easier time with domestic policy, but not always. He went loud with the accusation that employees of the Federal Savings and Loan Insurance Corporation, one of an array of federal offices that were popping up all over following the New Deal, were enjoying holidays and weekend trips veiled as official business. Thousands of dollars were at stake, the congressman said on the floor of the House.[345] Church charged that this was a mere symptom of mismanagement that had caused a $100 million ($2.2 billion in 2023) loss in the federal Home Owners Loan Corporation, of which the insurance entity was a part.

The congressman demanded an investigation, and while the issue lingered in the press for a month or so, the chairman of the banking and currency committee, an Alabama Democrat, did nothing of the sort.

Church got involved in gnarlier issues as well, such as the Agricultural Adjustment program, which paid farmers to raise fewer crops as a way to stabilize prices.

Initially, this was popular with farmers for obvious reasons, and since Church had a good number of rural constituents in northwest Cook and Lake Counties, he was less-than-strident in what was regarded in Evanston's conservative circles as a socialistic program. He went after this one in what he hoped would be a risk-free critique, saying that the program was too complicated and doomed to failure. "Most Congressmen could not hope to have full knowledge of its many ramifications," Church wrote in one of his op-ed pieces.[346] So when a Palatine constituent was confused by the government's indecipherable regulations, he could nod and think approvingly of his congressman.

TO NORWAY WITH COLLEAGUES AND FAMILY

Somewhat out of character, given Church's interests as a legislator, he joined forty-two other senators and representatives as delegate to the Inter-Parliamentary Union's thirty-sixth annual meeting, held in Oslo in 1939. With tensions in Europe beyond the boiling point, this was regarded as more than the usual goodwill meeting with legislators from twenty-two countries. Rather, it was an opportunity to discuss and perhaps to witness what was behind the impending Second World War. Church found considerable pessimism among delegates that war could be avoided, and he found reason for America to strengthen the isolationist resolve that was shared by many Republicans in the delegation.[347]

Peace by then seemed like a futile hope, though the leader of the US delegation moved to propose a resolution that the Union urge "upon the governments of Great Britain, France, Germany, and Italy an immediate consideration of a moratorium on war for thirty days or more with a view to the settlement of international disputes by arbitration."[348] The resolution came to nothing.

Marguerite and seven-year-old Marjory accompanied Ralph to Oslo, partly to enjoy Europe and also for Marguerite to witness the workings of the Inter-Parliamentary Union. It is not impossible that Ralph joined the delegation because of her encouragement. Since Europe was already on a glide path toward war, sightseeing outside of Norway was not possible. Moreover, discussions of the assembly of legislators from many countries concluded without much dissent that any talk was coming too late to avoid a catastrophic war.

A TRY FOR THE SENATE

By the beginning of his third term, Church had the sense that the country was growing weary of the New Deal and its relief and regulatory programs.

He said he saw evidence that the nation wanted a slowdown to the endless bureaucracy, a view he expressed in a 1939 op-ed in which he insisted that the rubber-stamp days of the Congress were over. Even Democrats were voting against more spending, Church said, "because a congressman is sensitive to public opinion."[349]

Not too unreasonably, Church thought that the electorate at large was moving in his direction. It was true that the Republicans were making inroads into the Democratic majority, gaining seventy-two seats in the House and seven in the Senate in the 1938 midterms. In Illinois, there was a certain weariness of Chicago-machine Democrats as well. Then in 1939, Illinois' popular senator Ham Lewis, an elaborately toupéed Spanish-American War veteran and a Democrat, died unexpectedly. As Republicans discussed how they might flip the seat to their side, a number of names were proposed—among them Ralph Church. Church liked the idea but would not step into the 1940 special election rashly, not least because it would mean sacrificing his House seat. If anyone's counsel was key to the decision, it would have been his wife's, with her finger on the pulse of the North Shore vote and the women's vote in particular. Publicly, he claimed there was a popular groundswell encouraging him to run. "With over 100 strong, confidential letters still coming to me every day, urging me to run for the US senate, it is increasingly difficult to resist the pressure."[350]

He did not resist. When he announced his candidacy for the Senate, he said his personal preference was to stay in the House, but "in a time of such national crisis it would be totally selfish for me to consider my own preference.[351] He sounded confident if not like an out-and-out front-runner.

There was an impediment to Church's plan: his primary opponent, Charles Wayland "Curly" Brooks. Brooks had made several runs for office so far in Illinois—for governor and for congressman-at-large—and lost. But he was a loquacious and popular speaker, a skill inherited from his father, who was a pastor. Because he had no constituents, no committee assignments, and a thin political record, he was able to speak expansively and unchallenged on the moral bankruptcy of the Roosevelt administration. Brooks was a custom-made candidate in other ways too—a war hero with a Distinguished Service Cross from World War I, and an ultra-strict isolationist. "Two things stamp out liberty," he said during the campaign. "One is concentration of power. The other is war."[352] Because he shared these characteristics with the *Tribune's* Colonel McCormick, he could expect more than a fair shake in the "World's Greatest Newspaper." McCormick's affinity for Brooks brought the candidate lavish coverage if not an outright endorsement. And it created substantial headwinds for Church.

Evanston Republicans likely believed that Church's record, and his careful balancing between American First and preparedness, would appeal to broad spectrum of voters. These supporters insisted that no one was more careful in staking out positions that consistently put a thorn in the side of the administration. There was also his basic industriousness and the pride he took in never having missed a roll call during his tenure in Congress. There were plenty of reports in the press in 1939 when Church was carried into the House chamber stretched on a wheelchair. He had just had a "repair operation," as he called it, but he refused to spoil his record for never missing a vote.[353]

If leaving Washington to campaign in Illinois was hard for Ralph, it made his wife's role more important than ever. She traveled back to Illinois often, especially in the month or two before the primary, sometimes driving the 700 miles straight through herself by car, sometimes by plane. She would stop in at the Church campaign headquarters in Chicago, and she did what she had done in previous campaigns, which was among other things to speak to small groups and impress them with her authenticity.

"What this country needs most, thinks Marguerite Stitt Church, is a good dose of middle-class government," the *Tribune* put it after an interview with her. It was one of the first times that Chicago at large had a chance to admire Mrs. Church as Washington already had. "A small, trim woman, alert but poised in manner," was how the reporter described her. "She has glossy brown hair. She wears inconspicuous dark attire."[354]

Ultimately, however, an active wife and perfect attendance record could not ease the way against "Curly" Brooks, who was stumping all over the state. His unrelenting isolationism got his appearances splashy coverage across the pages of many papers, especially the *Tribune*. Church, in the meantime, was speaking on the radio from Washington, still careful not to be absent for any vote, no matter how trivial. Church got fair press, but it was often to explain with academic precision why the New Deal was an economic threat to all Americans. Brooks meanwhile accused the Roosevelt administration of all manner of political sins, including fear mongering, socialism, and what seemed like the end of the world if Illinois did not put a stop to it.

In the end, on April 9, it was no surprise to even casual political observers that the more extreme Republican would prevail in the primary. Brooks defeated Church by 185,000 votes.[355]

Even in defeat, Ralph was stoic. He promised support for the Republican, and he continued his perfect record of answering the roll call, even though he would be going home after the first of the year. This, of course, did not just reflect his sense of duty. It reflected that at the age of fifty-seven he was not finished in politics. He kept speaking to the press and to Republican groups, and kept the Republican torch lit in the votes that remained through the summer and fall.

It was equally significant that Marguerite did the same in Ralph's lame-duck period. Her campaign schedule may have fallen off for the general election, but by November she was doing yeoman's work for the national GOP by traveling, in one instance, to Altoona, Pennsylvania, to speak on behalf of Wendell Willkie. Willkie was opposing Roosevelt that year, and despite polls making the incumbent the prohibitive favorite, she insisted that the administration had not "proven successful." Moreover she resented the idea of a third term, which no other president had ever attempted. "Roosevelt is not an indispensable man," Marguerite said.

Speaking of such things so far from home suggested that both she and her husband, although unsuccessful in his Senate run, were not leaving politics.[356]

CHAPTER NINE

LIFE IN WASHINGTON

THERE WAS NO DOUBT THAT Ralph Church would reenter politics in 1942, and those who were paying attention only wondered what office he would run for. In fact, Church seemed to be wondering the same thing early that year. For months, observers had speculated that he would run for his old seat, ceded in the last cycle to George A. Paddock of Evanston, an investment banker.[357] But the lure of higher office, even after his Senate defeat in '40, remained a shiny object seemingly within reach. Senator Curly Brooks, having won the special election against Church, would be up for reelection in '42. Was Brooks vulnerable? Perhaps he was. America was now foursquare behind the war effort that Brooks had vehemently opposed. Church, once an isolationist too, had shifted more easily to support the administration against the nation's enemies.[358]

Church filed his petitions to be a candidate for his old House seat on February 7, 1942, the first day to complete paperwork to get on the primary ballot. But rumors persisted that he would take another run at the Senate. This was hardly a secret, as he had been collecting signatures for a Senate petition as well. Things took a turn when a so-called "Draft Church for the Senate" letter went out to the papers and was published under the letterhead of something called the College Alumni Republican Club of Illinois.[359] It was a little mysterious, as some members of this organization, which did exist, said they were surprised, and that they believed Church himself had written the letter. While disavowing authoring the letter, Church trundled his Senate petitions to Springfield, this time just a few minutes before the final deadline. He became a candidate for two offices and had not yet decided which track to follow.[360]

February 28 was the last day to withdraw from either race. He took the train to Springfield that day, and it was said that he had two letters in his pocket. Just ten minutes before midnight, he delivered the one withdrawing his name from the Senate ballot. His reasoning involved State Treasurer Warren Wright, who was running for the Senate too. When it became clear that Wright, who had already run a successful statewide race, decided to stay in, Church opted out.[361]

The House campaign started with Church in a frankly shaky position. It was hard to argue against the incumbent Paddock, who compared Church to the schoolboy holding out for the most desirable date to the prom, then being jilted by his first choice and settling for his second.[362] Paddock wanted deeply to continue as congressman, he said. That was only the beginning of the race between two Evanston Republicans, which might have been polite and even substantive, as both had congressional records behind them. Instead, it descended into weak accusations and half-truths.

Paddock went after Church's thin list of accomplishments in Congress. The incumbent said quite rightly that Church had introduced no bill of substance in his six years in the House.[363] He had rarely even spoken on the floor beyond calling for a point of order or other objection. It was not hard for Church to make the same charge against Paddock's two years, as both were essentially backbenchers in a minority party with little direct influence on policy. For his part, Church asked voters to remember Paddock and a bill which was proposed the year before to increase pensions of members of Congress. The bill wavered in both houses, and when it received too much light of day, was withdrawn. The fact that it was never enacted did not stop Church from upbraiding Paddock, who "did not lift his voice or his vote in protest," the challenger said.[364]

Pale issues may have moved some voters in the district, but not many, and the candidates knew it. Instead, they devoted much of the campaign to lining up supporters and listing them in articles and ads. Paddock enjoyed the support of the district's "regular" Republican organization, which included no less than Evanstonian Charles Dawes, former vice president. This may have reflected, in part, Church's "most unpopular" label among his colleagues in Congress. In any case, Paddock also had the full-throated support of several Republican congressmen currently in the House, and these included Joseph W. Martin, minority leader from Massachusetts.[365] Some of Paddock's fellow-members on the Interstate and Foreign Commerce Committee also endorsed the first-termer in his race against a man with whom they had served previously. It appeared that Church's many points of order, not to mention his attempt on the scalp of Adolph Sabath, may have been coming back to bite him.

The 1942 Paddock/Church campaign proved two points that have driven American elections historically. One was that voters cared little about policy position as long as the candidate toed the correct ideological line. The other was that having the endorsement of other politicians is small beer compared to true grassroots support. And grassroots support is what the Churches had worked too hard to secure in more than two decades of engaging the local area. While the Republican Women's Club of Evanston formally favored Paddock, as the GOP organization did, it took only a moment for a robust group of Republican women to emerge and point out that Church had "made a constant and notably successful fight against pernicious New Deal measures and for national defense."[366] It proved that Church's conservative credentials had been incised on the voting DNA of this extremely conservative district.

In the end, on April 15, 1942, Church's victory over Paddock was a surprise and also decisive: 39,000 to 33,000. Church lacked establishment support, according to the Tribune, but "relied principally on his personal effort . . . aided by a large North Shore following."[367] Church carried Evanston, home to both candidates.

As usual in the period, the general election in Illinois' Tenth was anticlimactic. The Democratic candidate was J. E. Bairstow, corporation counsel of Waukegan. Bairstow repeated the criticism that Church had done little when serving in Washington. When he did ask for recognition on the House floor, Bairstow said, the Congressman's remarks were embarrassingly short, not to say inconsequential. Church replied to that one by saying that brevity is a virtue in any congressman, and that he should be given credit for practicing it.[368] People who knew the loquacious Church, who would go on to win the general election easily, must have smiled when they heard that.

POLITICS AND THE FAMILY

In the interregnum between Ralph's first four terms and his last four, the once and future congressman practiced law in Chicago, plotted his return to politics, and watched some important family events from a slightly closer vantage point than he had in the past. Son Ralph Jr. was already at Princeton, and the younger two finished school in Washington that spring—William graduating from St. Albans, and eleven year-old Marjory finishing the year between the Potomac School in Washington and Roycemore School in Evanston. They were living for the time being on Kalorama Road in Washington, a well-located house ample enough to later serve as a consular office of the Thai Embassy.

At Princeton, Ralph Jr. was a member of the Whig-Cliosophic Club, considered the nation's oldest "literary and debating society," which was more debating than literary, and more political than anything else. In fact, James Madison and Aaron Burr were members of the predecessor organizations, the Whig and the Clio, respectively. It was one of many clubs around which Princeton social life revolved, but young Ralph's choice of this one may have reflected a political edge to his interests if not his true talents. His major was mechanical engineering, which led to his later career in patent law, which he practiced with distinction in Chicago.[369]

Ralph Jr. entered the navy shortly after graduation and shipped off to Annapolis, where he completed a course in naval engineering. He let no time pass between the end of that latter accomplishment and the beginning of his next, which was his engagement to Evanston girl Janet Richardson, daughter of the Chicago-based executive of the *Atlantic Monthly*.[370] Even while Ralph Jr. was graduating from naval training, a series of luncheons for Janet was already beginning.[371] The marriage would be on a Monday. The only problem was that Ralph Sr., slated to serve as his son's best man, scheduled his travel home from Washington too close. Determined to maintain his perfect roll-call record in the House, Ralph Sr.'s plane—and accordingly, plan—was diverted because of inclement weather. Grounded in Indianapolis, the Monday marriage went on without him.[372] According to the Chicago Tribune Press Service, Church "telephoned his greetings to the bride and bridegroom," then boarded a plane back to Washington.[373] Once again, the business of politics came first.

If Ralph was clumsy, he seemed so mostly when compared with his wife. Marguerite's profile was rising. It became a matter of the public record that she was a college friend of China's first lady, Madame Chiang, which came up in the press as tensions intensified between the Chinese Nationalists and the communists. Madame Chiang came to Washington several times in the '40s to affirm US support for Taiwan, and she often socialized with Marguerite. In May of 1966, for example, they together attended the weekly luncheon of the Executive Club of Chicago.

Marguerite spearheaded the Mayling Soong Fund at Wellesley in her friend's honor. In 1947, she and Marjory, by then a Wellesley student herself, attended the fund's lectures.[374] In a thank you note made public, Madame Chiang called Marguerite "the epitome of brains, beauty and charm," memorable praise from a woman who was impressing America with the same qualities herself.[375]

Between 1946 and 1948, Marguerite worked tirelessly to raise funds for her alma mater. She served then as chairman for the National Special Gifts Committee of the Wellesley Seventy-Fifth Anniversary Fund Campaign—

and secured $3 million ($47 million in 2023) of the $4 million ($63 million in 2023) in funds raised for the college—a testament to her influence and ability to win friends in high places.[376]

Perhaps Marguerite's most prominent role in Washington D.C. came as a member and later president of the Congressional Club, a social organization for congressional spouses. Early in her Washington years she made a well-recognized appearance, introducing the music program, at a luncheon there. Eleanor Roosevelt was guest of honor, and Mrs. Charles Evans Hughes, wife of the former Republican presidential candidate, would have been the second-ranking guest.[377] Known for her "good humor" and "poise" among other qualities routinely listed in Washington society pages, Marguerite was also tapped by the club to teach what she had been doing with more frequency herself: public speaking.

In 1947, Marguerite taught a ten-week public speaking course through the Congressional Club. The organization described itself as having "formed in 1908 to provide a non-partisan setting for friendships among the wives of the House and Senate members in Washington, D.C."[378] Running concurrent with Marguerite's lectures were classes held by another congressional wife—Mrs. Lyndon B. Johnson—who ran the interior decorating group.[379] About her own classes, Marguerite told reporter Jane Eads that "women have begun to realize that they must join in the policy-making of the day and that before they make policies and help bring about their enforcement they must first learn to think clearly and to express their thoughts convincingly and appealingly." She said that 80 percent of American women "could become good speakers and enough can be done for the others to at least help them express themselves clearly." She concluded by saying, "Every woman in the United States should be able to express herself."[380]

The Congressional Club was expressly non-partisan, which by the post-war years made its affairs notable and rare for their spirit of reaching across the aisle. By the time that Marguerite was installed as club president in 1949, it was a sign of the club's prestige or Marguerite's popularity, or both, that

President Truman and his wife accepted an invitation to a white-tie formal at its stately neoclassical clubhouse. In a photo of the Trumans and Churches at the event, the president appears charmed by something Marguerite has said. Congressman Church, Truman's implacable political enemy, is smiling too, but well off to the side.[381]

RELISHING THE POLITICAL LIFE

Ralph Church continued for the next four two-year terms much as he had done in the past. He did not miss a single roll call or vote. He railed against the New Deal and President Roosevelt whenever possible. And on weekends when he returned to the Tenth Congressional District, he spoke (without brevity, it was said) to community groups in Evanston, Rogers Park, the North Shore, and up through Lake County. The women's groups remained his truest base of support. A fawning *Tribune* article about Church at home captured various themes of his electoral success. It portrayed the porch in front of the house of Church Street as a welcoming meeting place for supporters. One picture showed neighborhood kids playing in the log cabin in the backyard. Another had him lined up with the heads of women's groups from Evanston, New Trier Township, and other places in the district. His image as a tireless worker for the district was never really challenged, and when an election was nigh, no one spent more time shaking hands on commuter train platforms than one of the most conservative members of the US House of Representatives.[382]

There were times when the congressman addressed the broader issues of the day, though it was rare that his initiatives were not overridden by the Democrats, who held the majority throughout Church's tenure except for the term of 1937–1939. In any case, he appeared happy in the role of castigator, often on the subject of petty government waste, but also, in one case, of a question of potentially higher drama: his broadside charge that the attack on Pearl Harbor could have been avoided. He was not shy about blaming President Roosevelt's lack of preparedness. He was more specific when he outlined in some detail how Australian intelligence knew of the coming attack but had not gotten the information to anyone in Hawaii or Washington who could do anything about it. Church also accused an Army Air Force officer at Pearl Harbor who, when informed of an abnormally large radar signal hours before the attack, told colleagues to "forget it." The lieutenant was later promoted several times, a knife that the congressman attempted to twist in the reputation of the administration, though without discernible effect.[383]

It turned out that making partisan political points on the conduct of the war was ineffective. In fact, Church could be thankful for that reality, as he had a liability of his own. That was his leadership of the congressional push in 1939 to leave the island of Guam unfortified. Eventual war with Japan was not considered a certainty at the time, and Congress said no to funds requested to improve the military infrastructure of the Guam harbor. It was one of the few times that Church was identified as a leader on a successful House vote, though the consequences were distinctly unsuccessful.[384] The Japanese took Guam almost simultaneously with its attack on Pearl Harbor.

In the 1944 election, Church's opponent in the general election, Curtis S. MacDougall, a professor at Northwestern, used Guam as a cudgel against the incumbent. MacDougall was not alone, as the *Chicago Sun*, the *Chicago Times*, and the *Chicago Daily News* were among papers (typically at odds with the *Tribune*) that went after Church on this point as well. "There is a zealous effort to find goats to sacrifice on the altar of responsibility for our early disasters in the Pacific," wrote the *Daily News*, referring to Church's efforts to assign guilt for Pearl Harbor. "It is significant that some of the most zealous witch hunters are those who are faced with necessity of clearing themselves from a measure of responsibility," it continued, apparently referring to Guam.[385]

MacDougall was a professor of journalism and was encyclopedic in his recounting of these events and others that challenged Church's political career. McDougall's lengthy releases were precise and sometimes incriminating, but the results proved in the end that voters were less interested in policy than in Church's longtime identity as a Republican. In fact, the professor was well known as an author and as a previous editor of the *Evanston News-Index*. His campaign had the support of many liberal leaning people at Northwestern, which had a rock-ribbed Republican administration. The professor's energetic campaign made it appear there might be hope for the Democrats in '44, but in the end there was not, as Church defeated MacDougall easily.

If even MacDougall could get nowhere against the incumbent's perennially safe seat, it stood to reason that no one could as long as Church stayed on the far-right track. The script did change; Church was clever and had his ear to the ground. At some point when it got rusty to criticize Roosevelt's New Deal, and later Truman, Church found another target closer to home. That was the corrupt-unto-clownish city hall administration in Chicago. Edward J. Kelly was now mayor and was effectively consolidating the Democratic political machine in the city as it would operate for decades to come.

It was called the "Kelly-Nash" machine, after the mayor and the manipulator behind him, and Church gained ink using Kelly-Nash as an adjective for everything unsavory in politics. In one case, it had become aware of the machine's fingers in a federal program providing milk to Chicago public school children. The scheme, as Church described on the floor of the House, was for the denizens of Chicago City Hall to somehow skim a penny or two from each half-pint. The take, according to the congressman, was about $250,000 a year ($4.3 million in 2023).[386]

In truth, there was some derision pointed at Ralph Church for carrying on about school milk while soldiers were dying in Europe and the Pacific. Drew Pearson took particular outrage in recounting the small mindedness of some congressman when monumental questions of world security were otherwise at stake.[387] But columnist Pearson, who was born in Evanston to a father who taught at Northwestern at the time, didn't know Evanston if he thought he could move the town to disparage Ralph Church. The writer's efforts had little influence where it mattered.

Any position that reinforced the conservative line, especially alloyed with fiscal watchdogism, was what the majority of Church's constituents expected from their congressman. The fact that Church hounded the hated Democratic machine in the political jungle of Chicago won him approbation and, every two years in this period, elections.

NEW ISSUES FOR OLD CONSERVATIVES

With the end of the war, the labor movement gave the Republicans another load of political ammunition, as a pent-up pressure in union-management relations caused an enormous strike wave. President Truman's liberal support for unions was a strong talking point for the GOP in the 1946 election, and it helped turn a major victory for the Republicans. For the first time since 1931, the Republicans took the House. They installed Joseph W. Martin of Massachusetts as speaker, and one of their first orders of business was a set of labor relations laws packaged as the Taft-Hartley Act.

Church was well positioned on this one because unions, and opposition to them, resonated in his district. Church did not hesitate to go after opponents as allies of labor, and Marguerite, with a family history marked with clashes with unions, offered no visible opposition. In 1944, Ralph's frequent surrogate and later law partner George Robnett wrote in a lengthy letter in the *Tribune* that McDougall's support from labor unions represented "active and militant support of the Communists."[388] Another letter to the *Tribune* accused the MacDougall campaign of using "cliches which have become part of the esoteric language of the Communist." One so-called incriminating phrase, "the fight against fascism," would seem mild today, and probably less than incendiary at the time as well, unless you were very sensitive to Soviet propaganda.[389]

Church himself went after the head of the Amalgamated Garment Workers' union during the latter's testimony before the Campaign Expenditures Committee, on which Church sat. As the congressman asked questions of Sidney Hillman, he characterized his union's political action committee as "communistic" and a "racket." Hillman shot back that he resented those charges. "You are speaking of a workers' union," he said. He did imply that he appreciated the opportunity to testify before Church's committee, as other House committees, such as Un-American Activities, often said the same things without giving him the opportunity to defend himself.[390]

The Taft-Hartley Act, which was designed to control union activity, remained a good talking point for Church when he spoke to reporters. His district had light industry and a modicum of union strife in this period, but if there was any thought that union members voted in the Tenth, Church did not worry about them. Again, there was some opposition to Church's reelection in 1946, but it had nothing to do with Taft-Hartley or the labor movement. Primary rivals appeared that year, and the strongest was Hugh Riddle, a former fighter pilot who believed he could debate the incumbent on foreign affairs. His positivity (if not outright support) towards the United Nations gave Church's side the opportunity to call him an "internationalist," not many steps this side of "Bolshevik."[391] The result in the general election was the same as before: in Church's favor.

Amid the yuletide season, on December 21, 1946, Marjory Williams Church, then a senior in high school, made her official debut—an event typically recognized as an upper-class woman's formal introduction to society, with historical roots signaling a woman's readiness for marriage. In honor of their daughter, Ralph and Marguerite hosted a formal tea in their home, and the papers, of course, made note of Marjory's attire: "a gown of white satin and gold lamé, [and she carried] an old fashioned bouquet of French violets centered with a full blown yellow rose."[392]

By 1948, redistricting made the new Thirteenth Congressional District look even stronger for Ralph Church, as it cut out potentially Democratic precincts in Chicago and added townships as far north as the Wisconsin state line. Several primary candidates appeared that year, including John Nuveen, an investment banker. Opponents tried to capitalize on the feeling that Ralph Church had been in office too long and was little involved with the party leadership. This charge came largely from New Trier Township, where the resident oligarchs were corporate leaders who would continue, in years to come, to propose candidates from their own social circle for the seat. But Evanston, Church's bulletproof base, was more populous, relatively more middle-class, and quite happy with their conservative friend. The Republicans lost their congressional majority in '48, which had been fragile, but they did not lose Church, who won by a two-to-one margin over his Democratic opponent that year.

Despite his string of electoral victories, Congressman Ralph Church never seemed to take his seat for granted. Perhaps he could have been less obsessed with his attendance record, less eager to shake hands on the railroad platforms. But this was the formula that had worked from his earliest legislative campaigns. He, along with a significant majority of his constituents, believed in stricter budgets against the perceived fiscal neglect of the Democrats. His simple political approach was to repeat his principles and show up to vote for them, albeit as a member of the minority. Other Congressmen could work on the abstract principles of public policy—though this would be a minority position too. When Church boasted in 1948 that he had not missed a vote in his five terms in Congress, the God-fearing people of Evanston, not to mention the farmers up in Lake County, liked that.

A DRAMATIC EXIT

By 1950, Ralph Church showed no signs of slowing down, but there was concern for his health. His personal secretary said that he simply "couldn't rest," and carried the weight of his work wherever he went.[393]

He had suffered heart issues for a decade, and doctors had advised him "to avoid excitement and tension."[394] But there was always work to do. There was always a conservative position to stake out, and that was what he was doing on March 21, 1950, when he was testifying before the Executive Expenditure Committee, not normally a hot ticket on Capitol Hill. But Church had to weigh in on President Truman's plan to eliminate the office of general counsel of the National Labor Relations Board. He saw this as a weakening of provisions of Taft-Hartley, which Truman had tried and failed to veto outright.

On the third floor of the New House Office Building (renamed Longworth House Office Building in 1962[395]), the committee was assembled in a meeting room overlooking the Capitol Building with a crowd of 100 in total. Colleagues later said that Church seemed fit as he entered the room. Church greeted the Democrats and Republicans of the committee, which included its chairman, Democrat William L. Dawson of Chicago. Church's prepared remarks were strong on the subject of enforcement of Taft-Hartley, but he was also conciliatory, suggesting that the general counsel move to another office, rather than abolishing the position altogether.

He had been speaking for twenty-five minutes when, mid-sentence, he began gasping for breath. The sixty-six-year-old congressman then slurred a sentence—"If the congress does not set it aside within the required sixty days, I venture the prediction that it will result in considerable . . ."—then stumbled over the word "litigation."[396] He tried to repeat it, but before he could get through another sentence, he slumped and collapsed in his chair.[397] A member of the gallery jumped up and caught Ralph before he hit the floor, as Chairman Dawson yelled, "He's sick, he's sick."[398] Representative John W. McCormack of Massachusetts, a member of the committee, urged others to "stretch him out on the floor," then attempted to administer smelling salts.[399] Another member, Franklin Delano Roosevelt Jr., rushed to open a window to get air in the room.[400] Representative Arthur L. Miller of Nebraska, a physician, was called, but it was already too late. Miller pronounced Church dead of a heart attack at 9:50 a.m. before he could even be removed from the room.[401]

The event sent a shock through Capitol Hill. Almost immediately, flags on the buildings were lowered to half-staff. One hour after Ralph's death, Representative Leo E. Allen, also from Illinois, rose to the floor of the House and announced the tragedy, followed by almost forty members' spontaneous eulogies.[402] Then, a quiet descended, and the House was adjourned for the rest of the day, out of respect for Ralph E. Church. No one called "point of order" against the recess.

In days to come, many spoke fondly of the gentleman from Evanston.

Acting Senate Minority Leader Leverett Saltonstall spoke "of the high regard in which [Church] was held by the citizens of Evanston." To him and his colleagues, Church was "a hardworking, energetic, sincere man" who was "always frank in his expressions" and "presented with great courage and sincerity."[403] Democratic Senator Paul Douglas of Illinois echoed these notes of service in his remarks, commenting on "the conscientiousness with which [Church] approached all" and the "real sorrow" he felt at the passing of a "good citizen."[404] Representative Dewey Short from Missouri added to the praise, describing Church as a man with "a high sense of public duty" that was "honest, industrious, courageous," and notably "always willing to help people regardless of their race, party, or creed."[405] Representative McCormack described Church "a lovable character, a strong debater, and an able legislator; a man of definite views, and . . . possessed of intellectual honesty."[406] Representative Allen spoke particularly poetically, echoing the sentiments of the men who spoke before him, saying Church "passed away as a soldier fighting on the battlefield of peace for principles he regarded as vital to the welfare of his country."[407]

The many kind words cast his way were sincere and reflected the spirit of Congress at the time. Ralph Church was a battler on the House floor, but his integrity, many intoned, outshone partisanship.

In what would amount to a rather prophetic observation of Marguerite's upcoming, unexpected, and brilliantly successful political career, Representative Edith Nourse Rogers of Massachusetts spoke of a comment Ralph made one day before his death, sharing that he "spoke of women in politics, women that were holding office, and women that were doing work for the benefit of the country and the world," and on how "his admiration for his wife and his anxiousness to help her, for he knew she had helped him," was "one of the reasons he was so courteous and just and fair to women."[408]

On March 24, 1950, Ralph E. Church was laid to rest at Memorial Park in Skokie, Illinois.[409] His wife would join him here forty years later, but not before she continued the work he'd left without warning and created her own legacy of congressional service, the likes of which few had ever seen.

Reproduced with permission from Evanston History Center. Shared in The Chicago Tribune, April 4, 1940

Above: Ralph Church, age 10

Below: Ralph (front row, second from left) and the 1902 Danville High School football team

Reproduced with permission from Evanston History Center. Image appeared in the Danville News

Marguerite, 1922

Marguerite, circa 1925–1935

Image from a 1924 campaign flyer for Ralph

Ralph, November 1934

Photo courtesy of Library of Congress, Harris & Ewing Collection

Ralph, November 30, 1937

Photo courtesy of Library of Congress, Harris & Ewing Collection

Above: Ralph (center, seated) with other members of the Naval Affairs Committee, 1939

Below: Ralph at home in Evanston, 1940. Notice the ship's clock (later stolen) in the background

Photo courtesy of Library of Congress, Harris & Ewing Collection

Photo courtesy of Library of Congress, Harris & Ewing Collection

Ralph (right) chats with Dock J. Williams, former president of Chicago's United Packing House Workers Local 25, 1944

Photo courtesy of Wellesley College Archives, Library and Technology Services

Above: Newly elected to Congress, Marguerite passes the presidential gavel of the Congressional Club to Mary Lou Martin (Mrs. James C. Davis) January 21, 1951

Below: The women of the 82nd Congress, at a party thrown January 1951 by the Press Club of Washington. Left to right: Front row: Marguerite Stitt Church (R-IL), Ruth Thompson (R-MI) Second row: Cecil Harden (R-IN), Edith Rogers (R-MA), Margaret Chase Smith (R-ME), Frances P. Bolton (R-OH), Reva Zilpha Beck Bosone (D-UT) Rear: Edna Kelly (D-NY) Katharine P. St. George (R-NY)

Photo courtesy of Wellesley College Archives, Library and Technology Services

Reproduced with permission by Chicago Tribune/Tribune Content Agency, LLC - Waukegan News-Sun/TCA. Photo courtesy of the Evanston History Center

Above: Marguerite with cub reporters, including the first Black citizens welcomed into the Members' Dining Room in the House. 1952

Below: Marguerite at the Taipei Airport for a farewell to visiting Congreemen, December 6, 1955. Left to right: Karl Rankin, Geraldine Townsend (Mrs. George A. Fitch), Marguerite Stitt Church, Madame Chaing Kai-Shek

Photo courtesy of Wellesley College Archives, Library and Technology Services

Photo from the Martin Luther King, Jr. Memorial Library, Washington, D.C. and/or Collection of the U.S. House of Representatives. Photo courtesy of Evanston History Center.

Marguerite's Congressional Photo, 1960

Reproduced with permission from the John F. Kennedy Presidential Library and Museum

Above: Marguerite with President Kennedy and others at a swearing-in ceremony in the Oval Office for delegates to the United Nations, 1961

Below: The United States delegation to the United Nations in the General Assembly Hall at the United Nations Headquarters in New York City. Left to right: Secretary of State Dean Rusk, US Ambassador to the UN Adlai Stevenson, Representative Marguerite Stitt Church of Illinois. September 25, 1961

Reproduced with permission from the John F. Kennedy Pressidental Library Museum, Boston. Photo by Cecil Stoughton, White House Photographs

Photo courtesy of Wellesley College Archives, Library and Technology Services

Above:: Marguerite visits with Pat Nixon after the First Lady was installed as the honorary president of the Girl Scouts of the USA, 1970

Below: Marguerite's belated 91st birthday party with 400+ attendees, including, from left, Rep. John Porter and Marguertite's successor, Rep. Donald Rumsfeld, who was then an advisor to Reagan on national security affairs.

Photo by John Dziekan. Reprinted with permission from the Chicago Tribune/Tribune Content Agency, LLC. Originally run in the Chicago Tribune October 25, 1983

CHAPTER TEN

A QUIET ENTRANCE

THERE SEEMS TO EXIST NO public report of Marguerite and her family's response or reaction to her husband's sudden death. However, Una Corley Groves worked from the Church home every day in those years, later becoming Marguerite's secretary in Washington, and in 2018 she recalled Mrs. Church's steadiness and stoicism after her husband's sudden death. When asked if Mrs. Church broke down or exhibited a show of emotion, Groves said, "No. Never. There were times you knew she was deep in thought, but there was never a time she didn't have control. I don't think you'd ever find her surprised at anything." Groves continued, "She ran everything herself. She built herself. And she just kept moving forward."[410]

When Ralph died, his congressional secretary in Washington, Helen Nelsch, was left to run his office. As Groves explained, Marguerite had to step in swiftly to assist. Helen would need immediate direction now that Ralph was gone. "Back then, Helen Nelsch was what you'd call a typical Washington secretary," Groves said. "The job was her life, and she was completely devoted to Mr. Church."[411]

Immediately, Marguerite faced questions of political triage—the first of which was the primary election, coming in less than a month. Ralph Church's name could not be legally removed from the ballot, and party leaders in Illinois were quickly in discussion of how to address the problem. None of this concerned Democratic leaders in Washington, who understood that flipping Illinois' Thirteenth Congressional District from GOP to Democrat was unlikely if not impossible.

As early as March 22, the day after Ralph's death, the *Chicago Tribune* mentioned Marguerite as a potential successor.[412] The funeral was held on March 24 at the First United Methodist Church of Evanston, just down the street from the Church home, where Republican committee officials surely paid condolence calls while also perhaps tenderly navigating the subject of her running for his seat.[413] Ralph's honorary pallbearers included General Charles Gates Dawes, the former vice president of the United States, and Roy O. West, the former secretary of the interior under President Coolidge. Mourners honored Ralph "as a man who lived in Evanston ever since his college years, as a 'public servant' able and honorable in all his undertakings, and as a private individual who brought to his career clean hands and an upright heart." The church choir "sang 'Be Still, My Soul,' 'America the Beautiful,' and 'The Strife is O'er, the Battle Done.'"[414]

By early April, the *Tribune* described sentiment building for Marguerite, who, according to the paper, "has let it be known she would serve if called."[415] However, not everyone responded favorably to this declaration, and in particular the district's farming areas "brought rumblings of dissent." There, the *Tribune* reported, "opposition to women in politics is deep seated."[416] Additionally, the New Trier Women's Republican Club—one that previously opposed Ralph—announced William Montgomery McGovern as a write-in.[417]

As Republicans continued to encourage her to run, Marguerite departed for Washington on May 16 to attend Ralph's memorial on Capitol Hill and to tend to her Congressional Club duties.[418]

Stopping to answer reporters' questions on the tarmac, she spoke not of grief but rather what needed to happen in Washington. "In the latest attack on the American taxpayer," she told the *Tribune*, "he is now even being asked to take over 8.4 billion dollars ($107 billion in 2023) in debts of Great Britain.

National bankruptcy is the only logical result of the continuation of [the Marshall Plan].[419] She continued: "The whole world goes down with us. Doomed would be even the starry-eyed folk who believe international love can be created with American taxpayers' money."[420]

Her aptitude for the job did not go unnoticed, as evidenced by Dr. Kenneth Colegrove, professor of political science at Northwestern University and adviser to General Douglas MacArthur. In Colegrove's letter to William N. Erickson, then-president of the Cook County Board of Commissioners, he wrote: "Marguerite Church is an unusual woman. She would be able to represent this district with unusual prestige and competence."[421]

Upon her return from Washington, Marguerite spent the evening of June 9 as one of sixteen candidates allowed to speak for ten minutes each in Waukegan, Illinois. Marguerite made a strong impression. William Busse, who'd served for more than fifty years on the GOP county committee, said, "Mrs. Church made the best speech I have ever heard made by a congressional candidate in Illinois—man or woman." The *Tribune* said, "She blended sorrow, gratitude, tribute to her husband, party principles, and determination to aid the Republican cause regardless of the choice of a nominee."[422]

In the *Tribune*, reporter Joan Beck wrote that Marguerite was well-suited to her new role as candidate. "Speech making, campaigning, and political conferences have been as much a part of Mrs. Church's marriage as marketing and cooking," credited Beck, who worked mostly in the women's pages at this time, but who would break through gender barriers herself at the *Tribune* in decades to come.[423]

Beck acknowledged that Marguerite winning the election was likely, and she asked the candidate how having a *Mrs.* Church in Congress would be different. Marguerite acknowledged that her gender was on balance an advantage in a district where Evanston, with a deeply feminist history, was the largest population center. Beck drilled down, asking if she would take more interest in women's affairs than Ralph did.

"That's almost impossible," the candidate replied in her husband's defense. "We've both worked closely for many years for women's interests in government. You know he was a leader in the Illinois suffrage fight when he was in Springfield. I don't see how I could do more than he has for women."[424] While Marguerite's observations may have, in fact, been true, it seems any efforts Ralph made to support women's suffrage were made quietly. In fact, there is scant record of Ralph Church publicly supporting the women's vote when it mattered to the suffrage question, though it is likely he did so at home. "But women are still so new in Congress," Marguerite told the reporter, "that I'm excited about the possibility of being elected."[425]

For perspective, while Beck's column outlined Marguerite's political course of action, another column on the same page, by Antoinette Donnelley, outlined the "second of a series of daily articles on Fatties Anonymous, a new group movement for weight reduction."[426]

A STOIC STRENGTH

Despite the popular press labeling Marguerite as a "typical wife," it seems the Republican committeemen recognized her political value. And while they favored Marguerite for her similarities to her husband—her conservatism and her tireless hard work—over time she would demonstrate significantly different stripes. Ralph's career was driven largely, even conspicuously, by political calculation, even if his tactical sense was less than deft. (Witness his indecisiveness when moved to run for higher office.) For Marguerite, sheer principle appeared more prominent in her makeup. When her succession of her husband was first discussed, she expressed no hard certainty that she was the right person, and she seemed sincere when she said the voters should decide.

After her husband's death, too late to remove his name from the primary ballot, she knew the likely scenario. It was that Ralph's name would garner the winning number of votes by a large margin, which it did in April. Then the committeemen of the district would have to name someone to replace him, which they would do in June. Marguerite was quiet but not invisible in the intervening period. One major event was a May 11 fashion show at the Tam O'Shanter Country Club in Arlington Heights, held during a large meeting of the district's Republican Women's Organization, with members coming from thirteen townships in Cook County and all of Lake County.[427] Marguerite was the featured speaker, and when she got up to speak, she hardly mentioned the possibility that she might be moving into her husband's seat. Instead, she stressed the importance of women getting out and voting. The values of democracy and freedom, not to mention Republicanism, depended upon it, depended upon women, she implied. Turnout was key, she said, to preserving the way of life that they all held dear.[428]

Any successful politician has a base, and Marguerite's was composed of conservative women in a white, wealthy district. They were fired up by their new leader, and she knew how to keep them that way. Without breaking character, refined and supremely self-confident, she threw a little red meat to the women who broadly agreed that the Truman administration's "stupid foreign policy and ridiculous overspending" must be curtailed, as one attendee remembered her saying. Nevertheless, her attack was softened by gentleness. "Upon hearing her, and watching her as she spoke," said another voter who wrote of the meeting, "her personality of ease, grace, upright honesty, and simplicity presented itself as a human and genuine force of remarkable statesmanship."[429] She seemed very much to be calling on the voters' better angels, mixing sharp partisan whistles with softly worded appeals in support of freedom, democracy, and no more Democrats.

The GOP hierarchy of the district named Marguerite Church their candidate for Congress in June 1950. After some wrangling that was largely performative, she was elected by the committeemen to take her late husband's place in the general election. There was agreement that Marguerite was Ralph's equal, politically speaking, given her involvement in his campaigns and congressional work, not to mention her obvious erudition. She would keep the district safe for Republicans.

After her acceptance of the nomination, the *Tribune* ran a story headlined, "Grateful, Calm, Mrs. Church is Foe of Truman." Described as "gray haired and slight," Marguerite noted the Truman administration's "intellectual dishonesty and insincerity which President Roosevelt started." The reporter then noted the sadness as Marguerite added, "'Thrilling as it would be to become a member of Congress, please believe me when I say it's something I never wanted for myself. I would much rather have been the wife of the representative of the district for the rest of my life."[430] That same day, reporters captured her smiling face as she boarded an American Airlines flight to Boston. She would be attending Marjory's graduation from Wellesley without Ralph, celebrating her daughter's successful double major in political science and international law.[431]

Later that month, with plenty on her mind, it seems Marguerite "refereed" an explosive exchange at the Congressional Club. On June 21, 1950, the *Austin Statesman* ran a startling headline: "Harmonious Rage Envelops Dear Ladies of Staid Congressional Club." Clare Booth Luce, a former congresswoman from Connecticut, unleashed some fury to an assembled group of club members, telling "the ladies whose husbands were even then toiling in the congressional vineyards that the legislative halls up on the hill were filled with laggard lame-brains, backward dimwits better suited to pick and shovel work and with clods given to sloth and excessive indolence." Never had the ladies of the club been so "fused as one in a monumental non-partisan rage at this attack on their respective spouses."[432]

The reporter said Luce was faced by "some hundreds of women, each of whom was praying for the strength to get up and tell Luce a few things for her own good." But then, someone who was described and never named but could only have been Marguerite "beat them to the draw." She was "the wife of a Republican congressman who had spent most of his life in the House of Representatives." The reporter then described Marguerite immediately, if not brilliantly, disarming the crowd by acknowledging all sides of the argument. "'Dear Ladies,' the little woman purred. 'I do not think we should have it in our hearts to be angry with Luce for her frank estimate of Congress. After all, during her years in Congress, Luce doubtless saw only the frivolous side of our husbands. Thank you.'" The reporter then explained, "That folded up the meeting. Everyone felt the mousy little woman had said it for them, only better."[433] Marguerite's response only highlights how experienced—and well-prepared—Marguerite was to deal with the often highly combustible personalities in Washington.

MUTED FEMINISM AND OTHER ADVANTAGES

Marguerite's eventual success as a congressman (as Marguerite preferred to be called) was sustained by some special conditions that worked strongly in her favor, including the suffrage movement, controlled by white, middle class women. For example, Evanston, as the district's largest city, was ultraconservative but also deeply imbued in women's rights—albeit for white women—reaching back to the Women's Christian Temperance Union. The WCTU "was rare for an organization run mostly by white women in the late nineteenth century in that it included both white and Black members. However, this does not mean that Black members were always treated equitably."[434]

In 1885, Frances Harper, superintendent of the organization's "Department of Work Among the Colored People," published a piece in the WCTU newspaper The Union Signal titled, "Work Among The Colored People of the North," urging white women to devote more resources and time to the efforts of organizing Black women, a sentiment shared by many.[435] However, one example of racism's stain on feminism at that time was evidenced in the advocacy of the Rev. Dr. Anna Howard Shaw: a white physician, Methodist minister, and president of the National American Woman Suffrage Association. Shaw perpetuated ravages of racism as well as classism when she said, "Instead of recognizing [Civil War veterans'] service and rewarding the loyal women, the cry went forth: 'This is the negroes' hour. Let the women wait'—and they are still waiting. As they wait, they are not blind to the fact that this nation did what no other nation has ever done, when it voluntarily made its former slaves the sovereign rulers of its loyal and patriotic women."[436] Feminism in Evanston, in all of its manifestations (conservative and progressive—and yes, infused with white, middle class racism) was nevertheless bred in the bone, such that when Marguerite embarked on the run for her recently deceased husband's seat, she found that her gender, while in the political minority, was now viewed as a unique advantage.

Marguerite knew from experience that women had power, and she fully intended to invoke and employ it. She said, early on, that she understood that she would be held to a different standard—not higher or lower, but different. She said to the gathered crowd when accepting the GOP nomination in 1950, "If a man had been nominated and made a mistake, you would have said 'He is stupid.' If I make a mistake you will say, 'She is a woman.' I shall try never to give you a reason to say that."[437]

Though she benefited from and encouraged a rising respect for women and their capacity, Marguerite never considered herself a feminist. Many women of her time—particularly conservative women—did not embrace the label, viewing it as too radical. Marguerite was a juxtaposition. She saw most issues from every angle and could simultaneously believe in the traditional ideals with which she had been raised while also embracing a limited progressive outlook toward her gender. Consider her statement to the press that it was easier for women to campaign, as "I just have to keep house, while my husband had to manage a legal firm besides."[438]

Still, crediting gender as an advantage was not a habit common across the board, as women legislators were regularly met with questions and surprise—if not worse. Marguerite's fellow freshman in Congress, Ruth Thompson of Michigan, recalled a time when she, as a former probate judge, answered a phone call and was asked by the male caller to speak to Judge Thompson. After Thompson clarified that she was, in fact, speaking, the caller reportedly asked with incredulity, "Are you a lady?"—to which Thompson replied with a laugh, "Well, I certainly try to be."[439]

Marguerite entered politics with other advantages as well. First, she was the widow of Ralph Church, who may not have been loved by his colleagues in Congress, but was adored in his district where he worked the train stations and coffee shops in a way that amazed his friends and dismayed his rivals. Nearly as well known as the Congressman was his wife, who organized political meetings all over the district and helped make her husband's seat one of the safest incumbencies in the nation. She had also served as her husband's legislative emissary, something that would serve her well as her service in Congress evolved. Something else working to her benefit was the fact that Ralph had left her an estate of $25,000, which is roughly equivalent to $318,000 in 2023.[440]

As fate would have it, Marguerite's election occurred at a period in history when more and more women were filling the halls of Congress. From 1917 to 1919, there'd been one woman in the 67th Congress; by 1951, Marguerite, elected to the 82nd Congress, served as one of eleven female members of Congress—ten representatives and one senator. Surely, Marguerite and her female colleagues felt moments of camaraderie and support—or at the very least, a sense they were not alone.

As a white woman, Marguerite's race afforded her access to the political arena much earlier than her non-white peers. By 1950, Marguerite was one of the first 50 women—all white—elected to Congress. Fifteen years later, in 1965, Patsy Mink of Hawaii was elected to the House as its first woman of color; twenty eight years later, in 1993, Carol Moseley Braun became the first Black woman elected to the Senate; fourteen years later in 2007, Nancy Pelosi was named the first woman speaker of the House; and seventy years after Marguerite's election, Kamala Harris was elected vice president in 2020—the first Black, south Indian, biracial woman elected to the office.

Marguerite also lived in a town whose population, though heavily and egregiously segregated, emerged as one that drew and kept increasing numbers of residents of color. According to historian Andrew Wiese, who was quoted in a piece by journalist Larry Gavin, "The dynamics of local race relations combined with the aspirations of [B]lack southerners to shape a housing market that both supported [B]lack home ownership and accommodated the growth of a large [B]lack community in an otherwise affluent and white suburb."[441] In the 1850s, Evanston was vastly and predominently white, but by 1960, Evanston's Black population had grown to 9,126. It's reasonable to conjecture that Marguerite's long-standing roots in such a racially diverse and progressive community may have elevated her standing as someone who knew how to speak and listen beyond the echoes of white suburbia on Chicago's privileged North Shore.[442]

As a woman, Marguerite was hardly alone in her interest in politics, but she was a rare exception in an already small pool of female legislators. Working to her favor was a pattern known as the "widow's mandate." From 1921 to 1951, twenty-one widows (including Marguerite) directly succeeded their late husbands in Congress.[443] From 1917 through 1976, one-third of the ninety-five women elected to Congress were widows "elected or appointed to succeed their late husbands."[444] And from 1923 through 2005, more than 82 percent of the House widows who'd been nominated to run for their deceased husband's seats had emerged victorious in their elections.[445] Unlike Marguerite, though, half of them served one term or less.[446] The widows were also thought to garner more press in the wake of their tragic circumstances.[447]

Unlike some women in Congress, Marguerite appeared all but immune to judgment or the glare of a personal spotlight. Patricia Schroeder of Colorado, after her 1972 election, was asked by one of her feminist House colleagues how she planned to excel in her career while raising toddlers. And Minnesota's Coya Knutson, a champion of educational policy and matters of agriculture who served from 1954 to 1959, saw her legislative career derailed when her husband, among other things, publicly endorsed her opponent.[448]

Marguerite was seen as an attractive political wife, balancing modesty and strength, and even more attractive as a widow. She claimed from the outset of her political career that she had had no intention to run for office, that she wanted only to honor the deep affinity that the voters and her husband had for each other. During her retirement, she was asked if she had ever considered the possibility of running for Congress. "Oh, never, never," she said to Fern Ingersoll during her 1978 oral history. Then, referring to Ralph, she added, "And I'm sure he considered it even less than I did. I had married him the beginning of his second term in the Illinois legislature, so my political life was one of adaptation to his life."[449] If she ever focused on personal advancement, it was done in the context of community service, which was almost always mentioned whenever her name came up in conversation or news reports. Also noted was her brilliance and her eloquence, compliments rarely cast toward male members of Congress unless they were on some stump or another.[450]

Good words about her rang true. She herself said repeatedly that she never anticipated that she would have a political career on her own account, and she insisted that she would gladly surrender it before voting against her conscience. Her sincerity was convincing and a great political luxury. "In my case," she said in her later years, "I had an asset which was a great source of strength to me. I had never sought the office. I had never expected to hold it. And any moment that I would have had to vote against my convictions, they could have taken it back."[451]

According to Groves, Marguerite was not only possessed with "an uncommon combination of intelligence, warmth, background, lifestyle, and ability to connect," but also her political life was always "in the background." While Ralph was alive, Marguerite raised their children, kept their home, and devoted her time to service projects, to women's clubs, to her alma mater, to the Congressional Club, and to furthering Ralph's career. "That's why she 'had it' when the time came," Groves explained. "All the women immediately swooped in and supported and lifted her up. She didn't have to worry about a thing. She had a complete organization. A network. It was all done. She was a producer of sorts. She produced herself."[452]

ELECTION VICTORY

On November 8, 1950, the day after her electoral victory, Marguerite told the *Chicago Tribune*, "I am thankful for the vote of confidence given me by all those who supported and worked for my campaign, particularly the women who got behind me wholeheartedly." She concluded by saying, "I am going back to Washington to get my office in readiness for the session . . . it needs a good sweeping, just like the Truman administration."[453]

Women had been crucial to Ralph's success and would be to Marguerite's as well. It wasn't just votes; she credited an intelligence and patience of women that stood in stark contrast to many congressional men. "The November election proved incontestably," Marguerite said in a press release, "that women, working together in common faith and unity, can be an irresistible force for victory. Now—doorbell to doorbell, telephone to telephone, individually and in groups—we must proclaim what we know to be so signally true."[454]

Marguerite neither rested on her laurels, nor on the legacy of powerful women in "Heavenston." From the beginning of her own congressional career, she exercised the political savvy cultivated by being alongside her husband in sixteen electoral campaigns. In late 1950, she spearheaded the creation of the Women's Republican Club, Thirteenth Congressional District of Illinois, as it was formally called. Groves, who grew up in the district, said this was previously an ad hoc group, and many of the women in it had been meeting with Marguerite Church regularly for years.

A special purpose campaign organization, this branch of the Women's Republican Club had only been active since the month before Ralph's death. The group formalized the month after Marguerite's election, during her election victory luncheon, with representatives from the thirteen Cook County townships in the district and all eighteen in Lake County. Among other functions, it provided a unified force that overcame challenges, or at least attempted to never let them grow ominous. The *Tribune* reported on Marguerite's election victory luncheon: "Mrs. Church told the group that the election in November definitely proved that women working shoulder to shoulder could produce Republican victories."[455]

Still, there were critics. For example, in 1951 a group of GOP women in New Trier Township made it known that they believed Mrs. Church had walked too easily into Congress, and they temporized about supporting her for a second term. Many had supported William McGovern for the GOP nomination in 1950, favoring his ferocious anticommunism to Mrs. Church's isolationism. But dissent in Winnetka and Wilmette was quickly silenced; one township, albeit the richest in the district, could hardly stand up to the other twenty-nine. "I believe that unity as well as union can produce untold and wonderful results," Marguerite said at one of the Women's Republican Club's first meetings. "I take delight in seeing what this informal association of undaunted Republican women who have proved what they can do, now banding together without any loss of momentum of enthusiasm into a permanent association."[456]

On November 12, 1950, under the headline "New Women in Congress; One Is Real Career Girl and Other Is Typical Wife," the House of Representatives's newly elected freshman female legislators were introduced to readers. "Both Republicans, the two women have completely dissimilar backgrounds—but both have long been interested in public affairs and quick to translate their interest into practical activity. Ruth Thompson, the lone spinster among the ladies of Congress, is a real career girl. Marquerite [sic] Church has for many years been a typical wife and mother."[457]

Aside from misspelling Marguerite's first name and omitting her maiden name, the column portrays the women in ways that, today, are considered blatantly sexist, burying and downplaying details and accomplishments including, among other things, Thompson's attendance at business college, her law degree, multiple terms as a judge and state legislator, as well as Marguerite's experience as a teacher and psychologist, her master's degree from Columbia, her governmental special studies on international affairs, and her presidency of the Congressional Club.[458]

On November 17, Marguerite flew to New York City to be with her sister, Edna, who served as president of the Methodist Home for the Aged, which was celebrating the 100th anniversary of its founding.[459] For twenty-five years, Edna served as president, a role their mother, Adelaide Stitt, had also held from 1926 to 1933.[460] The holiday season would be Marguerite's last before her twelve years in Congress began, and she enjoyed it with family while preparing for her freshman year in the House.

Early in 1950, prospects had looked good for women running for Congress. With an unprecedented thirty-seven women running for the House of Representatives that year, odds were that a record number would win and take office. By election night, however, results were less than stellar. "Women Candidates for Congress Find It Rough Going" was one headline the day after the election.[461] Only ten women made it to the House of Representatives, up by only one from the previous Congress, and one down from the 1944 cycle.

A women's wave in the House would have to wait. For now, despite talk of female empowerment, their numbers would rise only incrementally—and remain politically divided. With six Republicans and four Democrats winning in 1950, the consistent fire that brought women's suffrage three decades before was lacking in uniformity when it came to supporting women running for office.

UNMISTAKABLY REPUBLICAN

Marguerite knew that politics was not a breeze, especially as the general election had approached. "Every serious thinking woman in the country knows the United States is facing a crisis," she said on television a few days before the election. "The women are not going to trust the kind of leadership that put us where we are today."[462] Of course, she was talking about the Truman administration, fraught with military indecision and easily blamed for communist aggression in southeast Asia.

When possible, she left the tougher broadside to others, especially early in her career. On that particular television show, she shared the screen with Everett

M. Dirksen, the downstate congressman who was running for the Senate. "Young Americans are dying in Korea this afternoon trying to stem the red tide," Dirksen intoned, "while in Washington the Communists are sheltered and protected as they peddle our secrets to Joe Stalin."[463] The stridency of Dirksen seemed less surprising than the fact that he was appearing with Marguerite. His esteem for her husband might have been less than complete, as some years before he had called out Ralph's partisan strikes against Adolph Sabath as spoiling the vaunted collegiality of the House of Representatives. This, however, was something that his elegant widow would never do.

Marguerite easily won in November (so did Dirksen), and though the Republicans remained in the minority, Truman's popularity was plummeting. Republicans smelled blood, and Marguerite was not unwilling to circle the weakened Democrats. The Korean War was confusing many Americans in 1951, and the issue was heightened not by the politicians but by General Douglas MacArthur, commander in Asia, who lobbied publicly against the administration's conduct of a "limited war." We needed an all-out effort, the general insisted, and we needed to pursue the communists on to Chinese soil if necessary. Many Americans, who remembered the total victory of the recent world war, agreed. But Truman did not, and the president unilaterally dismissed the American "shogun" for continuing what seemed like insubordination. Much of the public was aghast, and the Republicans were quickly eager to inflame public opinion on this winning issue. While she remained characteristically unemotional, Mrs. Church, a deep-dyed conservative on most issues for most of her political career, had no compunction in joining this political chorus.

Support of MacArthur was so widespread that towns all over America organized rallies to symbolically welcome the general home after his dismissal. The day he landed in San Francisco, April 17, 1951, church bells rang and sirens blared all over the country, including in the Thirteenth Congressional District.

For Marguerite, it was an initiation in constituent relations, as a flood of protest came into the office. "Can't fire MacArthur," said one of thousands. "He's the genius of the world," said another. The office staffed up to handle these letters and respond to each, with Marguerite penning a note to the many recipients she personally knew. Groves was amazed by the responsiveness which became largely Marguerite's modus operandi as long as she was in Congress.[464]

Marguerite made sure that reports of local celebrations were accompanied by her views. In one case, she spoke through the publicity chairman of the district's Republican Women's Club. She lamented the loss "by one stroke" of "the greatest foe of Communism in all Asia." She added that if the Democratic leadership had not made such poor decisions in appeasing communists at Yalta and Potsdam, "we would not be facing the danger which is now on us."[465]

What was that danger? That, of course, was a moving target, which the congresswoman deftly shifted herself depending upon the issue or occasion. In that first year of service in the House, she left it to interpretation by those who shared her political principles in general. "A vote for Republicans is a vote for peace and freedom," she wrote in a communiqué that was published in the papers.[466] It took time, but she eventually joined other Republicans in defining what peace and freedom meant. An early line in the sand was on a new draft bill, the so-called Universal Military Training Act, which would require all draft-age men to serve at least twelve months. Marguerite joined her party in resisting what the Republicans said was becoming a "military dictatorship" if the Pentagon was given too much power. The Republicans prevailed in forcing the Democrats to moderate the bill.

There were other delicate moments when the Republicans had to gauge how far they could go to resist what they perceived as rampant spending. On another issue she played a role in the Republicans' staking out of their position, this time on foreign aid. As a campaigner she had complained of the Marshall Plan, which was designed by the administration to rebuild post-World War II Europe with American dollars. When she got to Congress, she learned that it was hard to resist a majority, but it was not impossible. It was still 1951 when her party discerned flagging support for Truman and proposed to reduce aid to Europe by $350 million ($4.1 billion in 2023), to just under $1 billion ($11.8 billion in 2023). It was the kind of issue that Marguerite could get her arms around, and given her knowledge of Europe it gave her a chance to distinguish herself on the floor in some measure.[467]

As the effort to reduce the aid appropriation gained steam, Speaker Sam Rayburn took the floor. He said that a reduction of a half-billion from the foreign aid was dangerous and might lead to World War III. This must have struck Marguerite as a strange conclusion, or at least an exaggeration, but she said nothing at that moment. She waited until another New Deal Democrat, Representative John Rooney of New York, got up and amplified the speaker's argument, saying that the arguments of Republicans would be widely distributed in Communist countries, and "are giving great aid and comfort to the politburo." Marguerite jumped to protest and demanded that Rooney's words be read back to the floor. They were, and Speaker Rayburn deemed them "too cruel," and ordered them expunged from the record.[468]

For her part, Marguerite insisted that too much spending was, on the whole, simply destructive. "I do not see what good it will do us to save the whole world and lose our own soul," she told constituents as she reasoned her view of foreign aid.[469] It was not that the freshman representative turned the tide, but her eloquence did more than cover for her internationalist soul while also preserving her reputation as a conservative Republican. It marked her as a voice to be reckoned with. "For clarity of statement and beauty of expression," said a Democratic member on that occasion, "there is no member of this body that excels the gentlewoman . . . and I salute her." The reduction of the appropriation made it through.[470]

THE DOLPHIN IN THE ROOM

Marguerite settled comfortably into the routine that would sustain her for most of her congressional career. She understood that a fiscal hawk ought to control her office expenses. There was a tendency by other members of Congress to spend money on their offices, but Marguerite's was more spartan. One colorful touch was a mounted dolphin that Ralph caught on a trip to Florida. Another was a green leather desk chair, soft and forgiving enough that she once quipped that it was designed for "the congressional spine."[471] As for a district office, she preferred not to spend that money and keep her Evanston office in her home, as Ralph had done.[472] With these habits, Marguerite could attack what she perceived as big-spender Democrats without fear of hypocrisy.

The decision to keep her office in the house on Church Street also suited her constituents who came to value the big stone porch where Ralph and now Marguerite would receive visitors when they were in town. Tending to the constituency and knowing the voters were some of Ralph's great strengths, and Marguerite redoubled these efforts. Groves remembered that the first thing Marguerite did when she got to either office in the morning was answer correspondence. When that was done, she spoke to her staff to make sure everyone was "on the same page" as to the small details of public policy and constituent services. Her view was that if the people she represented were unknown or unheeded, her work as their representative would be spurious.[473]

She is said to have personally dictated replies to an average of 600 letters per week, and was careful to hold a cardinal rule of never asking for a political distinction from those needing her assistance.[474] "Then," explained Groves, "she went to the House floor, and from there to any committee meeting." She continued: "Every day for Mrs. Church was filled. Her day ended around 7:30 p.m."[475] Ralph, too, was credited with these same overtime hours by his peers.

Marguerite's office staff was composed of four—an attorney, Asa Groves Jr.; his new bride, Una, who served as Marguerite's personal secretary; and two women who handled matters regarding Illinois' Thirteenth Congressional District. According to Una, one of these women was secretary Alice Veck, who was devoted to handling inquiries about military personnel in the district. Parents called often about the whereabouts of their sons or daughters and, said Una, "Some [of those calls were] indeed sad, and Mrs. Church herself handled those."[476] The other woman on Marguerite's staff—whose name Una no longer recalls—was "another gal who wanted to be secretary to the secretary to the navy."[477]

Una recalls that when she and her husband weren't managing Marguerite's DC office, they socialized with a group which included Marguerite and another Washington couple who, in turn, managed the office of Senator Everett Dirksen. Dirksen, born in Pekin, Illinois, "was wonderful," Groves recalled in 2018 of those gatherings, which included the then-senator and his wife, Louella. "Glowing voice. Spellbinding. Mrs. Church was the offshoot of that. She could do with her voice what he could do with his, which was to express, and put the right emphasis on the right word."[478] Groves said her husband, born in Madison, Wisconsin, and Marguerite's son, Ralph Church Jr., had been friends and attended Northwestern Law together. As she remembered, they had been two of the few Republicans in their class. "Let's just say, they had to be extremely careful with their words."[479]

According to Groves, her husband was instrumental in drafting legislation. "Asa prepared the fireworks bill for Mrs. Church," Groves recalled years later, referencing a bill that would prevent fireworks from being transported into states in which they were illegal. "Mrs. Church turned to him and said, 'We have to stop this.' It required infinite work and preparation."[480]

In addition to their time together in the office, Una and Asa Groves Jr. sometimes traveled with Marguerite. "We went to Florida two or three times on weekends . . . when Congress wasn't going to be open until the following Wednesday. We'd go on Friday and come home Tuesday. We usually stayed at a hotel at Pompano Beach. We'd always find a nice place to drink tea and talk and look around. She was very, very kind to me. She knew I admired her tremendously."[481]

The Groveses left Washington in 1954 and moved to Miami, where Marguerite would continue to visit with them regularly.[482] That year, Barbara

Anne Harrison Ludden became Marguerite's political and social secretary, traveling with Marguerite and managing her Evanston district operations for eight years, including during Marguerite's 1961 service as a delegate to the United Nations. Following Marguerite's retirement, Ludden served six and a half years as chief of staff for Marguerite's Thirteenth Congressional District successor, Representative Donald Rumsfeld. Rumsfeld would later serve as US Secretary of Defense under Presidents Gerald Ford and George W. Bush.[483]

Ludden's nephew, Steven Anderson, wrote in a 2019 email that when his Aunt Barbara "told her parents (my grandparents) that she would be traveling to Illinois to work for Mrs. Church, they objected. They did not believe that their unmarried, twenty-one-year-old daughter should be traveling and living so far away from home all alone." Anderson continued: "Barbara told this to Mrs. Church, who was quite understanding. Mrs. Church then insisted that my aunt live in her home in Illinois when she was there. That way, she would not be living alone in an apartment or a rented room. Mrs. Church even went so far as to speak to my grandparents and to ensure them that she would take good care of my aunt. That conversation soothed my grandparents' fears and they allowed Barbara to take the position." Anderson concluded, "My aunt treasured her time with Mrs. Church. She spoke of Mrs. Church glowingly as a person and a legislator and recounted how Mrs. Church encouraged her to expand her horizons and to push back against preconceived notions of what women could or could not, or should or should not, do professionally."[484]

CHAPTER ELEVEN

A PIONEER IN CONGRESS

MARGUERITE ENTERED CONGRESS ON THE verge of momentum for Republicans on a national basis. While it was not necessarily women who would turn the political tide, many voiced dissent against the status quo in the '52 election.

Her timing was fortuitous. The isolationist wing of her party was nearly extinct, and her internationalist instincts could develop. Marguerite expressed a desire to be on the foreign affairs committee to which she was appointed in her second term. But beyond the good fortune that matched her views to her time, she often looked good beside the uninformed bluster of many male colleagues. An example is in how she broke through the war of accusations that accompanied any discussion of Red China versus Nationalist China. She did not weigh in too heavily. She would mention that she knew Madame Chiang Kai-Shek, wife of the embattled Nationalist leader, from their Wellesley days. "We made fudge together," she told a reporter, which made her an authority without ranting or boring anyone.[485]

It was impressive to any observer. But it was left to journalist Esther Tufty, who once lived in Evanston, to say what was frankly, if silently, on the minds of many about the new congressman (as she continued to call herself, and as many women in the House preferred to be called). "Marguerite will not like this," she wrote, "but her friends have always said she would make a better congressman than her husband, who was a reactionary politically and not as gregarious as she."[486] In fact, Marguerite did not shy away from her husband's arch conservative positions, and one could label her a "reactionary" for many of her views as well. But she—the congressman known for her crisp, buttoned-up attire—often couched her views in the softly tailored suit of a moderate.

In most cases, she cleaved to views that were well-known conservative positions, often in the extreme. And like her husband, as a member of the minority, she found her most frequent legislative task was to pound away at the excesses of the majority. But her hammer was usually covered in velvet. Ralph's style was to cry "Corruption!" or "Point of order!" Hers was more likely to look askance at a rival congressman, or to ask a seemingly naive question which, if answered in the detail requested, revealed weakness in the argument that she opposed. She delivered these punches without rancor. "She's not as noisy as most congressmen. She prefers to listen," a reporter said.[487] Still, when necessary, Marguerite was ready and willing to speak up to anyone. One reporter described a luncheon during Marguerite's first term, in which Defense Secretary General George Marshall favorably discussed universal military training. Along with the low ebb of Democratic prestige, the surging power of women stood behind Marguerite as she questioned Marshall: "Now General, I am a military novice," Marguerite said. "So, would you mind pointing out to me on the map exactly what our military objective is in Korea?"[488]

Marguerite also saw certain congressmen advocating for women. Members such as House leaders Joseph W. Martin of Massachusetts and Sam Rayburn of Texas assigned women like her to positions of leadership, ensuring female perspective on historically male committees.[489] According to the oral history of Representative Chase Woodhouse of Connecticut, it was Rayburn who once said to Marguerite, "You get the same pay as we do, don't you?" She says Marguerite answered, "Yes sir, for a change." Rayburn then replied, "And you worked three times as hard to get here as any of us did."[490] Congressman Jerry Voorhis, a Democrat from California, put it another way, saying he marveled at the "precarious balancing act" congressional women played. They could not depend upon male chivalry from rivals—partisan politics was rough for women and men—but nor could they assume the role of backslapping compatriot either.[491]

Marguerite served during what congressional historians describe as the "second generation" of women in Congress, those elected between 1935 and 1954. This second wave of women had more members than ever with pre-congressional careers and experience in elective office, qualifying them for better committee assignments and more areas of legislative expertise.[492] Additionally, states US House of Representatives Historian Matthew A. Wasniewski, Marguerite and her female congressional colleagues shared a dedication to bipartisanship as well as bonds beyond gender, having come of age during the Great Depression, two world wars, and the global pandemic of 1918.[493]

REALITY OF CONGRESSIONAL LIFE

Marguerite understood the power of her perceived moral authority and used it in unexpected ways. In June of 1952, while still in her first term, she hosted a group of newsboys from the *Waukegan News-Sun*. She planned to take them to the members' dining room in the House of Representatives for lunch, and when it became known that at least two of the newsboys, William Matlock and Sam Whiteside, were Black, dining room staff cautioned Marguerite that she probably would not get them past the door. Black congressmen were admitted to the dining room by this time, but Black guests hardly ever. Racism raised its sharp pickets often in America's vaunted seat of democracy, but at this moment Mrs. Church would have none of it.

In her oral history years later, she remembered that she had no intention of leaving anyone behind. "I said, 'These two boys are part of a group of six newsboys and I certainly do not intend to tell them they can't luncheon in the dining room of their own Capitol.' And when that time came, I walked in with the two little negro newsboys on either side. I entered pleasantly and greeted people as I walked down without resistance."[494] In 1957, she would support the Civil Rights Act. But it was here, five years earlier, that she was already taking overt steps to advocate for minorities.

By the time the boys were seated, another barrier had been cracked. "We had a perfectly beautiful lunch," Marguerite said in the oral history. "I think one of the things I'm happiest about is that I had the courage, even though I didn't even think that it took courage. I had an inner insistence that it must be done."[495]

For Marguerite, the move to Washington was hardly momentous. She knew her way around, and when she took the seat to which she had been elected, she returned to an apartment she had shared with her husband in the Shoreham Hotel. For the public, however, her profile was a little higher than she was accustomed to, largely because of increased interest in woman legislators in Washington, which was rising faster than their numbers. That January, the ten congresswomen and one female senator were invited to a number of events honoring them, and at least one gathering was particularly revolutionary. That was a meeting of the National Federation of Business and Professional Women's Clubs, where its president, Judge Sarah T. Hughes of Texas, surprised many when she said that she believed that equal rights meant equal responsibility, and that women consequently should be subject to military draft. This no doubt straightened Marguerite's back a bit as she tried not to shake her head. She often said that "equal protection" for women must not mean sacrificing the privileges that their gender was accorded.[496]

Quite a few of the women in Congress were widows whose husbands had been legislators or served in governmental roles—surely creating a bond among some. Marguerite said she became particularly close to Edna F. Kelly, a Democrat from New York who was elected in 1949, nominated by party leaders eager for a woman to fill a vacancy left by Representative Andrew L. Somers of Brooklyn. Kelly, a widow, was the first Democratic woman to represent Brooklyn in Congress. She'd been encouraged to enter politics following the 1942 death of her own husband, a New York City judge. When Kelly arrived in Washington in November of 1949, she announced that she wanted to be on the Foreign Affairs Committee. Prominent members asked her to defer to a man, that man being Representative Franklin D. Roosevelt

Jr. She refused, rounded up her allies, and got her way. Edna Kelly was as knowledgeable about the world as anyone she knew, Marguerite said of her colleague and friend. "She's grand."[497]

One particular issue these women agreed on was their latitude to let some congressional gender lines remain. Despite their positions of leadership in government, Kelly and Marguerite refused to cross certain gender boundary lines. Kelly, in her 1976 oral history, described such a time when she received an invite to a social event. "It was a dinner that only men went to," Kelly said, "and by mistake they sent me an invitation." She said she called the congressman from whom it came and said, "'Don't worry, about it, Gene.'" Kelly later said, "I accept that there are places where women can be excluded. I am not a feminist that feels women should do the same things permitted men. I am strong for [women's] individual rights with dignity. That is why I initiated the equal pay bill" (which Marguerite supported).[498]

Despite her own recent widowhood, Marguerite heartily enjoyed her congressional life from the beginning. She had been accustomed to a modicum of notoriety as Ralph Church's wife, and especially as president of the Congressional Club. But now, it reflected fully on her and had a different tint.

Marguerite told one story, amusing and meaningful, that happened in the first couple of weeks after her swearing in. "Aren't you that new Congress lady I've seen in the newspapers?" asked someone at a grocery where she was doing her shopping. She said yes, pleased to be recognized. The stranger was evidently unfiltered. "Well, that face isn't handsome," he said, and then added, "but I think I can trust it."[499]

No longer with children to raise, Marguerite could travel between Washington and Evanston as she preferred, not based on school schedules and family responsibilities. Mostly it was weekends, when she made sure to stay home and receive constituents, political bigwigs or not, who wanted to meet and discuss any subject. The house was essentially her district office, as it largely was for her husband, and as she told an interviewer well into her retirement: "We loved people, and they recognized that."[500] Meetings on the stone porch were a tradition known by most people in the district whether they had been there or not, and of her constituents she would later say, "I had a very wonderful district which was interested that I did as much as I did. I always came home and told everything. I tried to make it seem very, very real. And I never thought I was contributing too much. But somehow or other, I was giving myself a very great deal as I went along."[501]

Marguerite clearly enjoyed routine. As she told one reporter, when in Evanston, she'd rise at six o'clock in the morning, fix her own breakfast of eggs, orange juice, toast and coffee, then read the paper. When in DC, she'd wake slightly earlier, around 5:45 a.m., eating oatmeal while reviewing her notes.[502]

Marguerite stayed very much on a track that she knew from her husband's years in Congress. Life certainly changed for her, but they were changes that she largely enjoyed. She never overtly bridled at her supportive role in Ralph's political career, but when the seat belonged to her, things changed in subtle and not-so-subtle ways.

For one, she enjoyed interacting with the Democrats in a way that Ralph tended to avoid. "Marguerite was social with everybody on both sides of the aisle," Una Corley Groves said years later.[503] In fact, it sounds like congressmen from both parties were social with her, in the sense that she was a novelty on the floor. She was a woman, and there were few of those. And she was genuinely charming, something that was not common in Congress either. In fact, Groves said she was personally "irritated" by Marguerite's democratic socializing, and believed, as many did, that walls should exist between the Dems and the GOP. Marguerite "got along with everybody," Groves said. "That was her nature."

LOSS

There was, however, one individual who reportedly struggled to get along with Ralph Church's successor—his secretary, Helen Nelsch. A former teacher from Springfield, Illinois, Nelsch began working with Ralph in 1934, just before he was elected to Congress from Springfield, and she ran his office as it pleased her. Not that she had an iron fist, according to Groves, who overlapped with Nelsch in Washington. But Nelsch had her way of managing the congressman's time in the office. Groves said in 2018 that "Helen was not used to taking direction from strong women. She built her life around Mr. Church, around being a Washington secretary. When we first arrived in Washington with Mrs. Church, Helen Nelsch became unsettled."[504]

In July 1951, just seven months after Marguerite came into office, Nelsch reportedly committed suicide. She was found dead in her Washington, DC, apartment, "a revolver clutched in her right hand."[505] It was a sad passing, one that the authorities ruled a suicide without suspicion of foul play. To this day, however, some of Nelsch's family members contend she was murdered, as noted in text typed at the bottom of a family member's clipping of her obituary.

Upon her return to Washington following Nelsch's death, Marguerite worked immediately with Congress to ensure Nelsch's family received financial support and recognition.

AUTHENTIC POLITICAL VOICE

In her first term, Marguerite was assigned to the relatively obscure Committee on Executive Expenditures and took it seriously by pushing plans to reduce what she saw as profligate spending by the Truman administration. Unlike her late husband, who often railed against government waste at large, Mrs. Church turned her attention to details and in fact contributed to getting results. Just a few months into her first term she set her sights on the Reconstruction Finance Corporation.[506] The RFC, created in 1932 as a financing arm of the government, was a relatively easy target as it was bloated and ridden by corruption. But it gave her a taste of success, not to mention its slow pace, as both sides of Congress eventually agreed that the agency ought to be abolished. Her views were heard by colleagues and by the administration as the Expenditures Committee led the charge to get the RFC curtailed and finally disbanded by 1957.

In subsequent terms she raised her profile in a more prominent assignment on the Foreign Affairs Committee. But she remained on the Expenditures Committee (later called Government Operations) and kept on the details of government waste. For example, she became concerned to learn that the government operated businesses in which private enterprise was engaged as well. Why, she asked, was the government running 186 laundries and eleven dry cleaning plants, mostly for the military but within a short distance of private laundries and dry cleaners? Why, in the Panama Canal Zone, were there two bakeries run by the US government, one for military personnel and the other for civilians? Early in her tenure she introduced seventy-seven bills in her first three terms, mostly to implement recommendations to improve government efficiency.[507] Most of these measures got nowhere, par for the course for any member of Congress. But the sheer number of bills, amendments, and resolutions she introduced—201—reflected her level of activity. By comparison, her husband introduced only twenty bills in his first four terms—and twenty-eight total over the seven terms that he served—which was, in fact, criticized as a thin record.[508]

People who knew her repeated that Marguerite was a natural politician. This was evident as she discussed various questions, and none more striking than the debate on isolationism versus internationalism, and how America would wield its political and military power on the world stage. Some of her views, such as opposition to the Marshall Plan, were isolationist, curious given her worldly and well-traveled past. In fact, her husband had straddled the issue himself, especially in his failed 1940 Senate race against Curly Brooks, an unreconstructed America First-er.

Marguerite was able to abide both sides of this and other questions with more aplomb, and in doing so she illustrated the difference between a striving politician and an honest one. In fact, isolationism was a losing cause, even in her own party. But she stayed on her own conservative course, supporting for example the candidacy of Robert A. Taft for president in 1952.

Taft, son of President William Howard Taft, was an unreconstructed isolationist, and he appeared to be moving toward the nomination early that year. Marguerite appeared with Taft in Illinois and the North Shore as he cultivated support among wealthy conservative influencers. She never bruited her support for "Mr. Republican," as Taft was called. That was because Dwight D. Eisenhower, an indisputable hero and probable favorite, was in the running as well. She was happy to be pictured with Taft, and also with many of the wealthy isolationists who were also her constituents. But she said little on these occasions.[509]

At the Republican National Convention that year in Chicago, Marguerite was a quiet supporter of Taft but outspoken on her disapproval of Truman-Acheson foreign policy.[510] But her real interest was in a Republican victory no matter who won the nomination. As women politicians were profiled in advance of the convention that year, it was clear that their gender would be more prominent than ever, and this was not lost on her. She was tapped to speak at the convention where she chose not to insert herself between Taft and Ike. Rather, she skewered Truman, a sure way to excite all Republicans. "We have gone far along the path of socialization," she said. "Nor has this happened by accident. On the contrary, since the early days of the New Deal in the '30s, there has been an enveloping trend toward socialization of industry and of every phase of American living. The recent seizure of steel by the president—unconstitutional as it was—is but one final step in a long slow relentless effort."

She continued. "In foreign policy or lack of it, we have been out-bargained, outmaneuvered, outsmarted. Despite expenditure of 100 billion dollars to Europe alone since 1939 . . . administration policy, indeed by its own efforts has elevated Russia to a world menace; tossed historically friendly China into the communistic camp; brought down upon our heads the suspicion and hostility even of those who we have attempted to help; bound us with unlimited military commitments; and invited—yea, produced—war in Korea. A war, let me add, never acknowledged nor honored in name; never declared nor authorized in Congress; a war which we were afraid to win under MacArthur when we might have won; a war which the administration cannot find the means nor the will to end."[511]

She avoided pushing her candidate, Taft, and delivered strong rhetoric to unite the party, not divide it. The actions of the current administration, she made clear, were painfully close to the one thing that we were all supposed to be fighting: socialism. This, it must be noted, from a woman who declared herself a socialist in college.[512]

That the congressman was a woman strengthened her hand rather than diminished it. "She has shown herself to have a real personality," said a male admirer in a story in the *Tribune*. "She puts a lot of punch into her speeches without losing her femininity."[513] She said nothing to offend anyone at the convention, or largely ever, while she also cultivated a not-so-secret political weapon. Voting women were a latent power in national politics, evident when a delegation of Republican women from her district visited Washington. "I gave up feeling futile and decided to fight," said one of these twenty-seven constituents whom Marguerite hosted in the nation's capital. Another said that the nation's survival depended on the "higher standards and greater integrity" that women could provide.[514]

Progress for women remained slow but steady, and there was real anticipation that their numbers would grow in Congress. In 1952, a United Press headline reported, "Women Take Growing Interest in Congressional Contests."[515] The numbers were not much larger than two years before, but women in power were talking more about how to get more women elected, and why. Representative Cecil M. Harden, a Republican from Indiana and a grandmother, said that women are a definite asset to Congress as "they tend to be more economy-minded than men."[516] Representative Ruth Thompson, a Republican from Michigan, said that the US lagged behind some countries, such as Sweden, where women's numbers were higher in their legislatures.[517]

Marguerite must have felt both heartened and disappointed by results in '52. In November, she won easily over Democrat Lawrence J. Hayes, an Evanston lawyer and the youngest candidate in the House race that year. He did not attack Marguerite directly, and he barely uttered her name in his impossibly uphill campaign. The media reported Hayes' campaign focused strictly on party lines, in the hopes of raising the Democratic voice.[518]

But Marguerite's success as a female candidate was not shared by many. If she was disappointed that most of the women nominees that November lost, including Republican Phyllis Schlafly, who ran in a downstate Illinois district, she did not say so publicly. Overall, she likely felt grateful that even with women in an infinitesimal minority in Congress—twelve that year—there was an increase of two and their collective voice was growing stronger than their numbers.

SEXISM IN THE HALLS OF CONGRESS

Sexism was present in the halls of Congress, recognized by female members privately but rarely if ever discussed publicly. One of Marguerite's colleagues in the House, Edna F. Kelly, offered in her 1976 oral history conflicting and enlightening views of Speaker Sam Rayburn, saying that he was "a gentleman" and a "great leader" but also recalling a time when he was "very angry" and "grabbed [her] by the arm" so hard that it caused "black and blue bruises" as he attempted to get her vote for Lyndon B. Johnson.[519]

Marguerite never claimed an experience like that, though she once described to a crowd, with a laugh, the guard who attempted to block her from attending a meeting with Army high-ups at the Pentagon. The guard told Marguerite she couldn't enter without credentials. When she explained she was Representative Marguerite Stitt Church, the guard continued to stand his ground. "Look lady," he said, "think up something else. Even I know there are no women in Congress."[520]

Such blatant sexism was not uncommon. Syndicated columnist George Dixon shared a story a couple of months after Marguerite was sworn in. He noted the supposedly humorous sight of Marguerite "sprinting so fast down Capitol corridors that her coiled crown of hair came tumbling down around her shoulders. The sprightly fifty-eight-year-old pulled herself to a halt in the speaker's lobby and worked furiously with fingers and bobby-pins before striding onto the House floor." What Dixon failed to mention was the absence of a women's restroom near the House floor. The nearest women's facility was located in Statuary Hall—requiring a five minute walk and shared lines with tourists. A women's restroom would be installed near the Senate floor four decades later, in 1993, and Speaker John Boehner finally oversaw the installation of one for female House members in 2011—nearly a century after Jeanette Rankin joined Congress in 1917.[521]

Casual demeaning of women came in many forms, and not without suggestions that women themselves were complicit. A syndicated article with the kicker headline "Blueprint for a Better Personality" focused on what women could do to be well liked. Mostly they included banalities about pouting and fluttering eyelashes. Slightly more insidious was the so-called fact that while men make impressions through their behavior, "women are more apt to do it through appearance." The article used members of Congress as illustrations, with a picture of Representatives Marguerite Church and Ruth Thompson with Senator Margaret Chase Smith, smiling broadly and shaking hands. "These ladies of Congress know the value of a friendly attitude," read the caption.[522]

Despite blatant sexism, Marguerite never lost her sense of fairness and integrity, as evidenced in 1959 when Congressman Otto E. Passman (D-LA), chairman of the foreign operations appropriations subcommittee, took to the House floor. Passman, speaking of the League of Women Voters (who'd supported more liberal funds for the Mutual Security Program), said that they were "a fine bunch of ladies, but they don't know anything about the program. They would be better advised to concentrate on matters they were more qualified to handle, like child rearing." Though Marguerite voted against the bill in question, she—being a member of the league for more than thirty years—defended the group during a floor debate with Passman. "There are many others besides league members who regret that it has been necessary to cut the appropriation for the development loan fund and the technical assistance program," Marguerite said. "The League of Women Voters is an organization dedicated to good citizenship and studious attention to government problems. It seeks to make its recommendations always on a nondiscriminatory, fair and sound basis."[523] As was her way, Marguerite gave little to no air-time to the criticisms, digs, and slights by others. Instead, she simply stuck to the facts.

Marguerite publicly registered no rancor about sexism, and she insisted that her policy was not to be militant about women's rights. When she took office, she was one of only six Republican women on the House floor, and while she did stand up for herself in matters of substance, her survival strategy was to graciously (if not self-deprecatingly) leave the men to themselves and focus on her work. For example, as the only woman member traveling with men on Foreign Affairs assignments, Marguerite later said, "I know I must have been, sometimes, a little bit of a burden. And I adopted only three rules: I would never make a complaint; I would never make a suggestion; and I would never come down to breakfast."[524]

Though Marguerite and Representative Katharine St. George would eventually introduce legislation to protect the rights of women, Marguerite, in her retirement, described her earliest years in Congress as having been an "unimpassioned disciple at that time," and said, "I'm for equal protection under the law for both men and women, period. But I think we ought to be very sure that in some of the methods we use to secure rights, we do not prove our own incapacity."[525]

It may be that the high praise that colleagues often lavished on her blinded her to discrimination, despite inequalities everywhere. In fact, she claimed to be treated well by men she worked with. "Well," Marguerite said in her oral history, recalling a conversation with a young woman she mentored, "I never considered that I was a woman in a man's world, but I will give you one piece of advice. One thing you must be very careful never to do is let any man know that you are smarter than he is [*laughter*]."[526] Oh, but how to interpret Marguerite's statement? Was it simply made tongue-in-cheek? Did she firmly believe women are the superior sex? And how much did her psychological and sociological training influence her opinion about gender roles?

Or was this kind of thinking ingrained, perhaps born of the widespread belief that men and women inhabited separate worlds? In fact, the separation benefited Marguerite in many ways, not least in the esteem, if not deference, paid to women in Congress. In her 1978 oral history, Marguerite recognized how others' perceptions of her relative naiveté worked to her advantage: "I was sometimes given the answer because the person I asked was astonished that I didn't know enough not to ask the question."[527]

She encouraged women to embrace their unique qualities rather than conform to those determined by men. As she explained in her oral history, she felt "no militancy" about protecting women's rights, and said, "I still hold on to my theory that whereas there should be no injustice for either man or woman, a woman has to be very careful not to lose the particular qualities she has, which are different from the masculine, by trying to emulate the other sex."[528]

Marguerite stayed largely on the sidelines in debates for a constitutional amendment guaranteeing equal rights for women. In 1953, the Senate passed a bill that could have placed such an amendment before the states. The measure was designed to outlaw discrimination in areas such as employment and pay and to protect any special rights that women had under various state laws, such as the right to alimony payments. As the bill would have been sent to the House, a reporter asked for an opinion from Marguerite. She replied she was "happy" with it, a safe call, perhaps, as the House was seen as unlikely to act on the bill at all. In fact, equal rights *for* women were controversial even *among* woman (as it would be when the subject gained momentum again in the 1970s). The American Association of University Women, for example, remained neutral with a statement that the role of women in society is complex and that the question of equality needed further study. That was fine with Marguerite Church.

DELEGATE FOR CHANGE

Mrs. Church was deeply interested in establishing "legislation that did something."[529] An early bill that she championed was to curtail "bootleg" fireworks—specifically, the transportation of fireworks into states in which their sale or use was prohibited, a cause she took up after the deaths of three youngsters in her district due to fireworks.[530] If she believed it could be accomplished quickly, she learned otherwise. When she introduced the bill in 1951, she could not even get it to the floor, largely because of the opposition of a member whose district had fireworks factories. The lesson here was that persistence paid off, as did a good editing of the bill's language. It took the better part of four years before Marguerite convinced the House to pass the revised bill, followed by the Senate into law.

It was during those months and years of rewrites that some members might have given up. But Marguerite, devoted to her cause, did not. A passionate storyteller at heart, she spoke to members on the House floor on July 20, 1953, relying on her signature calm to paint a captivating picture of the obvious dangers of fireworks: "On the fifth of July," she said, "I picked up my Chicago paper and read of a little boy in the south end of the city who had lost both hands through the premature explosion of his fireworks package, bought by coupon and received through the mail."[531]

The details Marguerite shared were incorrect, though the reality was still horrifying. The victim was a fifteen-year-old from Beloit, a suburb on the southern end of Wisconsin. Moreover, that explosion occurred not as a result of illegally purchased fireworks but of the boys' own chemistry set, purchased by his parents. He'd attempted to make his own sparklers and flares when his parents refused to let him purchase such things.[532] Was Marguerite aware that her details were incorrect, or was she uncharacteristically caught up in the emotion of the issue?

"I urge it now upon your thoughtful consideration," she continued, speaking before her congressional colleagues. "I know the need; I think that you do, too; and I would remind you that there has never been a time when the American people, certainly the American Congress, and, I will add, legitimate American industry, did not welcome just remediation of a problem which could well become a national disgrace."[533] Resistance continued from members, including Henderson Lanham of Georgia, who crowed, "Why, I thought the Republican Party had come around to the idea of fewer controls; they were going to see that the federal government no longer interfered in the private lives of our people."[534] Still, Marguerite did not back down, reminding her dissenters that the bill had been modified to keep all parties—including citizens and fireworks manufacturers—in mind.

Then John Vorys of Ohio spoke up in favor of Marguerite's bill, summarizing what others already surely felt: "Mr. Chairman," he said, "I am fully in sympathy with the humane and important objective of this legislation . . . Certainly it is proper for Congress to plug the loopholes to prevent bootlegging of fireworks."[535] That day, at long last, the ban on fireworks shipments into states where their sales were strictly controlled was passed. The new law officially went into effect on July 1, 1954.[536]

More than most junior Congressmen, Marguerite knew what she wanted to accomplish in the House, and how to go about it. She was vigilant about waste, and for that reason the leadership penciled her in for the Committee on Appropriations for her second term. Appropriations held budget purse strings, and it was where she might influence spending. But she declined the appointment, which was a surprise as Appropriations was a prestigious assignment. She later explained that she turned it down because she saw the offer as a gesture to honor her late husband.

But she wanted a place on the Foreign Affairs Committee. Aside from her longtime interest in the world beyond, Marguerite was convinced that massive foreign aid, especially that under the Marshall Plan, was out of hand. Foreign Affairs was a place where she could monitor the spigot, if not turn it off. So she lobbied the GOP leadership, pointing out her interest in the nations of the world was of long standing. She knew Europe as a school girl. She had accompanied her husband to the Interparliamentary Council in Oslo several years before. She mentioned that she was intimate friends with Madame Chiang Kai-Shek, which was hardly trivial, though she did this quietly. What became clear was that this congressman was notable for her worldliness. She got Foreign Affairs and quickly made her mark on the committee, while she also agreed to continue on Government Operation, where she served in her first term.[537]

It did not disappoint Marguerite that Foreign Affairs would involve quite a bit of travel, though she knew that information-gathering trips were hardly junkets, or shouldn't be, and were in no way like the leisurely travel that she was accustomed to. One of the first was to Europe to see how allies were doing in the work of reconstruction, nearly a decade after the end of the war. At stake were foreign aid funds that were being sent abroad under a variety of programs. After several weeks in Europe, she was concerned.

She came home convinced, along with her colleagues, that the development of defense infrastructure in France, Germany, and elsewhere was moving forward, but without the urgency that the Americans wanted to see. Europe's commitment to NATO was safe, naturally, as those countries were needful of American military support. The delegation was less sanguine about lack of progress in the details, such as a jet-fuel pipeline in France that the US had paid for two years before. An experienced member of the committee said that the problem was "the failure of the government of France to focus its attention on this major defense project."[538]

As Congressman Church witnessed and listened to her colleagues, she must have thought about what would motivate the French to move. The answer, obvious to her, was money, or having it held back. That logic came naturally to the fiscal hawk that she was and would remain. She was a new member of the committee, and remained largely silent on the issue for the time being. But she would not remain quiet for long.

CHAPTER TWELVE

THE "GENTLEWOMAN'S" MEASURED DISRUPTIONS

MARGUERITE STITT CHURCH BECAME A disrupter, well before that label was common or considered positive. In her first term in Congress with Truman in the White House, if her party needed an articulate, well-aimed critique of the administration, she was often there to eviscerate them for waste and worse. Then as now, the usual trajectory of political discourse easily descended to name calling: "corrupt" and "cheaters" and "Communists" were the usual epithets. Marguerite was softer, though not gentler. She warned in no uncertain terms to a group of Junior Leaguers that America was losing the Cold War. "All we have spent for material aid to other countries has failed to bring us friendships and we have seen 600 million persons go behind the iron curtain," she said. For most political ills she was wont to blame the Democrats, though in this case she went a little deeper, citing "lack of knowledge and citizens' indifference to danger" as causes of failure.[539]

By the time Eisenhower was in office, she did not mind giving Republicans at large credit for freeing industry from the grip of government. "We inherited a number of sins and it will take some time to be clear of them," she told an Easter-time luncheon of party women in the spring of 1953. "This is the most serious moment of our lives and it was a Democratic error that made it. We promised a free economy, and we almost have it . . . But we have to be patient. As every good housewife knows, it takes a little time to clean out the attic."[540]

Her persona, if not her message, was often related to gender, and it was a pleasant surprise to many. If observers expected submission from this gray-haired grandmother with the quiet, patient smile, then surely her direct and effective delivery only resonated more, especially when she expressed her dissent on issues.

In 1954 she joined the majority to open the Saint Lawrence Seaway in a multinational effort with Canada. A GOP House member rebuked her, saying that her husband would never have cast such a vote. She replied, "Neither would he have wanted me to vote for it if I didn't believe in it." Her critic was speechless.[541]

Marguerite established her identity as an independent politician. Ideologically, she was conservative like her late husband. But her style was diametrically opposed to his. Ralph was brash; Marguerite was mild in demeanor. He was a scold; she was, one might say, subtle. Observers often took Marguerite's measure as owing to her being one of the few women in the House. Almost all were impressed by what they saw.

It was not only a matter of style. There was a shift in substance, as well, which reflected Marguerite's willingness to address changing conditions in the world. She was overly modest when she said in the beginning of her tenure that she was in Congress to honor, or uphold, her late husband's legacy. She was a housewife, not a politician, was the message. This was not her milieu, she insisted, so if Congress required a compromise of principle she would willingly bow out. She made herself sound passive and indifferent to change, but that wasn't true. Rather, her ability to remain a step removed from the everyday political fray endowed her with vision that her husband never had.

Her voting record was usually that of a modern conservative Republican. But when she surprised her colleagues, it was not independence for its own sake. It was often because American interests had changed, and she saw it before many of her less discerning colleagues did. After all, she regularly polled her constituents about current events, opened up her Evanston house when she was back in the district, and made sure to personally greet all everywhere she went.[542] "People wanted to talk, and I always had time to talk," she said in her 1978 oral history. In specific, she "flew home almost every week and came back on the twelve o'clock plane on Sunday night."[543] Her commitment to her constituents particularly came through in an October 31, 1956, column, in which she said, "I consider my job in Congress a two-way street. In Washington, I represent the Thirteenth District and do what people here want done in Congress. But I have just as much duty to come home and explain to my constituents—not only actual legislation, but also about events and national currents behind such legislation."[544]

For Marguerite to defend her performance was relatively simple due to her inherent moral authority, plus the pervasive conservatism of his district. There were times, however, when politics appeared to overshadow even Mrs. Church's conscience. One such time was in 1956 when a massive $1.6 billion ($18 billion in 2023) school construction bill appeared destined for easy passage. It was then complicated, however, when Representative Adam Clayton Powell Jr. of New York proposed an amendment withholding federal funds from any segregated school districts.

Marguerite's record of supporting racial justice made her vote in favor of the Powell amendment, which passed, unremarkable. But her vote was shadowed by the fact that the amendment assured that the funding bill would go down, as Southern Democrats were certain to vote against anything that promoted integration. Thus, Marguerite's painless vote in favor of civil rights was followed a few days later by a fiscally hawkish vote against the amended bill, which was predictably defeated.

Few press outlets challenged her apparent hypocrisy, at least by name, despite the dire need for school buildings. The *Chicago Defender* did not let it pass, however, reporting in October 1956 that Mrs. Church "made an impassioned speech in favor of the Powell amendment to the School Aid bill, helped to get it passed by a whopping majority, then turned right around and along with other Republicans and Democrats helped to defeat the whole bill."[545] In

August the following year, the *Defender* called Marguerite out again: "Why did Rep. Marguerite Stitt Church of Evanston, Ill., repeat the same trick she did last year of first voting for the Powell Amendment and voting to kill school aid and how can she explain this tactic to the voters?"[546] In fact, Republicans' "fancy footwork," as the *Defender* referred to it in 1956, hardly moved Black voters in the Thirteenth Congressional District, a small bloc to begin with.[547] But the GOP, the party of Lincoln, was at this time attempting to maintain favor among Black voters nationally, though the party was already weakening with Black voters in Evanston and everyplace else. Within a decade, Black Republicans were a rarity.

Nevertheless, one month later, Marguerite's commitment to uphold civil rights was noted by Gerald D. Bullock, president of the Illinois Conference of Branches of the National Association for the Advancement of Colored People (NAACP). In his letter to the *Chicago Defender*, penned during the heated debate of the controversial civil rights bill and published in the paper's national edition, Bullock wrote, "On June 14, Mrs. Margaret [*sic*] Stitt Church, Congresswoman from Illinois, made the following statement: 'No government which denies the right to vote to any large segment or to any small segment of its eligible population can hope to survive.'"[548] Bullock added, "I concur in that statement. And as long as there is the minimum chance that this presently disgraceful bill may be revised, there must be no surrender."[549] Though her own voting record prompted uncertainty by some, when it came to voters' rights, Marguerite Stitt Church's position remained clear and unwavering.

In a fast-changing world order, Marguerite's foreign policy expertise was often exhibited in high relief, recognizing that America's responsibilities had changed after World War II. American conservatives, once isolationist, had supported the war effort as part of a solid national front. But now many reverted to form and tried to push America back from the rest of the world. "Mossback" Republicans, as many were called, distrusted Europe and insisted that NATO would not enhance defense but rather lead us into further conflict.

This was not Marguerite Church's position. It was true that the mossbacks were Marguerite's natural political allies in many ways, and it was also true that she had campaigned against the Marshall Plan when she first ran for office. Her support for the Taft in '52, moreover, put her in that old camp, but not for long and not immovably. What was obvious to her well before she became a congressman was that Americans needed to engage the world at large, even if they did not embrace it. As a conservative, she distrusted Soviets. But her approach, unlike many in the conservative wing of her party, was to "keep our friends close and our enemies closer," as the saying goes.

During a heated foreign policy debate in January 1954, Marguerite took the floor to challenge what she perceived as administrative inaction in "not combating the vacuum in the world with the true story of the American dream." She explained that what bothered her the most was hearing "talk only of military might. Nothing is being offered to fill the ideological void by selling the true dream of human dignity and freedom." It was reported that at that, a group of women seated in the gallery broke into spontaneous applause, and when rebuked, one of the chastised women snapped, "You can shush me, but you'll never stop that woman—nor can you ever silence truth and freedom."[550]

With this view and support she took her seat on the Foreign Affairs Committee, a prize, she admitted, that was not in great demand by her colleagues.[551] Years later, in her oral history, she said, "few people really wanted to go on the Foreign Affairs Committee. We were still rather insular in our relationships."[552] She wanted to see the world and influence it. The former she did on frequent information-gathering trips to many far-flung places. The latter she accomplished in committee meetings in which foreign aid and the spread of democracy were discussed and debated. Quietly and modestly, she was determined to place herself on the front lines of a world that was changing whether America was driving or not. "I never regretted my choice," she revealed.[553]

CONGRESSIONAL STUDY MISSIONS

Even Marguerite didn't know until later how demanding her work on the Foreign Affairs Committee would be. Almost immediately after she was assigned, the chairman invited her on a fact-finding trip to India, leaving almost immediately. She couldn't go, she said, because she had people from her district coming to DC, and she, like Ralph, had always made constituent relations a top priority. The problem was that when the members got back from the trip, the Indian-Pakistani conflict was discussed in committee, and "nobody wanted to hear what I thought about it because, you see, I had not been there," she said. "I made up my mind from then on, whenever it was suggested that I go, I would be there."[554]

In the early years of her tenure she took trips abroad about once a year. "Study missions" as they were called by congressmen, or "junkets" as they were called by almost everyone else, had a bad name, especially to taxpayers who footed the bill. And there were abuses, often by lawmakers who wanted a vacation, sometimes by others who misbehaved abroad. There had been a case in this period when a senator visiting Germany got visibly drunk after a toast and began singing "*Ach, Du Lieber Augustin*" at dinner.[555] Other diplomatic gaffes were less amusing.

But Marguerite never had to justify the practice. For her, study missions were nothing like luxurious vacations of her past. Especially trips of the subcommittee on the Far East and the Pacific, of which she was a member for ten years—they were hardly ever leisurely and "tough going very often."[556]

A 1953 tour to Asia made thirteen stops in three weeks, from Korea and Japan to the Marshall and Caroline Islands. The sheer distance of this trip, made with three other members, was remarkable as it spanned 30,000 "air mile[s]," as the press covered it.[557] She assessed the China situation, though it was certainly from Taiwan's point of view, as she stayed with her old Wellesley friend Madame Chiang Kai-Shek. "She seemed happier and in better spirits than I've ever seen her," Marguerite said of the First Lady of Nationalist China. "She has taken up brush painting doing beautiful scenes of China, mostly in black and white. She has established a whole new school of painting."[558]

Except for her old friend, the congressman was less interested in exalted leaders than everyday realities. In Korea she visited the places where tensions were still high even after the armistices in July of that year. "Some officials protested that this was no place for a lady," Marguerite told the Associated Press. "I told them that I was not a lady, I was a member of Congress."[559]

Most often, Marguerite was the only woman on these trips, save for a female staff member who accompanied the group. "I was just there, very grateful to be there," she recalled. And while Marguerite made a point never to react or call attention to others' negative behavior, she would describe—in later years—the sexism she faced while traveling the globe with contingents of men. In her 1978 oral history, she recalled one such incident from the first time she traveled to a "Far Eastern" country with the Foreign Affairs Committee.

At first, she was "greeted with all the respect and enthusiasm and hope" of their hosts, only to find their group delayed without explanation. She finally asked about the delay, and "the chairman said, 'Well, you see, they didn't know that your name meant a woman, and no woman has ever been in the throne room.'" Marguerite explained, "Of course, if I had been a perfect lady and not a member of Congress, I would have said, 'Well, you go right along. What difference does it make?'"[560] Yet that was hardly Marguerite.

"I was very conscious of the fact that I was representing one of the very greatest districts in the United States," she continued, "and that is not just local pride. I had no intention of ever letting my constituents think that their member of Congress couldn't enter any throne room." Eventually, she was taken to the throne room.[561]

As she toured other countries—Indonesia and the Philippines among them—what she saw was not always encouraging. Problems, she said, "were bigger than most people in the Congress or the country dreamed."[562] It reinforced her conservative instincts about throwing dollars at these troubled places.

American dollars were flowing to all corners of the so-called Free World, but Marguerite was not shy about voicing reservations. She told the *Washington Post*'s Marie McNair that she "goes along with the Hoover-Taft policy, believing in giving help abroad only when the people have proved a willingness to help themselves."[563]

Still, driven less by results than competition for influence with the Soviets, the Eisenhower administration continued to pump hundreds of millions into underdeveloped nations. How effective was all this aid in solving real problems? Marguerite could say that too many were not effective at all. In Asia, she studied where the money went for roads in Vietnam, grain elevators in India, and a fertilizer plant in Korea.[564] Construction delays were common, and that was for the successful projects. Indifference on the part of those responsible in countries which would benefit was standard. Corruption was almost a given.

As Marguerite saw it, poor performance was one question. The causes for it were another, and beyond the obvious obstacles of incompetence, she occasionally gained deeper insight into why foreign aid did not meet expectations. In Singapore, for example, someone at a meeting told her delegation that American dollars were doing more harm than good, for they came with the goal of "giving freedom to people before they had been trained and adapted to its good use."[565] Marguerite and her fellow congressmen mostly discounted this remark as another anti-American attack. But in years to come, she came to believe that the critique was largely true.[566]

Another study mission in the mid-1950s brought Marguerite to central Africa, where committee members drove past "ant hills higher than my head" to visit villages where they met people who were supposed to be benefiting from American aid. But this claim was misplaced, she could tell almost immediately. "These women," she found, "didn't want guns; they didn't want atomic plants; they didn't want navies." She told the story of someone from a primitive village who had gone for treatment to a hospital in a larger town, and while there learned how to sew. She had begun to make a business of it. It showed

Marguerite that all many people needed was "someone who could show them the next step up from where they were to where they'd like to be," she said. "That experience controlled my thinking for the rest of my time in Congress."[567]

Surprises abroad were not always negative. In 1956 she was in Afghanistan, "which, incidentally, is one of the two countries in the world I would most like to go back to," she said. "I remember the young escort turned and said suddenly, 'You know, Mrs. Church, you will never know what being with this group for four days has meant to me.'" The man said, "I never knew what it meant to be free until I heard you all laugh."

Marguerite came home with observations that ran deep. Her colleagues knew it. When she leveled dissent, which she often did against most versions of "dollar diplomacy," other congressmen listened, even if they were constrained not to agree. Most of Marguerite's votes against big foreign aid bills were unsuccessful; the momentum for these programs was too great. After putting in so many miles, however, her credibility was enough to at least moderate the efforts in some cases, if not to champion them.

GUNFIRE ON THE HOUSE FLOOR

Marguerite had successfully completed her first two special study missions for the Foreign Affairs Committee when, early in the second session of her second term, she and her colleagues found themselves sprayed with gunfire in what was described by the United Press as "a mass assassination attempt" when armed Puerto Rican nationalists stormed the House chamber on March 1, 1954.[568]

The House had just adopted a rule for consideration of a bill governing the admission of Mexican farm laborers when the shooting began. The chaotic episode played out like a movie's action scene, as observed by one *Chicago Tribune* journalist who stood less than fifty feet from the assailants—one woman and three men, all from New York. "The shots at first sounded like a string of firecrackers, as they made a rapid, cracking sound . . . The woman pulled out a Puerto Rican flag from under her coat and waved it.

They shouted "Viva Mexico" and "Free Puerto Rico."[569] Five members were injured, one critically. Representative Alvin M. Bentley, a thirty-five-year-old Republican from Michigan, was bleeding profusely as colleagues rushed to his aid. Marguerite, standing on the floor, at first didn't know what to make of the scene. "There she stood, in the midst of it all," Representative John Porter later recalled. "She wasn't hit, although a number of members were. Bullet holes can still be seen in the desk on the Republican side of the chamber."[570]

Rep. George H. Fallon, a Democrat from Maryland, was shot through the hip as he stood beside his seat directly across the aisle from Marguerite's desk. However, this day, she said, was the first time she'd ever sat somewhere besides her own seat. Instead, she was seated several rows back, next to Rep. Timothy P. Sheehan of Chicago.[571] The *Daily Herald* headlined the story "Congressman Church Was Last 'Man' Down," and Marguerite was quoted: "I have never before been under fire and I did not know what to do until Representative Sheehan called me to duck. I ducked. I was literally on the floor." She then described the following moments: "It was a very tense three minutes. It seemed incredible to us. No person was safe. We were all possible targets, because the shots were not being aimed at any one person."[572] The group was described as being affiliated with others who'd attempted to assassinate Truman, and another man associated with their efforts was accused of threatening to kill President Eisenhower. Four were arrested, and one had a note found in her purse which read, "Before God and the world my blood claims for the independence of Puerto Rico. This is a cry for victory in our struggle."[573]

In the aftermath of the shooting, discussion flew about American security, Communist plots, un-American activities, and subversive groups. Representative Harold Velde of Illinois said that the event "served to confirm the frequent statements that have been made by the House Committee on Un-American Activities concerning subversion within the United States."[574]

Six decades later, Una Corley Groves remembered the day clearly from her spot in the gallery audience. "There were crazy people—and they were killing people—but they didn't get her. I ran to the escalator and took the [Capitol] tram to the office, and so did she. She came running back to the office—we met on our way back. I said, 'I don't know what's happening.' She sat down at the telephone and made phone calls." When asked if Marguerite was shaken, Groves paused, then said, "No. I don't think so."[575]

A few hours after the incident, Marguerite spoke to an *Evanston Review* reporter from her room at the Shoreham Hotel: "Some good will likely come from this fanatic but carefully plotted gun attack on congressmen in the Capitol if it makes the public realize that there is a spirit of evil abroad in the world and that it is a real and direct peril to this nation."[576]

"The most terrifying part of it," Marguerite told the reporter, "was that we were subjected to this continuous fire and were completely helpless, like standing ducks, and nothing seemingly was being done to stop our assailants. They emptied their Lugers into that group of 243 congressmen and weren't overpowered until they started to reload."[577] According to Marguerite, who estimated thirty shots fired, the seats and floor were "a bloody mess" where the congressmen were hit.[578] "The whole incident was insane and pointless," she said. "We had nothing to do with settling the question of Puerto Rica's [*sic*] independence."

That afternoon, Marguerite's daughter, Marjory, unaware of the shooting, had tried to reach her mother, but the phone lines were jammed. When they finally connected, Marguerite "began giving her daughter reassurance that she was unhurt," though it took Marjory—who still hadn't heard the news—a few seconds before the tragedy finally registered.[579]

CASH BASH

Following the shooting, sixty-one-year-old Marguerite's fortitude and energy showed no limits. On March 15, she oversaw the dedication ceremony for two new training schools at Great Lakes Naval Training Center. Two months after the gunfire, on May 15, she was the keynote speaker at a grassroots conference at Howard University focused on combating juvenile delinquency. Later that month, her fireworks legislation became law; it officially took effect that July. That same month, she gave a speech during the last Northwestern University summer session lecture series, a talk free and open to the public titled "The Ramparts We Watch."[580] Northwestern's daily paper ran a story about her talk the next day, under the headline "Rep. Church Sees 'World In Flux', Says Truce In Korea Fruitless, NATO Needs Unified Germany to Succeed."[581]

Following her talk at Northwestern, Marguerite then attended a dinner in DC honoring Vice President and Mrs. Nixon, rubbing shoulders with Dulleses and MacArthurs and international heads of state. In August, the House passed a bill she had authored, requesting federal funds toward the "emergency" need for amelioration and prevention of beach erosion along the shore of her district.

It was the world's complexity that she grasped, complexity which was never addressed in standard political discussions because it did not cleave to easy labels. Politics and especially foreign policy in the early 1950s were cast as a fight to the death between the Soviets and the West. With few exceptions, her party's line was to spare no expense in countering Soviet intentions, as if it were a binary choice. She saw, on the other hand, a matrix of decisions needed to advance the cause of "freedom at home," which was as close to a first principle, an absolute, as she ever expressed. She made it crystal clear that she did not coddle Communists, though she had the grace not to mention Senator Joe McCarthy, who was still up and running in 1951. Her solution to geopolitics was not unrelated to her view of fiscal responsibility. She wanted to extract Communists from within the government, fix inefficient bureaucracies, and deal with dishonest leaders. "If our republic fails," she said, "it will not be because of aggression from without, but because of the sapping of resources and strength by an unwieldy, paternalistic government that is becoming less and less representative of the American people."[582] Most congressmen would not have based foreign policy decisions on domestic considerations. But Marguerite did, and she turned heads because her voice was new, different, and sincere.

If Marguerite Church believed that having a Republican in the White House would lead to deliverance for her views, she was not long mislead. She remained focused on the foreign aid issue as the Eisenhower administration continued to send money abroad at unprecedented levels, and, in her opinion, without clear objectives. There was opposition to Eisenhower's foreign aid programs, though not enough to have anything more than a moderate effect on curtailing them. If millions to an Asian principality went mostly in a dictator's pocket, or if the taxpayers were otherwise fleeced, Marguerite was there to say it was as corrosive to our own democracy as it was to the ones we were trying to help.

Eisenhower's overarching objective in the aid programs, the Mutual Security Act and Food for Peace among them, was to counter Communist aggression and maintain friendships with countries that might otherwise accept Soviet aid. These were broad objectives, and results were hard to measure with precision. But whatever responsibility Congress had to monitor it was largely abdicated. Dissent, therefore, could do little more than chip away at the edges of the administration's funding proposals. Less to India, said one congressman; more to the Caribbean, said another. It was all largely a waste of money, Marguerite consistently said, along with a few others on Foreign Affairs. It wasn't that Congress had no influence, but if Eisenhower found his package reduced marginally one year, he simply increased the request in the next. It was a dance that continued until Republican leader Joseph W. Martin bluntly told his party to cut it out. "The charge that we can't afford the mutual security program is hogwash," Martin said. "When the United States cannot afford its own security, it's time to haul down the red-white-and-blue and hoist the white flag."[583]

Marguerite's first significant turn against her own party came in 1955 when she joined four other members in signing a minority report of the committee after Foreign Affairs sent the foreign aid bill to the floor of the House. This minority, four Republicans and a southern Democrat, held that Congress should cut off further aid funds until it got a full report of the billions already spent in recent years. It was a futile gesture in terms of stopping the flow of dollars abroad because the aid bill was supported by both the Eisenhower administration and the Democrat-controlled Congress. On the surface, the dissidents appeared as if they would have little effect other than putting the committee chairman, a Democrat, in the strange position of defending the aid program from "attacks and onslaught" by members of the president's party.[584]

But Marguerite and her band of dissidents did not let up, and little by little they pushed some buttons that worked. She and four other GOP members of the committee attacked the $3.3 billion ($37.8 billion in 2023) aid package that year, calling it a "blank check" for the president to fund foreign aid programs. As the bill went to the floor for debate, they pointed to $40.5 million ($464 million in 2023) in "indirect" military aid to Yugoslavia, which they reminded everyone was a Communist country, albeit outside of direct Soviet orbit.[585] Money to Yugoslavia was part of the Eisenhower/Dulles "wedge strategy" in the Balkans, meant to pry Eastern Europeans from the Soviet bloc. Yugoslavia got its money that year, though the wedge strategy was soon to be abandoned. Marguerite could take a narrow slice of the credit, which would have been belated, like the small concession to the fiscal monitors.[586]

In 1958, the Foreign Affairs Committee minority stated again that the US had poured nearly $49 billion ($520.6 billion in 2023) into foreign aid without much payoff in terms of friendship toward America. Instead, the US had sent "massive amounts of assistance to those who are either neutral or who lean toward the Soviet Union," their report stated. Nor were they above citing shipments of aid that seemed not just wasteful but absurd, such as nylon stockings to Korea and musical instruments to Turkey.

Marguerite and company had hoped that Republicans, at least, would rally around them. They did so enough to pare $340 million ($3.6 billion in 2023) from what Eisenhower asked for. Congress passed an allocation of $3.6 billion ($38.2 billion in 2023).

To her credit, Marguerite Church never surrendered the issue, which was only partially an economic one. An editorial by the *Chicago Tribune*, which had transformed its implacable isolationism into relentless anti-Communism, praised Marguerite for supporting the view that aid represented appeasement to Communists worldwide. "What have we got to show for these enormous disbursements?" the paper asked. "Hostility from a great number of countries which are on the receiving end. Indifference to us and sympathy for Communism."[587]

Marguerite might have put it that way too, the words velveteen, the indictment ferocious. And her votes remained largely in line, notwithstanding her stands for civil rights and the Peace Corps, with what became the conservative wing of her party. She was always willing to take on the big dogs in this fight; she did not squander opportunities. In May 1959, former president Truman came before Foreign Relations to testify in support of Ike's foreign aid expenditures. Truman said that the necessity of foreign aid "is now recognized by most thinking people in both parties . . . That does not include America Firsters and the *Chicago Tribune*," he said, taking a shot at Congressman Church's hometown paper.[588]

Marguerite asked the former president if he thought "dollars alone" could win friends abroad and contain communism.[589]

"I don't want to go into personalities," Truman said. The room went quiet for a moment, confused, then broke into laughter when it was apparent that Truman thought Marguerite had said "Dulles" and not "dollars." The ex-president smiled. "Mrs. Truman says I need a hearing aid," he said, then agreed that dollars alone were not sufficient.[590]

Marguerite smiled back quietly. She had made her point, which was that dollars were all that anyone was getting, and that her hearing, not to say reasoning, was sound.

Four months later, Marguerite was the featured speaker at the membership tea of the Regular Republican Women's Club of Palatine Township, Illinois. The *Daily Herald* covered her September 7, 1959, speech at the Palatine fire hall, during which she was described as saying that "the tendency of this nation is toward a welfare state." The paper's account continued, "Mrs. Church said, if American people do not rouse themselves from the apathy they are in, they will find they have been led into socialism, as that is the definite trend of the Democratic party."[591] The paper describes that twice that year Marguerite had refused to vote in favor of a national budget increase: "Mrs. Church said she does not wish to return to Washington if her district doesn't want her to vote her convictions on efficiency and economy."[592] Marguerite's views on socialism had no doubt evolved since her time at Wellesley.

CONSCIENCE OF THE COMMITTEE

Did Marguerite's attempts to apply the brakes have much influence? Ostensibly, it was marginal; foreign aid was sent abroad in ever-increasing amounts in the 1950s. There was evidence, however, that House members were more circumspect in light of the dissent that she and a few others voiced. That power could be documented vividly in meetings occasionally, such as in a peculiar if inconsequential way in 1955. Marguerite arrived late during some testimony by diplomat Jack McFall, ambassador to Finland. At issue in this period was Finland's de facto capitulation to the Soviet Union while maintaining nominal independence. Whatever was on the table at the moment could not have been too serious, because when McFall noticed her enter the room, he interrupted himself to say, "I just want you to know, Mrs. Church, that the Finns are more advanced than we are in the matter of women's suffrage." Instead of asking just what he was talking about, "Mrs. Church threw the envoy a sweet smile which came close to paralyzing him," as recounted by a syndicated reporter covering the meeting.[593] But instead of getting off the subject, the ambassador made the absurd assertion that all the barbers in Finland are women.

Marguerite continued to be silent, but another committee member, Albert P. Morano of Connecticut, called out, "Do they use a straight razor?"

"Apparently it was involuntary," wrote the reporter. "Representative Morano seemed to be surprised to hear himself saying it." The repartee became more inane even by congressional standards, and it even "took a ribald turn," unspecified, and then "trailed off into embarrassed silence as Mrs. Church surveyed each man individually with a long, quizzical look."[594] It was an example of how the lady from Evanston maintained a certain moral authority over her male and often inappropriate and sexist peers, evidently a simple enough matter in a case such as this.

In fact, Marguerite brought not just a stateliness but probity to the process of statecraft that often required the gravitas that few could bring. And she showed repeatedly that she could go toe-to-toe with the blue bloods of American diplomacy—since she, herself, was one—and rarely more forcefully than in 1957, when the committee had former secretary of state Dean Acheson to discuss subjects including the difficult situation in the Middle East. Again, Marguerite seemed to see the complexities of political conflict in that part of the world, and to discount the tendency of both the Truman and Eisenhower administrations to react only to the Communist threat among Arab countries, leaving other conditions to chance. The concern was that America supported, openly or covertly, allies in countries like Egypt, Syria and Jordan that she regarded as either feckless or harmful.

In fact, the Eisenhower administration tended to justify its actions on the basis of "moral force." In a question about the Suez conflict, Marguerite asked Acheson, "If you deny the right of one nation to commit aggression if it has Soviet domination, do you admit that the nation which is your friend has the right to commit aggression?"[595]

"If you want an answer, I do," Acheson said. "I can see no morality in the statement that you must have the same rule for your friends and for your enemies." The ends justify the means, in other words. "'Morality' is a very slippery word in international affairs," Acheson added, to which Marguerite needed only to nod.[596]

Exchanges like these were not widely reported and usually escaped the attention of the voting public. But they were noticed by colleagues and by members of the administration, and they had the effect of raising her stature and heightening her influence when she spoke. As a member of the minority party, and often a nuanced dissenter within that minority, she had all too little influence on public policy. Middle East diplomacy continued sadly on Acheson's slippery slope toward generations of conflict. Nevertheless, when Marguerite spoke, many colleagues believed that she raised the level of discourse. She reminded colleagues that character counted. Her civilizing effect on the House of Representatives was as obvious as it was incalculable.[597]

CHAPTER THIRTEEN

LEAVING CONGRESS GRACEFULLY, UNQUIETLY

INDICATIONS WERE THAT ILLINOIS' THIRTEENTH Congressional District was beginning to change political stripes midway through the 1950s. Its population was growing, largely in the northwestern townships of Cook County, where people were moving from Chicago, and "many new residents are expected to vote in the Democratic traditions of Chicago."[598] This was a reasonable assumption, perhaps, though if white flight caused this suburban growth, it was not particularly good news for the Democrats. Another movement that had begun was a flow of ex-urban dwellers from wealthy South Side communities like Hyde Park and South Shore to the North Shore. This trend would in time shift Evanston itself from staunchly Republican to staunchly Democratic. But that would take ten or twenty years. Not now.

During the 1954 election season, women were making major political news. Four women, all Democrats, had run their own campaigns without having been widows.[599] The women—Iris F. Blitch of Georgia, Edith Green of Oregon, Martha W. Griffiths of Michigan, and Coya Knutson of Minnesota—joined the then-largest cohort of women in Congress to form what the press dubbed the "Sweet Sixteen."[600] In addition to the four newly elected women, eleven female incumbents from the House (including Marguerite Stitt Church) and one incumbent senator (Margaret Chase Smith), won reelection that year—eight Republicans and eight Democrats in all.

Back in 1954, 35 percent of all women who'd served in the House had succeeded their late husbands.[601] Yet despite the historic advance for the number of women then in government, sexism in the press held fast, with characterizations of women often including physical descriptions and judgments. For instance, a column in the *Corsicana Daily Sun* described Iris Blitch as a "striking brunette," while Coya Knutson, Edith Green, and Martha Griffiths earned only mentions as "teacher," "farmer," and "buyer of shot, shells, Jeeps and trucks."[602]

As of July 13, 1955, the House had received fifty-three bills to implement recommendations of the second Hoover Commission, many of which had passed through Marguerite's hands, then adjourned August 2 for the session. Two months later, on October 11, Marguerite departed on her special study mission to the Middle East, South and Southeast Asia, and the Pacific.

By the start of the second session of the Eighty-Fourth Congress in January 1956, Marguerite had moved to an eight-story, modern apartment building at 2122 Massachusetts Avenue NW near Washington DC's Dupont Circle.[603] Una Corley Groves—who'd typically driven the congressman to and from her various meetings in Marguerite's Cadillac convertible—would leave Washington, DC, that year with her husband, Asa Groves Jr., who'd also served on Marguerite's congressional staff.[604] Groves says their departure came after much handwringing over Marguerite's resistance to run for Senate—something Groves says she and her husband never understood.[605]

Marguerite's 1956 election reflected some sense of change along these lines, but hardly enough to alter the vote. Her opponent was a woman, which may have indicated greater openness to women in politics, though this did not stop at least two news syndicates from diminishing it as a "powder puff" race.[606] More to the point, it may also have reflected the futility of going against Marguerite Church and a dearth of candidates willing to try. Democrat Helen Benson Leys of Wilmette took a realistic view of her chances in one piece of campaign literature. "Political experts say I have no chance to be elected," she wrote. "They may be right." She asked voters to cast their ballots "for the lady no one expects to win."[607]

There was some indication that the issues were changing as well, though one can only imagine that few voters noticed. Leys—who worked the district hard, addressing thirty-five meetings a week—was a longtime PTA leader and believed the federal government must do more to finance overcrowded schools. Marguerite never voiced such a view, always wary to support any scheme to increase spending. Yet there's no record that Leys ever attacked her directly beyond saying, "We need a more constructive foreign policy."[608]

Marguerite seemed to spend little time thinking about her critics, and rarely if ever acknowledged them. Representative John Porter, in his congressional tribute to Marguerite following her death, recalls her advice about remaining quiet: "I visited during my first campaign in 1978, concerned about a letter to the editor misrepresenting a position I had taken. 'Ralph Church,' she said—she often spoke of her late husband as 'Ralph Church'—'would tell you, "Don't answer it." Chances are nine out of ten people didn't read the letter in the first place, and half of those who did, didn't believe it.' If you answer, she would say, 'You have to repeat the false allegation, and it will be made known to many who would never have heard about it in the first place.' She never referred to her opponents by name or otherwise and never answered their criticisms. 'Why advertise the opposition?' she would say."[609]

Instead, she remained focused on what mattered: her constituents and the work before her, steadily projecting a centered sense of self, showing others—particularly women—what it looked like to be a woman of confidence and self-assurance.

She proved again that she was a "tireless campaigner," wrote Joan Beck in the *Tribune*. "Mrs. Church knows thousands of her constituents personally," Beck explained, to the point that Marguerite "can't go into a restaurant, for example, without greeting the cook and dishwashers." Her accomplishments, Ms. Beck acknowledged, were less centered on the district than on the world at large, noting that "in 1955, she visited twenty-six foreign countries on a 30,000 mile world trip to study political and economic problems."[610]

One could wonder if her foreign affairs record really would trump Leys' focus on local problems. Fear associated with the Cold War was building, and Marguerite appeared to understand obscure corners of the world. Competence counted, and no one appeared more composed in addressing any situation the nation might face. But well beyond objective issues, she also rode a cult of personality as an elegant, patient, honest—not to mention right-wing—broker. The cult was sustained by the *Tribune*, the best-read paper in her district, which appreciated her votes as a fiscal hawk and latter-day isolationist, which the editors of the self-styled "World's Greatest Newspaper" valued greatly.[611]

In any case, Marguerite Church won with 71.6 percent of the vote in the general, which was better than 1954, when she got 69.6 percent against Evanston attorney Lawrence J. Hayes, and even better than 1952, when she won with 70.6 percent against Libertyville attorney Richard A. Griffin. Marguerite received the largest vote in any district contest for the office of United States Representative since 1936. As correspondent Esther Tufty wrote, while it was still a new and challenging phenomenon for women to run for Congress, "once elected . . . they seem to get re-elected, usually easily."[612]

A FOURTH TERM

Marguerite, age sixty-four, began her fourth term on January 3, 1957. She attended President Eisenhower's inauguration and is photographed wearing a ball gown at one of his four inauguration parties, quite a departure from the "look" most of the world saw.[613]

Marguerite, an advocate for women's specific empowerment, fought in 1957 to remove discretionary practices in appointments by introducing a bill proposing the amendment of Title IV, Section 165 of the Revised Statutes to eliminate a provision discriminating against the appointment of women to government positions, but "the [Civil Service Commission] had not deemed the status of women federal employees a problem" and the bill died in committee.[614] Frustratingly, even though a 1959 federal employment survey "found that women, still one-quarter of the federal labor force, continued to be clustered in the lowest grades," the commission did not identify discrimination as a cause. "More men than women were trained professionals and therefore were naturally classified in the higher grades," the report said, not bothering to look any deeper.[615]

A statement Marguerite shared about her own daughter with a reporter from the *Washington Post* suggests the evolving nature of how women referenced one another in society. Marguerite explained that Marjory was, at the time, studying at the prestigious Northwestern University, and added, "And she looks like she doesn't have a brain in her head!"[616] While she was clearly paying her beautiful daughter a compliment while also acknowledging her intelligence, this sort of comment points directly to society's and Marguerite's black-or-white thinking at the time. It wasn't easy for women to be seen as multidimensional: you were either a "looker" or a "brain," and that was that.

In August of 1957, at the conclusion of the first session of the Eighty-Fifth Congress, Marguerite opened up to a reporter, explaining she had no vacation plans that summer, though she would take her first vacation in seven years at the beginning of her upcoming 40,000 mile study mission with Foreign Affairs, of which she was now a ranking member. "I haven't had a real vacation since I've been here," she told the reporter. "Up to last year I had a boat, but I had no time to use it so I sold it."[617] Marjory and two of Marguerite's granddaughters lived at her home now.

Marguerite made the trip back and forth between Washington and Evanston about seventeen times during each congressional session.[618] Marguerite said that although she often made "bold" plans for her time off from Congress, "when the time comes, I just want to go home."[619] Her district, she said, is her life, and, "unlike the men in Congress, I have no other profession."[620] She converted two rooms of her home into office space, and typically arranged five to six speaking engagements every week between September through December.[621]

Even while serving in Congress, though, Marguerite found time to support her extended family and make lasting memories. One of her grandsons, Tim Church, professor emeritus in counseling psychology at Washington State University, was eighteen months old when his grandfather, Ralph E. Church, suddenly died. He still speaks fondly of Marguerite today. "I would visit Grandma's house during my visits to Evanston and remember some of the family dinners there and, of course, the collies that she always had as pets."[622] He recalls a time when he was in middle-school, flying with his grandmother to Washington, DC. "This was probably my first time flying on a plane," Tim Church said. "I spent time in her Congressional Office and participated in one floor vote in the House of Representatives." As he tells the story, "Grandma was a fiscal conservative, and when a voice vote was called for a spending bill, Grandma told me to shout 'No!'"[623]

Her grandson describes Marguerite as "extraordinarily articulate and a gifted speaker," someone who clearly enjoyed sharing stories of her life in politics and government. "I recall one time in high school when Grandma traveled on the family boat from Chicago to Sheboygan," Tim Church recalls. "I brought several of my high school friends down to the harbor, and they seemed mesmerized by Grandma's views and her many stories about politics and government."[624]

He fondly remembers how Marguerite encouraged her grandchildren, as well as her appreciation for tradition. "Grandma encouraged achievement by her grandchildren and was pleased and complementary when they did well academically or ran for elected offices in high school. I think she also took some pride in my service as a Supply Officer in the Navy, as this was somewhat of a family tradition, with Grandpa Church, my father Ralph, Jr., and my Uncle Bill also having served in some way in the Navy."[625]

SILENCE AND STRENGTH

By and large, Marguerite's electoral success in the district at least equaled that of her husband, the ultra-conservative Republican in a district that rewarded right-wing positions. The six-year-old Thirteenth Congressional District was largely the same geographically and politically as Ralph's former Tenth, though a savvy politician knows things do not stay the same forever. Time showed that Marguerite's true strength was exhibited not in her steadfast conservative positions but when she was willing to go against the flow. Another exceptional skill was that she viewed all sides of every issue, which was no doubt a benefit cultivated during her time as a collegiate debater. While this approach elevated her diplomatic prowess, it was something she eventually struggled with at the end of her congressional career. Marguerite couldn't help but see all sides of all issues and found it increasingly difficult to make fair decisions.

Moreover, her foreign aid votes were an example of independence, as she veered to the right on those. But another issue where she consistently bucked the main line of her party was on the subject of militarism. She was not shy about opposing it when most of the House of Representatives let the question go its own tragic way.

One of the first indications of her resistance to military adventures was in 1950 when she first ran for Congress. On a television broadcast with Everett Dirksen, who was running for the Senate that year, it was easy for both to assail the policies of Truman, whose Korean War had low public support. Marguerite said she wanted "to alert the country to what it means to live by the sword." She feared that the Democrats' war policies would mean a "loss of the essential things of home life through the imposition of controls," and that wartime austerity was hardly compatible with domestic tranquility.[626]

Conflict in Asia was an obvious threat to America's peaceful intentions. Indeed, Marguerite's consistent opposition to military activity was a careful dance because the Communist threat was never to be scoffed at, especially with Joseph McCarthy's fearmongering. In 1951 she couched her attitude in budgetary terms. "There is nothing you can't get [passed] in Congress under national defense," she said. But "bills involving vast expenditures are passed haphazardly." She was speaking to a group at the Union League Club in Chicago where the audience of mainly male business leaders nodded in agreement. Some were perhaps less sanguine when she insisted, "We can't have peace by just rattling a sword and by spreading gifts around the world."[627]

Sword-rattling grew louder as problems in Vietnam became evident. By 1954, American diplomats watched with alarm as the French retreated from Dien Bien Phu, where Communist Viet Minh forces were fighting toward the expulsion of western colonizers. As the battle was ongoing, Secretary of State John Foster Dulles appeared before the Foreign Affairs Committee to discuss how the United States should respond to this development. He implied strongly that if the Chinese got into the Vietnam conflict, that could trigger a like response from the US, and it was one that might not be confined to Indochina. Most members of the committee listened quietly as Dulles ramped up the list of fearful possibilities.

Marguerite alone seemed willing to bring the conversation back to present reality, in which any American involvement in Vietnam, even well short of World War III, was a serious matter. She asked if the United States had committed troops to Vietnam at this point.

"We have not," Dulles said tersely. Marguerite let it go at that. She implied, at the very least, that it would be a serious step, perhaps fateful, which it indeed turned out to be. If anything, she might have been more forceful about the administration's seeking congressional approval before taking any step of that sort.[628]

Not long after the exchange with Dulles, Marguerite was back in the district and speaking to her Republican Women's Club. She discussed Vietnam, saying, "There is no easy answer for Indochina, but I am sure the administration has made no commitment to send troops there." She believed that the president was "trying desperately to avoid commitment of troops without discouraging the French from continuing the war against Communists." Her message to the women was plain: "If we have to replace bloodshed in Korea with bloodshed anywhere else, I am not going to vote for it."[629]

It wasn't long, however, before the Vietnam War began. Not long after Dien Bien Phu fell, the French were forced to divide Vietnam between North and South, and they scheduled their departure by 1956. That left an American military assistance advisory group (MAAG) as the primary support that the South Vietnam regime had to fight communism. The slope was slippery, and as the United States slid into its awful war, most increases in American involvement were effectuated without any vote at all from Congress.

Marguerite appears to have been quiet for much of this unilateral escalation, perhaps because, or perhaps in spite of, the fact that some of these MAAG advisors were being killed. Like many in Congress, she did not raise a voice against what became the catastrophe of the Vietnam War. In her final term in Congress, she did what most had done during World War II and now toward Vietnam, which was to maintain solidarity in what was promoted as a national effort.

Nevertheless, she did have the opportunity to express her feelings about growing militarism in her time, not over Vietnam but rather over the ominous issue of nuclear war. In 1961, a group called Mothers Against Nuclear War met at the Winnetka Community House to hear a number of speakers, including religious leaders, address the dynamics that had led to "mutual assured destruction." When they adjourned, about thirty members of the group motorcaded to Marguerite's house. The congressman, who was out of town, had her staff leave out a laundry basket into which protesters were encouraged to deposit letters they'd written to her. Later, Marguerite received the women in her home, making it clear she'd heard their concerns. The women insisted that nuclear testing should stop and discussed the real possibility of an "accidental" nuclear exchange.[630]

As was her custom, the congressman asked probing questions and listened: "Do you blame Russia for what it has been doing?" she asked. The answer was yes. "Do you feel we can trust Russia?" No. Marguerite kept listening.[631]

"Just because someone stands up and carries a banner encouraging world peace doesn't make him a Communist," said one woman. Another said that the government needed to be influenced not by military leaders and politicians but by humanitarians such as Albert Schweitzer and Bertrand Russell.[632]

Marguerite appeared to agree, saying that many people did not share the view or consciousness of the nuclear issue, and women would have to "remain strong" for their view to prevail and to end the arms race.[633]

NOT A VICIOUS BONE

Sitting on her porch and going against the flow was one thing. Doing it in the halls of Congress was another. But Marguerite had an excellent chance to do so in debate over the Civil Rights Act of 1957. This was a civil rights bill brought forward by the Eisenhower administration largely to assure voting rights after *Brown v. Board of Education of Topeka* had ended legal school segregation in 1954. Southern Democrats were rabidly against it, and in debate they invoked "prejudice against the South" as the animus behind the bill. Marguerite believed that was nonsense and said so. On the floor of the House, she spoke of Emmett Till, the Black Chicago teen murdered by racist white men while Till was visiting relatives in Mississippi: "When the jury refused to punish those who took a young life, I knew that whatever my admiration for those from that part of the country, I would have to vote to protect not only lives but civil rights."[634]

By twenty-first century standards, this was hardly a provocative statement. In the mid-twentieth century, however, it induced Congressman Phillip Landrum of Georgia to get up and say that he had never heard one part of the country "denounced so viciously."[635]

Marguerite replied by saying that she did not have a "vicious bone" in her body.

"I had always thought so, too, until I heard the gentlewoman from Illinois today," said Landrum, to whom Marguerite evidently gave the last word in the exchange.[636]

Marguerite had her finger on the nation's moral pulse, it seemed, but she remained a politician who avoided certain confrontations. One such question was the case of Taiwanese naval officer Hsuan Wei, who in 1954 was in the US for training, part of a military exchange program. Hsuan had professed unhappiness with the dictatorial regime of Chiang Kai-Shek back home and then disappeared before he was set to return to Taiwan. He soon made his way to Evanston, where he enrolled at Northwestern, and he asked for political asylum.

Before the State Department could rule one way or another, the navy, which also had jurisdiction, arrested him in Skokie and shipped him to San Francisco. The plan was to deport him back to Taiwan, but Hsuan and his lawyer protested that this constituted a potential death sentence. The Associated Press reported Wei saying, "I am convinced that if I returned I would be executed."[637] Fortunately for Hsuan, legal complications between the State and Defense Departments (as to which had priority) were such that Hsuan was returned to Evanston temporarily, where he continued as a graduate student in the engineering school.

The young man's life was very much in the balance when the Student Government Board at Northwestern took up his cause, as did the *Daily Northwestern*. Roscoe Miller, the university's president, followed suit by asking Marguerite Church to meet with Hsuan. Miller believed that the best chance for Hsuan was special legislation by Congress enabling him to remain in the United States. If Miller understood that Marguerite was a close friend of Madame Chiang Kai-Shek, he did not mention it, nor did it discourage him from making the request.

Aside from perfunctory statements from Marguerite, she did not move on the Hsuan case. Nor did she make a public statement as to why not, which provided an opening for Congressman Sidney Yates from the North Side of Chicago and an adjacent district to do so.

As he took up the case, Yates invoked the name of Abraham Lincoln who, as president, defended a condemned Union soldier. The congressman recounted that Lincoln asked, "Heavens. Has this man no friends?"

"No, Mr. President, not one," was the answer.

"Very well, I shall be his friend," replied Lincoln.[638]

Marguerite's silence became a campaign issue for Lawrence A. Kusek, who ran as a Democrat in the Thirteenth in 1958. "It is sad to note," Kusek said, "that in seeking to get asylum, Hsuan Wei has not received any help and assistance from Mrs. Church, in whose district he lives."[639] Perhaps Marguerite believed that Congress would not pass legislation on Hsuan's behalf and did not want to enter a losing battle. If Marguerite discussed the situation with her friend Madame Chiang, it was not made public. It may be that delays in Hsuan's deportation, which went on for years, were engineered outside of public view.

In any case, life became nerve-racking for the young man after small legal successes were followed by reversals. In what seemed like a final act, a deportation order was signed in 1961.[640]

Strangely, the press, which had covered the affair in detail for years, lost track of Hsuan. That is, until 1967, when a *Tribune* columnist found him teaching math at Ithaca College in New York.[641] In the end, evidently, the immigration service found it convenient to quietly admit Hsuan, who insisted that, despite his dissent toward Nationalist Chiang Kai-Shek, he was also an ardent anti-Communist.

DISTRICT SHIFTS LEFTWARD . . . SLOWLY

So even for the gentlewoman from Illinois, politics were getting more complicated if not rougher. Even if she avoided much contamination from the Hsuan Wei affair, it cannot have pleased her to be caught between service to a constituent and loyalty to Taiwan, not to mention to her friend Madame Chiang. Of course, it did not move the numbers very much, as she defeated Kusek in the 1958 election with a 67.1 percent majority. But the next time around looked, as it had looked in the past, like it might be harder. It was 1960, the year of the fresh face of John F. Kennedy, and in the Thirteenth Congressional District Marguerite had an equally fresh face as an opponent. Democrat Tyler Thompson was a minister, a professor at Garrett Seminary, and a candidate with a story: He had been captured by the Japanese while serving as a missionary in Singapore during World War II.

Thompson, who was also president of the Illinois chapter of the American Civil Liberties Union, acted as if the Democrats had a chance for an upset as he got the support of Adlai Stevenson, who lived in the district, as well as Mayor Richard J. Daley and the president of the Evanston chapter of the NAACP—even though Black voters had been Church Republicans in the past. As Thompson stumped, he implied that the conservative leaders of the district were tired and outdated. He made a point of ripping an anti-communist seminar program called Education for American Security conducted by an ex-FBI man at Glenview Naval Air Station. Its political agenda represented a "startling and alarming example of McCarthyism," according to Thompson.[642]

During an October 1960 campaign rally, Marguerite urged less dependence on federal controls to minimize spending. She was quoted in the *Arlington Heights Herald* as saying, "While there are needs that must be met, a local state or community can meet its needs cheaper, without the cost of supervision through a federal agency, while preserving the pride of independence."[643] Adding praise for her Republican colleagues, the paper reported that Marguerite "stated that Richard Nixon's greatest attribute is the ability to make a sound decision based on information," and that "Henry Cabot Lodge, according to Mrs. Church, offers invaluable experience as a United Nations delegate plus an accumulated knowledge of the world's problems."[644] And about John F. Kennedy, Marguerite said, "Voters must make a choice on the ability of the candidate to keep his head and his maturity. Consider this:" she concluded. "Under which leadership can we sleep best at night?"[645]

One could sense a harshness that the Thirteenth District had not experienced in the past. Another incident in the cycle involved a Glenview resident, who was a member of the John Birch Society, mailing out unsigned flyers against Thompson, saying that the Democrat was red-tinged or a Communist sympathizer. Whether these flyers changed any voters' minds remained unclear. They did create a stir, however, because the Bircher who sent them was prosecuted in federal court for sending anonymous campaign literature in the mail, a federal crime.[646]

Yet another incident was covered by the *Chicago Defender*, with Thompson saying that "today he has been the victim of poison pen letters alleging he wants to move Negroes into every block" of Evanston.[647] Thompson told United Press International, "I feel sure my opponent knows nothing about these letters," which were reportedly mailed, unsigned, to twelve of his campaign workers and included text that read: "You live in a privileged neighborhood. Do you want colored people next door?" and "This man Thompson is working toward putting colored people in your block and mine—not his own, he moves out when he gets them there!"[648]

The rancor of these incidents made the papers, but again, they did not alter the usual result. Marguerite won the general election with a 66 percent majority thanks to a combination of her customarily tireless campaigning and undeniable seniority. Marguerite handily defeated Thompson, earning the largest number of votes nationwide for a House of Representatives candidate.

While the Democratic party lost twenty seats to Republicans, they still retained their majority in the House.

Weather almost ruined John F. Kennedy's 1961 presidential inauguration and its festivities, snarling traffic and crippling travel in late January. As the Army Corps of Engineers worked with plows, flamethrowers, and tow trucks to clear the streets of snow and abandoned cars, Marguerite, despite her disfavor of many of Kennedy's policies, did her part to ensure the show went on. She sent a police car to rescue one stranded auto carrying composer Leonard Bernstein and actress Bette Davis, marooned somewhere on Massachusetts Avenue, then invited the two to freshen up in her Shoreham Hotel apartment before heading to that evening's Armory Gala. However, according to recollections years later by Representative John Porter, some A-listers were more inclined than others to show their appreciation for her gestures.

As Porter recalled, "Washington was struck with a terrible snowstorm and everything came to a halt. Into [Marguerite's] Connecticut Avenue apartment came Leonard Bernstein and Betty [*sic*] Davis. Leonard in need of a razor so he could shave, Betty [*sic*] in need of stockings since hers had a run in them. Mrs. Church provided the razor and the stockings. Bernstein sent her a dozen roses, but she never heard from Ms. Davis."[649] On January 24, Marguerite wrote back to Bernstein: "The flowers are a happy reminder of circumstances which might—without them—today appear to be sheer fantasy. I do appreciate your thoughtfulness. Surely this Republican was glad that she was able, at long last, to provide one police car for the good of her country—and for the rescue of people like yourself who were giving so much."[650]

OUT AS SHE CAME IN

John F. Kennedy's election as president meant that Republicans' influence would shrink, and that Marguerite's often-dissident voice within the minority would be even more isolated. But she was accustomed to having marginal influence on the results of legislation, and if having Kennedy in the White House discouraged her, she did not show it. She went after the new president as she went after the big spenders in her own party.

In the Foreign Affairs Committee, she unsurprisingly complained about the size of Kennedy's foreign aid allocations and their apparent lack of purpose.

The Kennedy administration had promised that things would be different, naturally, but Marguerite said that it sounded like the old song, "Waltz Me Around Again, Willie," a hit from fifty years before.[651] The reference pointed less to her age than to her experience.

Marguerite continued efforts to curb wasteful spending in government, but especially under this administration they were not always met with success. According to a March 15, 1960, newspaper column found in the Wellesley College Archives, she had tried to prevent an effort to allow senators and congressmen to blanket postal areas with "junk mail" for free. "The lady never had a chance—and she knew it," the column read, adding that Marguerite had attempted to "slay congressional dragons" but "got her feminine ears pinned back by the leadership in the House of Representatives." The column reported Marguerite's response to the defeat: "What made me angry was the quiet way in which it was done," she said, describing "three or four lines" "buried in a post office and treasury appropriations bill." She concluded, "But it was worth it. I went down fighting, and it was a blow for freedom."[652]

If Marguerite's frustration ever revealed itself, it was also apparent in some of her speaking engagements, which she was still invited to make all over the country. At one, she complained about the alleged voter fraud in her own state that supposedly tilted the Electoral College to Kennedy, and she provided details of a story alleging that Chicago vote totals were purportedly held back until the Democratic moguls knew how many more Kennedy votes were needed to win the state.[653] In a speech to a meeting of the Republican Women's Conference about a month into the new administration, she said that it was "the old new deal, the old bad deal wrapped up in a youthful, attractive package."[654]

Kennedy's politics were fair game, but personal attacks, to which Kennedy was vulnerable, were out of bounds to the gentlewoman from Illinois. According to Una Corley Groves, Marguerite and most people in Washington were aware of the president's amorous indiscretions, and she, like most people in the Capitol, made no public issue of it.[655]

But her respect for the presidency also put her at odds with her more acerbic Republican House colleagues. In a debate preceding a vote to increase the size of the White House police force, she believed things were getting too personal toward the president. The measure's sponsors claimed extra force was needed due to, among other things, "the great increase in the number of tourist visitors—from 720,000 a year to two million since 1952—as well as the addition of new executive office and the enlargement of such functions as presidential news conferences."[656] Marguerite disavowed comments of others of her party—including those of Representative H. R. Gross of Iowa, who called Caroline Kennedy's ponies (named Macaroni and Tex) "Macaroni and Spaghetti"—as well as references to "police all-night twist parties" at the executive mansion and protection of Kennedy's "ancestral estates." Marguerite bid these critics to desist such scurrilous attacks out of respect for the office.[657]

As she accepted being a member of the minority, she did not mind being an unpredictable one. In 1961 she surprised colleagues and constituents with her refusal to support the renewal of Public Law 78, which governed the seasonal migration of Mexican farmworkers into the US. The legislation, dating to 1951, governed conditions that were now considered unacceptable to many people sympathetic to the migrants, and Marguerite agreed. Her conscientious dissent was elegant in its simplicity. "I am unwilling to accept the fact that we cannot give more protection to the imported Mexican laborers," she said as the issue came to a vote, "and particularly more protection to our US migrant farm laborers. Merely to extend this act without consideration of connected problems that must be faced, is not adequate or responsible action."[658] Although it did not change anything, as the so-called "bracero program" was extended for another year without any provision to improve worker conditions, Marguerite once again stood for human rights.

She also urged women to embrace unity amidst changing times, to look forward and not back, and to take personal responsibility for the fate of the nation. In April 1961, speaking to women from her district at her ninth annual Easter brunch, Marguerite mentioned the coming changes to their district of nearly one million, urging the group to stay united. She implored, "I ask you for the sake of the country that you not splinter yourselves in the face of impending redistricting in Illinois."[659] A reporter from the *Evanston Review* wrote, "The congresswoman said Washington has an exciting atmosphere because of a new sense of perspective and a more audacious approach to problems." Noting Marguerite's reference to "great organic change" and progress due to "population mobility, migration and congestion," the reporter captured perhaps her most telling statement: "The world is leaping ahead down unknown paths. We can't step aside, no matter how much we long for the good old days." She cautioned the women of her district to note the real "war" going on that "is not between people or nations, but between different codes" of financial conservatism and regimentation. Lambasting the "paternal approach to government," she said, "We must face up to the fact that this is not just a national problem, but one on the world level. What we do individually will lead to national survival or national bankruptcy."[660]

Marguerite had certainly assumed a unique position in the House. Not only was she one of the few women in the body, she often took surprising positions that went against the usual Republican line. She sometimes alienated colleagues in this. And while her positions sometimes had the effect of moderating laws that were otherwise unacceptable to her, her conservative views—and one could say ultra-conservative views—remained in the minority. But she never seemed weary in this, and her predictable steadfastness often made her influential. She could moreover take satisfaction that even when overruled, her positions in support of human rights, for example, pricked the conscience of her colleagues and became politically mainstream in the fullness of time.

In a manner of speaking, she will be remembered for her courage to be a socially progressive lawmaker despite her attitude of—and affinity for—conservative politics.

Nevertheless, she is established, respected and also—apparently, now—considered a "fashion plate." In January of 1959, Marguerite was named to "Chicago's 10 Best Dressed" list in the *Chicago Daily Sun-Times*.

She told a reporter she was "unaware that she had even been nominated for the contest," and, when asked about her fashion sense, responded as straightforward as her style: "I wear tailored suits. My evening clothes are designed in simple lines with the emphasis on fabric." Listed among socialites and fashion plates, it's easy to imagine Marguerite's quick wit and self-deprecating manner as she first learned the news and responded, most likely with well-concealed amusement: "This is an unexpected honor," she said. "I am overcome."[661]

According to political commentator George Dixon, Marguerite was at the 1960 Republican National Convention in Chicago, preparing to introduce National Chairman Thruston B. Morton, when one of the show's organizers—a "Hollywood ringmaster," according to Dixon—directed Marguerite toward the makeup tent for a spruce-up. Marguerite declined. Dixon said she replied, "'I don't want to be made up for my speech.'"

According to Dixon, Mr. Hollywood countered with, "'You want to look rested, don't you?'"

"'No,'" Dixon says she replied. "'My district expects me to look harassed.'"[662]

CHAPTER FOURTEEN

SEPARATION OF CHURCH AND STATE

A NUMBER OF CHANGES WOULD come in Marguerite's final term in Congress. One of them was foreshadowed in her attitude toward United Nations Ambassador Adlai Stevenson as he testified before Foreign Affairs. The administration asked Congress to approve a loan to the UN peacekeeping operation that was active in the Congo. As many UN member nations were not paying their share, especially the Soviet Union, Stevenson was asking for funds to keep the peacekeepers afloat. He ran into a predictable buzz saw of criticism, not least from Democrats such as Representative Wayne Hays, who said that "when the American people learn that we are paying mercenaries to murder white missionaries, the people are not going to like it."[663] Hays' hyperbole in this was over the top, but Stevenson corrected Hays only in that UN forces were not mercenaries, rather peacekeepers.

Anyone might have wondered what Marguerite would say on the issue, as she normally resisted sending money abroad under almost any circumstance. In this case, however, she said in committee that she understood that the International Court of Justice was going to rule and advised the General Assembly take those nations' votes away if they didn't pay up. She counseled that Congress should wait on the court's ruling before turning the request down.[664] A month later, the court was indecisive, but the committee and the House approved a loan, though with restrictions to keep the eventual figure lower than the $100 million that was asked for.[665]

Not much later, President Kennedy asked Marguerite to be one of the five members of the delegation to the United Nations, something of an honorary position for a member of Congress but one that interested her greatly. She was one of forty-nine women representing thirty-six nations, the largest number of female delegates in the group's history. She would be serving with women who were lawyers, prominent educators, directors of corporations, and at least one foreign minister, Golda Meir of Israel.[666] Marguerite did not make policy in this role, though she did bring some luster to the UN, which needed it. House members knew that she was seasoned by her many fact-finding missions abroad, and her tacit endorsement of the UN suppressed right-wing distrust of the organization. As for why Kennedy appointed Marguerite to the United Nations, one newspaper editor took a guess: "She has fought so hard against some of his favorite legislation in Congress; he was convinced that such a fighter for what she thought was right would fight just as hard in the world court for democratic principles."[667]

The one time she invoked her UN role on the floor of the House was when she asked for a resolution to protest consideration of membership for mainland China. She asked that "the United Nations not be threatened by the admission of a nation which defies our principles of freedom."[668] While she had not been to Red China, as it was called, she had been to Taiwan, not just to visit, but to stay with the wife of the ruler of Nationalist China. Her position prevailed in the General Assembly, as the US led the fight to exclude the Beijing government.

Though her role at the UN was primarily an observational one, what she observed and shared after her retirement was not sugar-coated. "I am a United Nations supporter," she told the *Arlington Heights Herald*, "but much is yet to be done to make the organization the peace-keeping influence its founders envisioned."[669] She said, "My most memorable impression is also my most disappointing impression," and added that the United States' behavior in the organization "betrayed longstanding national principles in favor of appeasement." She may have been referring to the tendency to not challenge the Soviets when they moved on innocent countries and suggested she would have been tougher if she were crafting policy, or even articulating it. But that was not how it went at the UN: "The United States delegates do not vote their personal convictions, rather by order from Washington," she explained. If ever there was a recipe for the status quo, that was it.[670]

Some members of the hard-core right wing of her party believed that some of Marguerite's votes betrayed the GOP. To them she replied—and repeated—that she became a member of Congress to vote her conscience, not necessarily her party. She added, of course, that her principles had not changed, and in those terms she justified another surprising vote.

When she joined the majority to create the Peace Corps in 1961, Marguerite said there was something deeply American in the effort. "I am not afraid to try this program, experiment though it is," she said on the House floor on September 14, 1961. "I willingly again admit the possibility of failure. But here is something which is aimed right—which is American, which is sacrificial—and which above all can somehow carry at the human level, to the people of the world, what they need to know; what it is to be free; what it is to know; what it is to have a next step and be able to take it; what it is to have something to look forward to, in an increase of human dignity and confidence." She then added, "I would not urge anyone to change his or her vote by what few words I utter. But I would like to attest again my own faith in the hope of this program." Then, acknowledging numerous failed attempts at peace in the world, she added, "Truth and hope remain—the dream of peace on earth and good will to men still exists. The crusades are still going on."[671] The theme of peace only echoes those words of her much earlier 1939 Zonta article.[672]

A WAR FOR PEACE

The idea of the Peace Corps had been batted around Washington for years, at least since the 1950s, when Nelson Rockefeller and Senator Hubert H. Humphrey were advocating for and alluding to its merits. Rockefeller thought the United States "needed to demonstrate to the world its positive characteristics and ideals rather than only stressing what it was against.[673] And Humphrey "suggested a people to people program that emphasized education, healthcare, vocational training and community development. He touted the program during his failed campaign for the Democratic presidential nomination in 1960 and was the first to use the name 'Peace Corps' in a June 1960 Senate bill."[674] In 1952, Democratic Senator Brien McMahon of Connecticut proposed that young "missionaries of democracy" be sent abroad to provide technical and educational assistance where needed in developing countries. In 1957, Humphrey, also a Democrat, introduced a bill to create the Peace Corps.

It did not pass, but in 1959, members of the House and Senate proposed to seriously study the subject. When finished, the report was endorsed by Marguerite's Foreign Affairs Committee as well as the Foreign Relations Committee of the Senate. During committee discussions, Marguerite "wanted to be certain that volunteers would be trained in 'facts about this country, facts about its purpose, and particularly an enthusiasm for human freedom.'"[675] As Marguerite said in committee, "If this Peace Corps concept fails, more fails than the program itself. An ideal falls or a hope falls, a dream becomes unrealizable."[676] With Kennedy in the White House, the idea took off, initially with an executive order in March of 1961, and then when funding was approved in the fall.

The Peace Corps was not without its critics. Richard Nixon, as a candidate for the presidency in 1960, called it a "haven for draft dodgers," though Nixon did support the program after he became president.[677] A number of congressmen hammered the proposal as a place where stealth Communists could promote their ideology, and some critics called it an "espionage agency."[678] Other conservatives simply saw it as a socialistic tax-and-spend travesty. Sargent Shriver, a diplomat who would become the first director of the Peace Corps, also noted that conservatives disliked the term "peace." As Shriver said, "They maintained it sounded wishy-washy, vague, and weak."

And the left, he said, disliked the term "corps," believing that "it sounded militaristic" and "like a scourge." Ultimately, as Shriver recalled, "I decided we'd use both words, put them together, and get the best out of both of them: Peace because that was truly our business; and Corps because it showed that we were not individualists, but a group!"[679]

As one of Marguerite's fellow House Members, Catherine May Bedell of Washington, remembered it, negative views about the Peace Corps were gaining in the House. And that's when Marguerite Stitt Church spoke—and spoke in favor—of the program.

"I saw one person make the difference," Bedell recalled, years later. "I felt that it was Marguerite Stitt Church who really could be given the credit for seeing that the original Peace Corps program passed the House of Representatives."[680] As Bedell explained, "you quite literally could see people who had been uncertain or perhaps who had already decided to vote against the Peace Corps sit there, listen to her very quietly, and start to rethink."[681]

"When she spoke, people listened," said Una Corley Groves in 2018. "There was no conversation during her lectures. There were no people whispering to each other. There were people concentrating on what she said."[682]

Among the opposition were twenty-nine Democrats led by Otto "the Terrible" Passman of Louisiana, an implacable enemy of foreign aid and integration. Passman might have reasonably hoped that Marguerite Church, usually a reliable conservative vote, would join him.

Largely, however, the Peace Corps was promising the kind of in-the-weeds assistance that Marguerite believed was lacking in most of the aid programs that she consistently opposed. Opponents who derided the program as a "utopian brainstorm," she insisted, were misguided.[683] It would be "as American as Boston baked beans and apple pie," she said.[684] It was also noted that thousands of voters in her district responded to her questionnaire on the subject, with 61.9 percent in favor and 27.1 percent opposed, the rest having no opinion.[685]

After Marguerite's plea on the floor of the House, the $40 million ($410.7 million in 2023) allocation breezed through the House by a vote of 287 to 97.

Marguerite's crucial championing of the Peace Corps bill in 1961 truly secured Marguerite Stitt Church's place in history as a pioneer, or what Groves would later describe as a "producer."[686] Relying on her unique skills and experience, she'd been able to *listen* to others' needs around the world, articulate enough to express those needs to her colleagues, and (despite tremendous resistance) passionate enough to ensure the passage of the first international *service* program of its kind, which focused on two of her greatest personal interests: social and economic development. Through the Peace Corps, women would work beside men, elevating and empowering citizens beyond borders, addressing critical international needs that Marguerite herself observed during her foreign tours, including so many of them expressed by the women she met.

RETIREMENT

At the end of 1961, Marguerite announced that she would not run for a seventh term in 1962. Perhaps significantly, the press release was mailed not from Evanston, not from Washington, but from New York, where she was attending a conference near the Hudson River that December. She was working—in her own words—"harder than I had ever worked in my life," serving as one of five US delegates to the United Nations General Assembly and as a ranking member of the Foreign Economic Policy Subcommittee.[687]

Away from Capitol Hill, she seemed to find herself realizing new opportunities. Much like her role as US representative, her position as a UN delegate, which began on September 19, 1961, hadn't been one she'd sought, but rather, one that found her. She'd been surprised to learn through newspaper stories that she'd been appointed, and was forced to cancel her biannual "study mission" as the ranking Republican member of the House subcommittee on foreign economic policy and the subcommittee on the Far East and the Pacific.[688]

Marguerite was nothing if not flexible—and loyal. Of her decision to accept the appointment, she said, "The next session of the General Assembly . . . will be, because of the implications of world crisis, one of the most significant ever faced."[689]

Life as a UN delegate looked unlike that of a typical American grandmother. Her day typically began at 7:15 a.m., reading congressional mail. At 9 o'clock, she read reports from the sessions the day before. The procedures in the UN, she said, were much more formal than in Congress, noting, "You must send your name if you wish to speak."[690]

And it was while at the UN that her privilege and positional bias were, perhaps, on display when Marguerite was challenged to a debate by Bulgarian delegate Decho Stamoliev, who pointed to racial problems in the US "and charged that there is discrimination and even slavery in the United States." An undated article reports that "Mrs. Church countered that if all nations had done as much as the United States to eliminate discrimination, 'we would all rejoice.'"[691]

As she later recounted in her 1978 oral history, it was on one particular night in early December of 1961 that she'd been walking up New York's First Avenue and experienced a most unusual feeling, something she described as "a strange sense of freedom." She said, "I couldn't define it or analyze it, but I found that I was thinking, reacting, from a broader viewpoint, without the daily pressures to which I had so long been accustomed."[692]

Marguerite, noticing the possibility of life beyond her role as a member of Congress, seemed to have a decision to make.

Unsure if she'd retire or not, she decided to think things through, and later described the pep talk she gave herself: "'Well, you know, if you just had sense enough and courage enough, you might have this freedom for the rest of your life. You've never taken time to be away.'"[693]

The following day, she sent the retirement announcement to her secretary, Barbara Ludden, but instructed her to hold it until Monday. During that weekend's conference, as Marguerite later recalled, she kept thinking about the idea of life beyond Congress, revealing, "I was engaged in another one of those interminable discussions where you'd see things from every angle, and because there is no answer, you don't find it . . . and [I] thought, 'You know, maybe you were meant to have that thought of retiring." As she recalled, she went home and, after some thought, "wrote a little statement that I wasn't going to run again."[694]

Marguerite told reporter Lois Wille of the *Chicago Daily News*, "As far as I'm concerned, I'm still ripe for all sorts of living. And eager for new work. I never intended to stay in Congress forever and ever. If you're there too long, you have no desire or initiative when you leave.'"[695]

Sixteen years later, she reflected on that decision to leave Congress: "I have never regretted it," she said, adding, "I think everybody should walk out when they can still walk, when they can still live, still think, and somehow or other make adjustments for themselves—and let the Congress have new leadership.[696]

Her decision was final, and her simple message, signaling the end of a remarkable political partnership-turned-career, ran in the December 8, 1961, *New York Times* under the headline, "G.O.P. Woman Surprises:" specifically stating that she thought it "'appropriate' that a new Representative be elected for the new Thirteenth District."[697]

Tributes and accolades flowed in abundance once Marguerite announced she'd retire. The Illinois Merchants Association declared her a representative "who, during her twelve years as a member of Congress, has adhered so faithfully to her beliefs in the basic concepts of this republic and who has provided so perfect an example of the invaluable contribution which women can make to the conduct of government."[698] And when the United Republican Fund announced a dinner to honor Marguerite for her service, president Fred M. Gillies said 2,000 would attend the group's $100-per-plate ($1,017 in 2023) dinner and paid her a compliment—as so many about women were—based against the male standard: "Mrs. Church took her place as a congressman from Illinois' populous 13th District in a way that would have done credit to the most experienced man."[699] To be sure, Marguerite did not miss the opportunity to reference men when discussing her own strength as a member of Congress. One reporter wrote that Marguerite said of the void she'd leave upon retiring, "It will take three men to take over our district."[700]

After her announcement to retire, Marguerite told Bruce Ladd of the *Arlington Heights Herald*, "I have never found that being a woman hampered my ability to be effective. I have sought to act as a 'congressman,' not a woman."[701]

As the press scrambled for reasons behind her retirement, Ralph Church Jr. told the *Chicago Tribune* that, among other things, his mother would be seventy by the end of her present term, a good turning point for anyone.[702]

What went unsaid was that politics were continuing to change on the North Shore, with more actively progressive voters—still not a majority, but certainly more vocal.

Moreover, Illinois was about to get a thorough redistricting, one long overdue as the Thirteenth Congressional District had grown to nearly a million people. Marguerite's current district would be included in parts of three new ones. The new Thirteenth would still be centered in Evanston, where the liberal wave was still more than a decade in the future. But it seemed like a good time to bow out. Doing so would, in effect, ensure that Ralph E. and Marguerite Stitt Church, together yet apart, were the only two to shepherd that district.

As Marguerite told one reporter: "I think the Thirteenth will always be, very peculiarly, our own—my husband's and mine."[703]

It was an elaborate exit for Marguerite, with a number of honorary degrees coming her way in her final term, including one from Northwestern in June of 1962. At commencement that year, she joined several other conferees on the dais, including future Nobel Prize winner Saul Bellow and the Museum of Science and Industry's president, Lenox Lohr. It was Marguerite's speech that drew the most attention in the press, as it cleaved hard to her conservative foundations and less to her uniquely progressive and internationalistic approach.

In her speech to the 2,500 graduates, Marguerite posed soul-searching questions that focused on America, revealing her dedication to fiscal conservatism, freedom, and faith.

"The United States must develop a clear, consistent policy based on our self-interest," Marguerite told the crowd. "By self-interest, I mean our determination to be free, and to preserve the freedom of our people. Our allies and our opponents must be made aware of our aim and of our will to achieve it."[704] To anyone who claimed the "force of human freedom" or "the great principles on which this great country is built" to be outdated or untrue, Marguerite had but one direct response: "Those who would have you believe these concepts are false or antiquated are those who trifle with your freedom."[705]

Marguerite was the devoted Republican and isolationist when she said that the national debt constituted an existential threat to American freedom. She also wondered if the Ten Commandments were obsolete; this was a rhetorical question but hardly nonpartisan, as evangelicals had mobilized against Kennedy's election and would continue in politics for decades to come. Marguerite expressed the fear Americans felt about the country becoming a socialist nation. The audience at Northwestern, then a largely conservative institution, agreed with her on these points, as had Evanston and the district for years.

Then she asked, "Have we become so concerned with causes that we have lost sight of our principles?" as the *Tribune* reporter at the commencement paraphrased. It was a distinction that got the attention of anyone who was listening. Causes, she implied, were the stuff of politics. Principles were sometimes harder to follow. Marguerite said that her principles were built on "the force of human freedom . . . the determination to be free and to preserve the freedom of our people." Freedom was what defined her as a congressman. Now, as she was retiring, she was asking the graduates to behave based on what defined *them*. She did not say it with words in the speech, but her career full of action proved that if decisions were hard and surprised friends and rivals alike, those who used courage to stand up to their personal convictions were the most free and successful[706]

CRASH COURSE IN LATIN AMERICA

As part of President Kennedy's efforts with The Alliance for Progress—as well as to scout the newly posted volunteers of the US Peace Corps—he sent Marguerite on a trip to Latin America, which many criticized as a "junket" for "lame ducks" and other bureaucrats.[707] Marguerite would be a part of an Inter-American Affairs subcommittee studying conditions in several Latin American countries. Scheduled for November 11 through December 14, 1962, it would be the last trip she'd make as a member of Congress. The itinerary was to take Marguerite and a congressional delegation (CODEL) through Ecuador, Peru, Colombia, Panama, Costa Rica, Guatemala, and Mexico, though the trip was fraught with misadventure, almost from the start. In Peru, Marguerite took a fall, causing an ankle injury, something she was often prone to. She arrived in Ecuador on crutches, prompting Representative-elect Donald Rumsfeld, her successor in the 1962 election, to stand in for her scheduled activities as she recovered.[708]

Marguerite was then involved in a serious car accident in Guatemala on December 4, having just arrived in the country one hour earlier.[709] She and the CODEL were headed in two cars to a meeting with Guatemalan President Miguel Ydígoras Fuentes when a Guatemalan driver ran a red light, forcing Marguerite's car into a light pole.[710] She was traveling with three other members of their delegation. Marguerite suffered a broken leg and fractured ribs in the accident, but she was hardly the only one injured. Her colleague, Representative Armistead Selden of Alabama, sustained a broken rib and a cut over his right eye, requiring seven stitches. Also injured was Rosita Bennett, a congressional staff member, who suffered a crushed nose.

The worst one injured was congressional staff member Albert Westphal, who sustained a severe head wound requiring seventy-two stitches and multiple blood transfusions.[711]

Journalists captured Marguerite's return to the US, wheelchair-bound with a cast on her leg, smiling, gracious, and wrapped in a fur stole, shaking hands with a colleague at the end of their harrowing journey.

No physical limitation had ever seemed to stop her before, and Marguerite would continue to stand up for others—albeit not physically for the time being—for many years to come.

A LEG TO STAND ON

On the eve of her last night in office, January 8, 1963, Marguerite was honored at a testimonial dinner at Northwestern University, her late husband's alma mater, by an admiring crowd of more than 600. She arrived in a wheelchair, still recovering from the fractured leg and cracked ribs she sustained during her final congressional trip.[712] That evening, a reporter from the *Evanston Review* captured Marguerite in a moment of lightheartedness, joking with well-wishers as she poked fun at her own well-known fiscal conservatism: "This is the first time I've been any place since I met my comeuppance in Guatemala City," she said. "Foreign aid got a lusty kick after all."[713]

In the university's filled-to capacity Patten Gymnasium, Representative J. L. Pilcher, a Democrat from Georgia, said of Marguerite, "She is one of the greatest statesmen I have ever known—a Republican second, an American first, and a very gracious lady," adding, "There's not much difference between you Midwest Republicans or us southern Democrats."[714]

The program featured several previously recorded tributes, including one from former President Dwight D. Eisenhower, who said of Marguerite: "She has been a gracious, diligent and forceful member of Congress, and a valuable asset to the Republican party." He continued, "Indeed, regardless of party, every person who believes in good government and every person who believes in the value to America of independent and intelligent judgment will miss

Marguerite Church in the Congress."[715] It was, perhaps, not lost on many that Marguerite had, during her first term, investigated Ike's reorganization of the Council of Economic Advisors.[716]

Another recorded tribute came from the former First Lady of the Republic of China, Madame Chiang Kai-Shek:

> *"Of all the congressional and civic leaders and other friends who are joining this testimonial dinner in honor of Mrs. Church, I believe that I am the only one who was fortunate enough at one time to have attended her lectures. She instilled in us, her students, a deep appreciation of Christian principles. Since then in her public life she has been guided invariably by these same moral and spiritual values. To her I would like to express my admiration for her courage in exemplifying what she taught."*[717]

As noted by the *Chicago Daily Tribune*, seventy-year-old Marguerite rose from her wheelchair to stand at the podium, aided by a cane, addressing her admirers with characteristic self-deprecation: "I apologize for my ignominious entrance," Marguerite said. "I've never been known to hide by [*sic*] condition, so I have to admit I am the lamest duck that ever lived."[718]

Marguerite's remarks that evening reflected her love of country, not to mention the pride she felt having served in Congress and her gratitude for having served: "Thank you for the life you let me lead during the last twelve years," she told the crowd, declaring the United States to have "the highest ideal of government ever maintained by mankind."[719]

Following this emotional statement, Marguerite then spoke of her late husband. Ever the masterful orator, she must have sent her adoring crowd roaring with laughter upon retelling one of Ralph's tongue-in-cheek quips: "You would never be any good at this," Marguerite said Ralph once told her, jokingly, "You haven't got the mind for the job."[720]

By all accounts, though, she had the ideal mind—and heart—to perform the job successfully, and she made sure to thank those Evanstonians, in particular, who recognized it and encouraged her to run. She especially thanked her

"Church for Congress" campaign manager, Irl H. Marshall, as well as May Emerson Carney Middleton (Mrs. Edward L. Middleton), and her best friend from Wellesley College, Gladys Dowley (Mrs. Dunbar W. Lewis), the two of whom she referred to as her "amateur crew."[721]

And always, it seemed, the love for her husband was apparent. "I think I was grateful, first of all to the district," she said, "not because they were sending me [to Washington], but because it showed me what respect they had had for the kind of congressman who had served them for so long."[722]

As for Marguerite's successor, Donald Rumsfeld, he and his wife, Joyce, were appreciative and aware of Marguerite's efforts and effect. "In a roomful of people, she would be noticed," Rumsfeld explained in a 2021 interview. Growing up in a district solidly passed from Church to Church, Rumsfeld saw the strength and opportunity of the unmoving seat and leaped at the chance when Marguerite retired. His "driving force" was their example.

She was also his driving force quite literally. In 1962, when the Rumsfelds' "financial capabilities were less than modest," Marguerite offered to drive Joyce to Washington and help her find a residence. "It was a truly gracious thing for her to do," Rumsfeld shared, elaborating that Marguerite's "previous contact with Joyce had been next to nothing."[723] The 750-mile trip was done in one long stretch, as "Mrs. Church always did it that way."[724] "I'm glad I knew her," Joyce remembered, noting in particular Marguerite's "grace and sophistication."[725]

Marguerite, in her seventies, still had plenty of road ahead.

MRS. IRONPANTS AND FAMILY

Having served twelve years in Congress herself—and thirty-two years as her husband's political partner before that—Marguerite could now shift her attention to her children and grandchildren as she never had before, though she stayed active in numerous organizations and responded graciously—and honestly—to inquiries from her former constituents and the press.

Months after leaving Washington, when asked by the *Arlington Heights Herald* about her time at the United Nations, the normally upbeat Marguerite spoke frankly of her enormous disillusionment and concern. "My most memorable impression is also my most disappointing impression," she said. "The time is long overdue when the U.S. must take a stand in the UN supporting the principles upon which this nation was founded even if it means defeat on a major issue. The U.S. has never been defeated on a major issue in the UN." Just as damning, the column said, "Mrs. Church stated she has never seen 'politics' played like they are being played under the Kennedy Administration, and her experience in Washington dates back 25 years."[726]

Six days after President John F. Kennedy was killed, Marguerite publicly upheld her stand on 1964 presidential delegate Barry Goldwater. The *Chicago Tribune* reported her saying, "We shouldn't let the period of respect seem to weaken our convictions. All of us should watch very alertly to see whether there will be profligate spending and whether America's interest will be put first." She continued, "You don't deal in personalities, but you don't sacrifice issues. Republicans owe it to the country to stand for positive things which the United States needs."[727]

The Churches' eldest son, Ralph Jr., followed his parents—at least for a short time—into politics, serving as the Thirteenth Congressional District Republican state central committeeman in 1964.[728]

There was relatively little reported about Marguerite's interactions with her middle child, William, beyond her dedication to provide for him. Groves said William "used the bedroom above the garage. He seemed to be a deeply troubled individual," and added that "Marguerite's psychological training was poured into raising him."[729]

The press did, however, note many instances when Marguerite and her daughter Marjory spent time together, such as in 1969, when they co-hosted an "old fashioned Christmas open house" in Marjory's home on Burnham Place in Evanston. The event—complete with a buffet supper of turkey, ham, and scalloped oysters—included Marjory's four daughters, all in red velvet, and her son, then aged ten, in a nifty red tie.[730]

Despite her 1963 retirement from Congress, Marguerite never stopped working. Throughout retirement, she remained an active force with the Republican party as well as the Wellesley Alumnae Association, and, from 1970 to 1971, served as a member of the White House Conference on Aging's National Planning Board through the US Department of Health, Education, and Welfare.

She served in countless national roles as writer, lecturer, board member, advisor, committee member, political backer, and member of numerous political task forces.

Close to home, during her 1967 address to the Evanston Historical Society on Abraham Lincoln's birthday, she spoke fondly of her late husband and her entry into politics.[731] While speaking at the fiftieth birthday party of the Women's Republican Club of Evanston—a group she helped to found—she wore a button that said, "Red Hot Republican." During that 1971 celebration, Marguerite spoke of the club's first meeting, and how she'd pushed her son, Ralph Jr., in a baby carriage over to the Shumway House (in 2023, The Mather Senior Living Community) at 1605 Hinman Avenue: "I kept the carriage outside and opened the window in the meeting room five or six inches so I would hear him if he cried."[732]

Family tragedy struck once again on March 15, 1972, when Marjory's son, Todd Wood, then thirteen, was killed near Evanston's Nichols Middle School. Police and the press reported that he and eight boys were approached by a female motorist who exited her car and reprimanded them. According to a press release, the boys had been throwing snowballs at cars and fled from the motorist up an embankment to the Chicago Transit Authority tracks just as a train approached. As the boy ran alongside the train, his jacket was caught, and he was dragged about fifty feet.[733]

Marguerite's grandson was pronounced dead at the scene, a devastating loss for the family and particularly Marguerite, who'd worked tirelessly in Congress to keep children safe from harm.[734]

Another blow came two years later when Marguerite's sister, Edna, died in the Churches' Evanston home at the age of eighty-four. As was her way, Marguerite did not comment publicly on either of these losses, rather keeping personal matters personal. Still, records from the First United Methodist Church in Evanston indicate she received Reverend Dow Napier Kirkpatrick at her home when he paid Marguerite condolence visits following each of the deaths.[735]

As always, Marguerite persevered, moving herself—in ways both literal and figurative—onward and upward through her innate sense of duty. One month after her grandson's death, in April 1972, Marguerite accepted an invitation by the newly appointed president of the Evanston Young Republicans, D. Daniel Baldino, who'd recently launched the organization's quarterly speaker series. During a 2021 interview, Baldino recalled Marguerite's speech, as well as the woman herself. "Marguerite spoke on public service and civic engagement," Baldino said of Marguerite's talk, which was given, as they often were, in the living room of a private home. "She was outgoing, but in a very genteel way. She was a lady, very reserved, but hardly stuck up or haughty. People looked upon her as an icon—a kind of grande dame. But really, she was just a nice person."[736]

In 1975, the year after her sister Edna's death, Marguerite served as a chairman of the President Ford committee.[737]

And, the following year, while on a trip to Puerto Vallarta, she didn't pass up a chance to dine high atop a cliff. As Representative John Porter of Illinois' Tenth Congressional District explained in his tribute to Congress honoring Marguerite, she kept up with everyone, at the age of eighty-four, ascending almost one hundred steps to a restaurant.[738]

One of Marguerite's last public appearances was during a ninety-first birthday celebration held in her honor. During that 1983 event, thrown by the Women's Republican Club of the Tenth Congressional District and held at Allgauer's Restaurant in Northbrook, Illinois, two of Marguerite's children, Ralph Jr. and Marjory, looked on as Senator Charles Percy of Illinois presented the former congressman with a box of long-stemmed roses. Blushing, she accepted it, then said to her admirers, "You'd better all be careful or I might run again."[739]

Letters of praise were shared on behalf of President Ronald Reagan, Vice President George Bush, and former Presidents Richard Nixon and Gerald Ford.[740] Representative Philip Crane told Marguerite, "I don't mean any disrespect, but when I got to Congress, I learned that your Democratic adversaries still referred to you as Mrs. Ironpants," adding, "They said you either devastated them with your gentle rhetoric or your charm, but either way, you were invincible."[741]

That day, Donald Rumsfeld, who had succeeded Marguerite after her retirement from Congress in 1963, said he felt "fortunate that with four billion people on earth, my life has intersected with hers," describing Marguerite's life as a "rising road."[742]

Crane suggested she was herculean while "preserving always her ladylike qualities," calling her "an early pioneer in women's liberation, assuming a role of leadership in every aspect of our society."[743] And Porter added, "She reminds us, in a time of widespread cynicism, that there are honorable and caring people in public life. Mrs. Church will always stand in my mind as the personification of the ideals of this nation, as one to rekindle our spirits and beliefs."[744]

Despite the hardship, the sorrow, and the many challenges she faced throughout her ninety-one years, she was still an optimistic, gregarious woman, celebrated by the group whose mood that night ranged "from carnival to spiritual."[745]

"I am humble and grateful for this tribute," Marguerite told that crowd of 400 Republicans—mostly women—"and I wonder at times—as I have throughout the years—how it all happened to me. I never took myself too seriously," she said, "and I never planned to be in public life. It just happened, and I did what was necessary."[746]

WORTHWHILE STRUGGLE

Marguerite lived until the age of ninety-seven, dying in her sleep in her home on May 26, 1990. The first song played during her memorial service at the First United Methodist Church of Evanston was not a hymn but rather a patriotic song—"America the Beautiful"—originally penned during the first year of Marguerite's life by fellow Wellesley College alumna Katherine Lee Bates.[747] Marguerite is buried next to her husband, Ralph, in Memorial Park Cemetery in Skokie, Illinois, under a majestic tree.

In the three decades since her death, Marguerite Stitt Church has been remembered for many things, including her fiscal conservatism and her shaping of legislation which, in her words, either "did something" (e.g., protecting citizens by restricting the transport of bootleg fireworks) or "established policy" (e.g., placing the budgeting system of the federal government on an accrued annual expenditures basis). She was lauded for her fresh outlook on social welfare issues, particularly civil and equal rights, but above all else, Marguerite Stitt Church lived to serve and encourage others, particularly women.

Even as a member of the twentieth century Republican party—one that leaned toward fewer governmental controls—Marguerite rarely hesitated advocating for common sense legislation that reflected a more progressive ideology when she saw it morally necessary. Counter to a traditional, Republican, "fewer controls" approach, she'd successfully authored a bill banning the transport of fireworks into states where they were prohibited, and had, on at least one occasion, opened doors—quite literally—for some Black citizens when others in the nation refused. She also spoke out for women when it was hardly the popular thing to do and advocated for the spending of millions to establish the Peace Corps despite her personal record of fiscal conservatism.

Marguerite's confident, direct, and sometimes unconventional approach was never seen as "political posturing," because what you saw was what you got—a delivery that simultaneously appealed to her constituents and disarmed her adversaries.

She was a woman of humility, of optimism, and of unwavering love for the life partner whom she'd suddenly lost, and she demonstrated these traits through actions rather than any political spin. Her steadfast approach never did change—nor did her energy seem to wane—even after she left Congress.

As Representative Fred Schwengel said following her retirement announcement, "on the basis of education, of experience, of predilection for public service, and of performance, this Representative from Illinois is what political scientists must regard as the ideal public servant," and added, "the substantive story of this career is a story of enormous energy and activity and all of it with results which mean much to the society of our time."[748] Schwengel, who founded the United States Capitol Historical Society, recruited Marguerite in 1962 to assist him in envisioning its future and to serve on its first board of directors.[749] Marguerite even donated $3,000 of her own money ($30,499 in 2023) in 1962 to help establish the society.[750]

What was it that inspired Marguerite most? According to former Congressman Samuel H. Young, "her trinity for a successful life were faith, home, and love. That's the way she lived her life."[751] Marguerite confirmed that herself in her 1978 oral history, saying she was motivated by "a tremendous love of what I always say is a very great country. Not great for its wealth or its might or its power—though I'm glad we have all three—but great because of the basic principles of justice and equality, freedom under the law, which distinguish us in many ways from so many other lands."

Marguerite also explained the "thrill and sense of inner satisfaction" that she got from her position, from "an opportunity to make decisions. . . . I still think the struggle is most worthwhile."[752]

As one of the first fifty women elected to Congress, she served for twelve years through multiple crises. When she entered Congress in 1950, Marguerite and her ten female colleagues made up 2 percent of all members; by the time she left, twelve years later, the women in Congress had nearly doubled.

Marguerite Stitt Church made the most of her position and was often described with terms like "accomplished" and "trusted." While she was known for her charm, dignity, and prestige, she was, most of all, a woman who rose to the occasion and was deeply cherished.

On March 21, 1950, as news of Ralph Church's sudden death that morning spread through the halls of Congress, his colleagues took to the floor of the House of Representatives and spoke about their fallen comrade, describing him with equal parts admiration, affection, and awe.

Ralph Church was a man of his own making, with a down-to-earth approach and love of people that fueled his authentic passion for no-nonsense legislative work. And it was this authentic passion that preserved his humility, guided him through many disappointments, and kept him fully engaged in the service of others until his last, legislative breath.

When Capitol Hill learned that Marguerite had died, legislators were once again moved to speak extemporaneously of a dedicated servant named Representative Church, echoing many of the same sentiments used four decades earlier, including tireless integrity, effective leadership, and an inexhaustible devotion to country.

For more than four decades, from 1919 to 1962, the remarkable lakefront city of Evanston and the world at large grew and benefited under the enduring partnership and efforts of Ralph E. and Marguerite Stitt Church. And their legacy should inspire and educate for decades and more—together, they offer lessons of service, heart, and advocacy that exist nowhere else.

TIMELINE

May 5, 1883	Ralph E. Church is born in Catlin, Illinois.
September 13, 1892	Adelaide Marguerite Stitt is born in Manhattan, New York.
1903	Ralph graduates from Danville High School.
1907	Ralph graduates from the University of Michigan with a bachelor's degree.
1909	Ralph graduates from the Northwestern University Law Department with his thesis, "What Is the Place of a Contract—Where It Is in Fact Made, or Where It Is Performed?" He is admitted to the bar and begins practicing law.
1910	Marguerite graduates St. Agatha Day School for Girls and begins studies at Barnard College.
1911	Marguerite transfers to Wellesley College.
1913	Women gain the right to vote in some state elections.
March 17, 1914	Wellesley College Fire
1914	Marguerite graduates Wellesley Phi Beta Kappa. She majored in psychology, sociology, and economics.
1914–1915	Marguerite is a lecture assistant in biblical history at Wellesley and teaches Soong Mayling (later known as Madame Chiang Kai-shek, former first lady of the Republic of China).
1915	Marguerite enters Columbia University as a graduate student in the Faculty of Political Science, Philosophy, and Pure Science (currently known as the Graduate School of Arts and Sciences).

July 6, 1915	Marguerite serves as an emissary for her father in California with the New England Shoe and Leather Association. She participates in the first telephone call from San Francisco to Boston—the first time east and west are connected by wire—opening up an historic trade channel.
1916	Ralph attends Reserve Officer Training School at Fort Sheridan, Illinois.
1916	Ralph is elected to the Illinois House of Representatives.
circa 1916–1917	Ralph and Marguerite meet on a blind date in Chicago, visiting at the home of Alderman Oliver L. Watson.
January 1917	Ralph begins his first term in the Illinois House of Representatives.
1917	Marguerite completes her master's degree in political economy from Columbia University with her thesis, "The Impact of Metropolitan Newspapers on the Reading Public."
1917	Marguerite interrupts her PhD studies and works for the New York State Charities Aid Association in New York City as a consulting psychologist.
December 21, 1918	Ralph and Marguerite marry in New York City. They honeymoon in Boston and the southern US. They have two homes in Illinois: an apartment in Evanston (943 Judson Avenue) and another in Springfield (1006 S. 2nd Street).
January 16, 1919	The Eighteenth Amendment is ratified, establishing the prohibition of alcohol in the United States.
1919	Ralph begins his second term in the Illinois House of Representatives.
1920	Responding to the United States Census, Ralph and Marguerite self-report their professions as "attorney" and "psychologist."

1920 · Ralph and Marguerite move to 517 Haven Street in Evanston.

1920 · Ralph E. Church Jr. is born.

August 18, 1920 · The Nineteenth Amendment is ratified, granting women in the United States the right to vote.

1921 · Ralph begins his third term in the Illinois House of Representatives.

1921 · Ralph offers an amendment to Illinois' Motor Vehicle Law to specify special provisions and penalties for the relatively new crime of auto theft.

1923 · Ralph begins his fourth term in the Illinois House of Representatives.

1923 · Ralph announces his candidacy for speaker of the Illinois House of Representatives. His support of Prohibition is one fatal flaw in this effort, as a staunch anti-Prohibition colleague is elected speaker.

1924 · William Stitt Church is born.

1925 · Ralph begins his fifth term in the Illinois House of Representatives.

1925 · Ralph and Marguerite purchase 1640 Sheridan Road in Evanston. The address is later changed to 300 Church Street.

1927 · Ralph begins his sixth term in the Illinois House of Representatives.

1929 · Ralph begins his seventh term in the Illinois House of Representatives.

1929 · Marjory Williams Church is born.

1930 · In the United States Census, Ralph and Marguerite's occupations are listed as "lawyer" and "legal secretary." Their household (worth $75,000, the equivalent of $1.4 million in 2023) now has a servant and nursemaid.

1931 · Ralph begins his eighth and final term in the Illinois House of Representatives.

1932 · Ralph becomes a candidate for the US House of Representatives but loses in the GOP primary to James Simpson Jr. in disputed vote. His run for the seat as an independent candidate is unsuccessful.

December 5, 1933 · The Twenty-First Amendment is ratified, repealing the Eighteenth Amendment and ending Prohibition in the United States.

1934 · Ralph elected to the first of his seven terms in the US House of Representatives, defeating Simpson in the primary and David B. Maloney in the general. During Ralph's service, Marguerite is active with the Family Welfare Association of Evanston, the Evanston Receiving Home of the Illinois Children's Home and Aid Society, and the North Shore Auxiliary of the Chicago Maternity Center.

1935 · Ralph is sworn in to his first term as a member of the Seventy-Fourth Congress. He is appointed to the Naval Affairs Committee. The Churches now own a house at 2334 California Street NW, Washington, DC, and their three children enroll in local schools.

1935 · Ralph attends ceremonies to reopen Great Lakes Naval Training Station in his district in North Chicago.

1935 · Ralph lambastes the New Deal's Resettlement Administration, a failed plan to move impoverished workers to planned communities, as "communistic."

1935 · Marguerite is selected to speak at the Institute of World Affairs in California. She delivers her address, "Feminine Force in a Changing World."

·

1937	Ralph begins his second term in the US House of Representatives (Seventy-Fifth Congress).
1937	Ralph shows his isolationist sympathies in an op-ed piece in Illinois newspapers opposing the Roosevelt administration's proposed sale of arms to China to defend itself against Japan.
1937	Ralph seeks an investigation of fellow member of the Illinois congressional delegation, Adolph Sabath, a Democrat. He earns bipartisan opprobrium for challenging a popular member of the House.
November 1937	Ralph is labeled in the press as the House's "most unpopular member," in part for delaying Thanksgiving recess on a procedural point.
1939	Ralph begins his third term in the US House of Representatives (Seventy-Sixth Congress).
1939	As a member of the Naval Affairs Committee, Ralph joins other Republicans in minimizing defensive measures for the US territory of Guam. He is later criticized for this when Guam falls quickly to the Japanese after the attack on Pearl Harbor.
September 1939	Ralph is carried on stretcher into the House of Representatives to avoid missing a vote and to continue his record of perfect attendance in the House.
December 1939	Ralph joins forty-one other members of Congress on the US delegation of the Interparliamentary Union meeting in Oslo, Norway. Marguerite accompanies Ralph on this trip.
1939–1945	At Ralph's request, Marguerite makes several inspection tours of Europe during the war.
1940s	Marguerite embarks on nationwide speaking tours on behalf of the Brookings Institution, a Washington, DC, think tank.

1940 · Marguerite participates in nationwide speaking tours on behalf of the Republican National Committee for the presidential campaign.

1940 · Ralph sponsors HR 8983, which is passed and signed to authorize the acceptance by the US Navy of the gift of the yacht *Freedom* from Chicago industrialist J. Sterling Morton.

February 1940 · Ralph becomes a candidate for the US Senate. He is defeated by Charles Wayland "Curly" Brooks in the GOP primary. Largely due to focusing his campaign on the open Senate seat instead running for reelection, Ralph loses his House seat.

November 1940 · Naval Air Station Glenview is created in Ralph's district with the government's purchase of Curtiss-Reynolds Field. Ralph, as member of the Naval Affairs Committee, is a key supporter of the new installation, which serves as a reserve training facility.

1940–1943 · Marguerite serves as president of the Wellesley Alumnae Association.

1942 · Ralph seeks and wins election to his former House seat, defeating George A. Paddock, who replaced him two years earlier, in the primary. His win is in spite of opposition by regular Republicans in the district.

1942 · Marguerite sees Madame Chiang Kai-shek address Congress.

1943 · Ralph begins his fourth term in the US House of Representatives (Seventy-Eighth Congress).

1943 · Ralph misses his son's wedding in order to maintain a perfect attendance record in Congress.

1944 Marguerite participates in nationwide speaking tours on behalf of the Republican National Committee for the presidential campaign

1944 ·	Ralph defeats Democrat Curtis MacDougall, a distinguished journalism professor at Northwestern, in a general election challenge.
1945 ·	Ralph begins his fifth term in the US House of Representatives (Seventy-Ninth Congress).
1947 ·	Ralph begins his sixth term in the US House of Representatives (Eightieth Congress).
1947 ·	With Republicans in control of Congress for the first time in a decade and a half, Ralph joins his party's majority and supports the Taft-Hartley Act, which restricts the activities of labor unions.
1948–1950 ·	Marguerite serves as president of the Congressional Club.
1948 ·	Ralph resists a challenge primarily from Republicans in New Trier Township and investment banker John Nuveen, winning the nomination and later election to his seventh term in Congress.
1949	Ralph begins his seventh and final term in the US House of Representatives (Eighty-First Congress) Redistricting means he is now representing the 13th Congressional District.
February 1950 ·	Marguerite leads the creation of the Women's Republican Club of the 13th Congressional District of Illinois.
March 21, 1950 ·	Ralph suffers a heart attack and dies while offering testimony before colleagues of the House Executive Expenditure Committee.
March 24, 1950 ·	Ralph is buried at Memorial Park in Skokie, Illinois.
June 9, 1950 ·	Marguerite is nominated by the Republican party to run for Ralph's seat.

November 7, 1950 · Marguerite defeats Thomas F. Dolan in the general election with 74.1% of the vote—and the highest ever number of votes for a Thirteenth Congressional District candidate.

January 3, 1951 · Marguerite begins her first term in the US House of Representatives (Eighty-Second Congress). She is the only woman from Illinois in Congress this year.

January 28, 1951 · Marguerite completes her service as president of the Congressional Club.

June 20, 1951 · After three children in her district die in a fireworks accident, Marguerite introduces HR 4528 to ban transportation of fireworks into states where they are prohibited.

July 28, 1951 Ralph's secretary since 1934, and now Marguerite's, Helen Nelsch, 53, is found dead in her D.C. apartment.

January 8, 1952 · Marguerite is offered a spot on the Appropriations Committee (like Ralph). She declines and remains on the Committee on Expenditures in Executive Departments (which later becomes the Committee on Government Operations, then the Committee on Governmental Affairs, then the Committee on Homeland Security and Governmental Affairs).

June 17, 1952 · Ignoring warnings, Marguerite brings Black citizens into the House Members' Dining Room.

November 4, 1952 · Marguerite defeats Lawrence J. Hayes in the general election with 70.6% of the vote.

January 3, 1953 · Marguerite begins her second term in the US House of Representatives (Eighty-Third Congress). She reintroduces her fireworks legislation as HR 116 and is the only female on the Republican Policy Committee.

January 16, 1953	Marguerite is named to the Foreign Affairs Committee. She also stays on the Committee on Government Operations during the first session of the Eighty-Third Congress.
April 3–21, 1953	Special Study Mission to Europe, examining the military aspects of the Mutual Security Program with regard to preparedness for meeting a possible Soviet attack. The trip concentrates on France and Italy, plus the French zone of Germany and airfields in Belgium and the Netherlands.
July 1953	Marguerite speaks passionately to Congress about her fireworks legislation. Though she misstates some details, the bill passes the House.
November 9–December 17, 1953	Special Study Mission to Southeast Asia and the Pacific. The 30,000 mile trip focuses on military, economic, and technical assistance programs under the Mutual Security Program.
March 1, 1954	Four members of the Puerto Rican Nationalist Party open fire on the House floor. Five congressmen are wounded, but Marguerite is unharmed.
May 1954	HR 116, Marguerite's fireworks legislation, passes. It takes effect July 1, 1954.
November 2, 1954	Marguerite defeats Richard A. Griffin in the general election with 69% of the vote.
January 5, 1955	Marguerite begins her third term in the US House of Representatives (Eighty-Fourth Congress).
July 13, 1955	The House receives fifty-three bills from Marguerite to implement recommendations of the second Hoover Commission.
October 11–December 15, 1955	Special Study Mission to Middle East, South Asia and the Pacific. The trip, covering 30,800 miles, is "a first hand study of United States problems, policies and programs, and to assess the strength and weakness of the various countries and the degree of Communist penetration in them."

February 1956	As Marguerite faces a female opponent for the first time, the press declares a "Powder Puff Derby" is shaping up.
November 6, 1956	Marguerite defeats Helen Benson Leys in the general election with 71.6% of the vote and earns the largest number of votes nationwide for a House candidate.
January 3, 1957	Marguerite begins her fourth term in the US House of Representatives (Eighty-Fifth Congress).
January 14, 1957	Marguerite introduces HR 2859, a bill "To exempt from taxation certain property of the National Association of Colored Women's Clubs, Inc., in the District of Columbia."
January 14, 1957	Marguerite introduces HR 2858, a bill "To amend section 165 of the Revised Statutes to eliminate a provision thereof which operates to discriminate against women in connection with appointments to Government positions."
May 1957	By now, Marguerite has introduced seventy-seven bills regarding the Hoover Commission report.
June 18, 1957	Marguerite votes in support of HR 6127, known as the Civil Rights Act of 1957. Leading up to the vote, she tells her colleagues: "No government which denies the right to vote to any large segment or to any small segment of its eligible population can hope to survive."
November 16–December 14, 1957	Special Study Mission to Near East and Africa. This difficult trip for Marguerite focuses on communistic interests and the success or inadequacy of US policy.
May 19, 1958	Marguerite submits her findings from the 1957 study mission: there is a need for missionaries and libraries. She builds a case for what will become the Peace Corps. Rather than money, Marguerite recommends technical assistance delivered by humans and the formation of women's groups.

June 1, 1958	Marguerite receives an honorary Doctor of Laws degree from Russell Sage College.
November 4, 1958	Marguerite defeats Laurence A. Kusek in the general election with 67.1% of the vote.
November 27–December 4, 1958	Marguerite attends Mexican President Adolfo López Mateos's inauguration as one of two delegates from the House of Representatives appointed by Eisenhower.
January 7, 1959	Marguerite begins her fifth term in the US House of Representatives (Eighty-Sixth Congress).
February 9, 1959	Describing the US railroad system at a "crisis stage" and operating at a loss, Marguerite introduces HR 4257, a bill "To amend the Internal Revenue Code of 1954 so as to permit railroad corporations to take full advantage of tax relief measures enacted or granted by the States and their political subdivisions."
October 20–December 4, 1959	Special Study Mission on Foreign Economic Policy. Marguerite travels 40,000 miles to seventeen countries.
November 16–20, 1959	Marguerite attends the fifth Parliamentarians' Conference of NATO and is the only woman of nine House delegates.
June 1960	Marguerite receives an honorary Professor of Laws degree from Lake Forest College.
November 8, 1960	Marguerite defeats Tyler Thompson in the general election with 66% of the vote and the largest number of votes nationwide for a House candidate.
January 3, 1961	Marguerite begins her sixth and final term in the US House of Representatives (Eighty-Seventh Congress).

February 28, 1961	Marguerite introduces House Joint Resolution 269, "Proposing an amendment to the Constitution of the United States relative to equal rights for men and women." It is referred to the Committee on the Judiciary, but it later dies.
September 12, 1961	Marguerite is sworn in as one of five House delegates to the sixteenth session of the United Nations General Assembly.
September 14, 1961	Marguerite debates the Peace Corps Act on the House floor with seven-term Rep. H.R. Gross (R-Iowa), who labels it a "kiddie corps" and "utopian brainstorm," likening it to "Hitler's youth corps." Following Marguerite's impassioned speech, many minds change, and the Peace Corps Act passes, 288-97.
September 22, 1961	Congress approves the $40 million Peace Corps bill. It becomes Public Law 87-293.
December 8, 1961	Surprising her fellow Republicans, Marguerite announces her retirement.
June 16, 1962	Marguerite gives the commencement speech and receives an honorary Doctor of Laws from Northwestern University.
July 17, 1962	Marguerite is one of fifteen men and women who meet to establish the United States Capitol Historical Society.
November 1, 1962	Donald Rumsfeld, a Republican hoping to succeed Marguerite, receives her endorsement.
November 6, 1962	Marguerite's Thirteenth Congressional District has been remapped into three smaller units. In the new Thirteenth, Donald Rumsfeld defeats John A. Kennedy, winning 63.7% of the vote.

December 1962 · Latin American trip through Ecuador, Peru, Colombia, Panama, Costa Rica and Guatemala, designed to lead to future learning about the Alliance for Progress and the Peace Corps. Due to an ankle injury sustained in Ecuador, Marguerite is unable to navigate a planned trek with her congressional delegation (CODEL) in Peru, so Donald Rumsfeld stands in for her—literally and figuratively. Days later, and just one hour after arriving in Guatemala, she and several colleagues are severely injured in a car crash. With a fractured leg, Marguerite spends some of her last days in Congress at the Naval Hospital in Bethesda, Maryland.

· In total, Marguerite sponsored 201 bills. Fourteen passed the House (7%). Twelve were enacted (6%).

1963–1972 · Marguerite serves on the national board of the Girl Scouts of the United States of America.

June 9, 1963 · Marguerite receives an honorary Doctor of Humane Letters degree from the National College of Education, of which she is a trustee.

July 1964 · Marguerite is a delegate and a platform committee member for the Republican National Convention in San Francisco, supporting Barry Goldwater. At the convention, she delivers a speech denouncing nuclear weapons.

1968 · Marguerite serves as a co-chair of the Nixon for President Committee.

1968 · Marguerite serves as a co-chair of the All-Illinois Committee to elect Richard B. Ogilvie for governor.

1975 · Marguerite serves as chairman of the President Ford Committee.

November 1978 ·	Marguerite is interviewed by Fern S. Ingersoll for Former Members of Congress, Inc., as part of its project, "The Modern Congress in American History."
April 22, 1985 ·	Marguerite receives the Abraham Lincoln Award from the United Republican Fund.
May 26, 1990 ·	Marguerite dies in her sleep at home in Evanston, Illinois.

NOTES

1 Harold Smith, "New Aspirants Mentioned for Church's Seat," *Chicago Tribune*, March 26, 1930.
2 Harold Smith, "Fear Spurs Aim to Name Church," *Chicago Tribune*, April 9, 1950.
3 "Mrs. Church Is Waging Brilliant Speaking Campaign; Able, Distinguished Candidate," *Evanston (IL) Review*, October 12, 1950.
4 Marguerite Stitt Church, interview by Fern S. Ingersoll, November 25, 1978, Former Members of Congress, Inc. oral history interviews, 1962–1985 (bulk 1969–1980), Manuscript Reading Room, Library of Congress, Washington, DC.
5 George Tagge, "Congress Race in 13th District is Free-For-All," *Chicago Tribune*, March 31, 1950.
6 Letter to the editor, "Sideshow: Blasts McGovern 'Red-Bait,'" *Daily Northwestern (Evanston, IL)*, February 21, 1947.
7 Tim Petrusak, "Professor William McGovern—His Search is Over," *Daily Northwestern (Evanston, IL)*, January 5, 1965.
8 Harold Smith, "Fear Spurs Aim to Name Church," *Chicago Tribune*, April 9, 1950.
9 Ibid.
10 Associated Press, "Widow of Rep. Church Wants No 'Write-In,'" *Woodstock (IL) Daily Sentinel*, April 3, 1950.
11 Harold Smith, "Strong Fights Enliven Race For Congress. Mrs. Church and Jonas Lead Battle," *Chicago Sunday Tribune*, November 5, 1950; "Official Vote of the State of Illinois Cast at the General Election, November 7, 1950, Judicial Election, 1950, Primary Election General Primary, April 11, 1950," compiled by Office of the Illinois Secretary of State (Springfield, IL, 1950), 55.
12 "Caucus to Pick Candidate for Church's Seat," *Chicago Tribune*, April 13, 1950.
13 "Spending Slash Urged by Widow of Rep. Church," *Chicago Tribune*, May 17, 1950.
14 George Tagge, "13th Dist. G.O.P. Aspirants Rake Foreign Policy," *Chicago Tribune*, June 4, 1950; George Tagge, "Stop Marshall Plan Now, Lyons Urges," *Chicago Tribune*, May 25, 1950.
15 Ibid.
16 George Tagge, "Congress Race In 13th District Is Free-For-All," *Chicago Tribune*, March 31, 1950.
17 Robert Howard, "Widow Spurns Write-In Bid To Succeed Church," *Chicago Tribune*, April 2, 1950.
18 "Grateful, Calm, Mrs. Church is Foe of Truman," *Chicago Tribune*, June 10, 1950.
19 Church, oral history.
20 "G.O.P. Names Church Widow For Congress," *Chicago Tribune*, June 10, 1950, p. 1.
21 "Grateful, Calm Mrs. Church is Foe Of Truman," *Chicago Tribune*, June 10, 1950, p5
22 Ibid.
23 Genevieve Forbes, "Mary Barthelme 'Real Judge' Now and Real Human," *Chicago Tribune*, November 8, 1923.
24 "Women Urged to Help Stop U.S. Spending, *Chicago Tribune*, May 12, 1950, p. 6.
25 Ibid.
26 Harold Smith, "Strong Fights Enliven Race For Congress; Mrs. Church and Jonas Lead Battle," *Chicago Sunday Tribune*, November 5, 1950.
27 Matthew A. Wasniewski, 2006. *Women in Congress, 1917–2006*. (Washington, DC: US Government Publishing Office, 2006), 285.
28 "Election Statistics: 1920 to Present," History, Art & Archives, United States House of Representatives, accessed March 8, 2019, https://history.house.gov/Institution/Election-Statistics/Election-Statistics.
29 "Mrs. Church Set to Carry Fight to Washington," *Chicago Tribune*, November 9, 1950.
30 Church, oral history.
31 Karen Cord Taylor, *Getting to Grand Prairie: One Hundred Londoners and Their Quest For Land in Illinois* (Francestown, NH: Weathergage Press, 2015), 7–14.
32 Ibid., 103.
33 Josiah Pierce to his mother and father, written on board the *Devonshire* 11–18 May, 1849, Maine Memory Network, Maine Historical Society.
34 Taylor, *Getting to Grand Prairie*, 91.
35 Ibid., 89–90.
36 Ibid., 89–90.
37 Ibid., 28, 67
38 Ibid., 91.
39 Ibid., 132.
40 Ibid., 1–5.

41 George W. Smith, *History of Illinois and Her People* (Chicago and New York: The American Historical Society, 1927), 265.
42 Wilfred B. Shaw, "James Burrill Angell and the University of Michigan," *Michigan Alumnus*, April 1916, 326.
43 "Ralph Edwin Church, '07,/'07-'08," *University of Michigan Alumni Magazine*, November 1935, University of Michigan Archive, Ralph E. Church file, Bentley Historical Library, University of Michigan.
44 "The University Students are Going to Put On the Greatest Minstrel Show," *Detroit Free Press*, January 13, 1907.
45 "Second Minstrels Are Better Than the First" and "Famous Negro Leader Will Lecture Monday," *Michigan Daily*, April 4, 1907.
46 "Officers Chosen By Junior Lits," *Detroit Free Press*, October 6, 1906.
47 "'Bob' Clancy Slated for President," *Detroit Free Press*, October 3, 1906.
48 "College Clubs Taking Active Part in Big Political Game," *Detroit Free Press*, October 4, 1908.
49 Ralph Church, "What is the Place of a Contract—Where it is in Fact Made, or Where it is Performed?" (law school thesis, Northwestern University, 1909), 1.
50 Ibid., 19.
51 Ibid., 20.
52 Charles N. Wheeler, "Wild Greeting for Roosevelt Like Old Days," *Chicago Tribune*, May 30, 1916.
53 Ibid.
54 Ibid.
55 Ibid.
56 Capt. Henry J. Reilly, "U.S. Lacks Many Men, Animals and Wagons For Army in Case of War," *Chicago Tribune*, November 29, 1915.
57 "Citizen Training Camp Brings Five Hundred Prospective Soldiers Together at Fort Sheridan," *Bell Telephone News (Chicago)*, October, 1915.
58 "Fatigue Fades at Rookie Camp," *Chicago Tribune*, September 28, 1915.
59 Ibid.
60 Smith, *History of Illinois and Her People*, 266.
61 "Ralph E. Church to Devote Time To Legislature," *Evanston (IL) News-Index*, April 5, 1918.
62 Ibid.
63 Joel Arthur Tarr, A Study in Boss Politics: William Lorimer of Chicago (Champaign, IL: University of Illinois Press, 1971), 135.
64 Ibid., 233.
65 Ibid., 236.
66 Lloyd Wendt and Herman Kogan, *Big Bill of Chicago* (Indianapolis and New York: Bobbs-Merrill Company, 1953), 79.
67 William R. Willcox, "Republican Catechism," *Evanston (IL) News-Index*, October 16, 1916.
68 Paid political advertisement, *Evanston (IL) News-Index*, September 13, 1916
69 Ibid.
70 David Schieber, Albert Hunter, and Gary Alan Fine; "Alcohol In Heavenston: Shifting Moral Orders and Economic Interests in a Suburban Community," *Social History of Alcohol and Drugs* 27, no. 2 (2013), 176–177, doi:10.1086/SHAD27020174.
71 Ibid.
72 Ibid.
73 Paid political advertisement, *Evanston (IL) News-Index*, September 13, 1916.
74 Editorial, "Vote For Carter and Church—One and One-Half Each," *Evanston (IL) News-Index*, November 3, 1916
75 William R. Willcox, "Republican Catechism," *Evanston (IL) News-Index*, October 16, 1916.
76 "Republicans Coming Into Their Own Now," *Evanston (IL) News-Index*, November 3, 1916.
77 "Garfield In Fine Plea For Hughes Votes," *Evanston (IL) News-Index*, October 17, 1916.
78 Ibid.
79 "Republicans Vote Straight and Save Time," *Evanston (IL) News-Index*, November 4, 1916.
80 The Week In Society," *Brooklyn Life*, July 10, 1920; "CHURCH, Marguerite Stitt," History, Art & Archives, United States House of Representatives, accessed November 3, 2018, https://history.house.gov/People/Detail/10940.
81 "Mountain Resorts Are Thronged," New York Times, July 19, 1903; paid advertisement, *Brooklyn Daily Eagle*, June 4, 1922.
82 "United States Census, 1870," database with images, FamilySearch (https://familysearch.org : 14 June 2019), New York > New York > New York City, ward 20 > image 2366 of 3801; citing NARA microfilm publication M593 (Washington, DC: National Archives and Records Administration, n.d.).

83 "A Timeline of the History of Belfast," Tim Lambert, accessed April 16, 2021, http://www.localhistories.org/belfasttime.html

84 "United States Census, 1900," database with images, FamilySearch (https://familysearch.org : 5 August 2014), New York > New York County > ED 524 Borough of Manhattan, Election District 9 New York City Ward 21 > image 4 of 34; citing NARA microfilm publication T623 (Washington, D.C.: National Archives and Records Administration, n.d.); "1900 Census Special Reports: Occupations at the Twelfth Census," United States Census Bureau, last modified March 1, 2016, https://www2.census.gov/library/publications/decennial/1900/occupations/occupations-part-5.pdf.

85 See note 82 above.

86 "Sanguinary and Horrible Murder of a Widow in New York—Particulars of the Tragedy," *Cincinnati Daily Press*, December 11, 1860.

87 "Testimony of Sophia Stitt About Her Missing Brother Wanted For Murder," *New York Times*, December 14, 1860.

88 Ibid.

89 "The Twelfth Street Murder," *New York Times*, January 28, 1861.

90 John Forsyth, Margaret Forsyth, United States Census, 1850, Connecticut, Hartford, Simsbury, August 19 (Image available www.familysearch.org)

91 "United States Census, 1850," database with images, FamilySearch (https://familysearch.org : 9 April 2016), Connecticut > Hartford > Simsbury > image 28 of 67; citing NARA microfilm publication M432 (Washington, DC: National Archives and Records Administration, n.d.).

92 "United States Census, 1880," database with images, FamilySearch (https://familysearch.org : 19 February 2021), Mary Forsyth, New York, New York, New York, United States; citing enumeration district ED 402, sheet 523C, NARA microfilm publication T9 (Washington, DC: National Archives and Records Administration, n.d.), FHL microfilm 1,254,886; "United States Census, 1860," database with images, FamilySearch (https://familysearch.org : 24 March 2017), New York > New York > 3rd Division 20th Ward New York City > image 49 of 204; from "1860 U.S. Federal Census - Population," database, Fold3.com (http://www.fold3.com : n.d.); citing NARA microfilm publication M653 (Washington, DC: National Archives and Records Administration, n.d.).

93 1870 United States Federal Census for Adelaide Forsyth, New York Ward 20 District 10. Digital image available at https://www.ancestry.com.

94 "United States Census, 1870," database with images, FamilySearch (https://familysearch.org : 13 June 2019), New York > New York > New York City, ward 20 > image 1625 of 3801; citing NARA microfilm publication M593 (Washington, DC: National Archives and Records Administration, n.d.).

95 Patsy Parker, "The Historical Role of Women in Higher Education," *Administrative Issues Journal* 5, no. 1 (2015): 3–14, doi:10.5929/2015.5.1.1.

96 Ibid.

97 "U.S. School Catalogs, 1765-1935," s.v. "Adelaide Forsyth" (born 3 Jan 1859), digital image available at https://www.ancestry.com.

98 Diana K. Kelly, "The Nineteenth Century Experience of Women College Students: A Profile of the Women and Their Motivations" (report, Fullerton College, 1987), 12, https://files.eric.ed.gov/fulltext/ED292745.pdf

99 Ibid.

100 Carl F. Price, *Who's Who In American Methodism* (New York: E. B. Treat & Co., 1916), 212.

101 United States Federal Census for Adelaide Stitt, 1900, New York, New York, Manhattan, District 0524, image available at https://www.ancestry.com; Stitt, New York, Manhattan, A. D. 21 E. D. 10, image available at https://www.ancestry.com; New York, New York, Manhattan Ward 12, District 0588, image available at https://www.ancestry.com; New York, State Census, 1915 for Adelaide Stitt, New York, New York, A. D. 15 E. D. 34, image available at https://www.ancestry.com; 1920 United States Federal Census for Adelaide F Stitt, New York, New York, Manhattan Assembly District 7, District 0572, image available at https://www.ancestry.com; New York, State Census, 1925 for Adelaide Stitt, New York, New York, A. D. 07 E. D. 34, image available at https://www.ancestry.com.

102 "Mrs. Adelaide F. Stitt, Ex-Head of the Methodist Home for Aged a Hunter Alumna," *New York Times*, June 19, 1944; Maria Perez, administrator and chief executive officer, Methodist Home for Nursing and Rehabilitation, e-mail message to author Christine Wolf, January 16, 2019; Constance Newell McClure, *Methodist Church Home for the Aged in the City of New York 1850–1950* (New York: J. M. Laverty & Son, 1951).

103 *The 160th Anniversary of the Methodist Church Home: Discovering the Past, Celebrating the Present and Looking Forward to a Promising Future* (Riverdale, NY: Methodist Home for Nursing and Rehabilitation, 2010), 10–13.

104 Ibid., 31.

105 Ibid., 24.

106 McClure, *Methodist Church Home for the Aged in the City of New York 1850–1950*; "Joseph Forsyth," *New York Times*, June 1, 1932.

107 "U.S. Passport Applications, 1795-1925," "Wm J Stitt" (born 28 Dec 1856), digital image available at https://www.ancestry.com.

108 "Edna S. Robinson," *New York Times*, July 24, 1974.

109 "Dissolution Notices," *New York Times*, January 7, 1922.

110 "Stitt Sole Owner of Adlers," *Glovers Review*, February 1922, 59; "Kleinhans & Co. Bankrupt," *Pittsburgh Press*, June 6, 1902.

111 "Resorts Along Jersey Shore are the Mecca for Multitudes," *Brooklyn (NY) Daily Eagle*, August 10, 1902.

112 "Today in History—June 2—Indian Citizenship Act," Library of Congress, https://www.loc.gov/item/today-in-history/june-02; "50 Years of the Voting Rights Act: An Asian American Perspective," Terry Ao Minnis and Mee Moua, Asian Americans Advancing Justice, August 4, 2015, https://advancingjustice-aajc.org/report/50-years-voting-rights-act-asian-american-perspective.

113 "The Women's Rights Movement, 1848–1920," History, Art & Archives, United States House of Representatives, accessed November 6, 2018, https://history.house.gov/Exhibitions-and-Publications/WIC/Historical-Essays/No-Lady/Womens-Rights.

114 Kevin Ramsey, "1998 Marks the 100th Anniversary of the Founding of St. Agatha Day School for Girls," *Trinity Per Saecula*, Spring 1998, 16.

115 Ibid.

116 Ibid.

117 Ibid.

118 Betsy Ancker-Johnson, ed., *Wellesley After-Images: Reflections on Their College Years by Forty-Five Alumnae* (Los Angeles: Wellesley College Club of Los Angeles, 1974); Adelaide M. Stitt college entrance examination 8426, Form R, St. Agatha School, Episcopal Diocese of New York Archives.

119 *Forum*, vol. I, no.1, April 1909, Episcopal Diocese of New York Archives.

120 Editorial, *Wellesley College News*, January 4, 1912.

121 "Stitt Sole Owner of Adlers," *Glovers Review*, February 1922, 59

122 "Trade Notes," *Notions and Fancy Goods*, July 1910, 56.

123 Obituary of James S. Stitt, *New York Times*, July 8, 1907.

124 "Polo In History," Milwaukee Polo Club, accessed April 19, 2021, http://www.milwaukeepoloclub.com/the-history-of-polo.

125 "Glove Cities," Glovers and Tanners, accessed April 19, 2021, http://www.gloversandtanners.com.

126 United States Senate Committee on Finance, briefs and statements on H.R. 3321, vol. 3, at 1650 (1913).

127 "A Broadway Store on Fire; Hard Work for the Firemen—the Loss about $170,000," *New York Times*, October 7, 1882.

128 "Loft Buildings," *Insurance Press*, December 17, 1913, 14.

129 "A Broadway Store on Fire; Hard Work for the Firemen—the Loss about $170,000," *New York Times*, October 7, 1882.

130 "Guaranty Fire To Start Soon," *Eastern Underwriter*, November 14, 1919, 11.

131 United States Senate Committee on Finance, briefs and statements on H.R. 3321, vol. 3, at 1650 (1913).

132 "The Glove Cutters' Strike of 1914," Herbert M. Engel, University at Albany History Department, accessed April 19, 2021, http://www.albany.edu/history/histmedia/engel1.html.

133 Ibid.

134 "The Glove Cutters' Strike of 1914: New York State Board of Mediation and Arbitration

Hearings, October 13, 1914—Morning Session," The Glovers of Fulton County, University at Albany History Department, accessed April 19, 2021, http://www.albany.edu/history/glovers/mediationhearings-october13am.html

135 Herbert M. Engel, *Shtetl in the Adirondacks: The Story of Gloversville and Its Jews* (Fleischmanns, NY: Purple Mountain Press, 1991).

136 "The Glove Cutters' Strike of 1914," Herbert M. Engel, University at Albany History Department, accessed April 19, 2021, http://www.albany.edu/history/histmedia/engel1.html.

137 Ibid.

138 "Coeducation at Columbia: 'Coed at Last': Columbia College and the Road to Coeducation," Columbia University Archives, accessed on April 19, 2021, https://library.columbia.edu/libraries/cuarchives/resources/coeducation/collegiatecourse.html.

139 "Chiefly about People," *Western Christian Advocate*, February 11, 1914, 18.

140 Course list of Marguerite Stitt, 1911–1914, Wellesley College Archives, Library and Technology Services.

141 "Biographies of Harriet Brooks and Kenneth Hare," Government of Canada, last modified November 2, 2017, https://www.canada.ca/en/shared-services/corporate/data-centre-consolidation/high-performance-computing/biographies.html.

142 Ibid.

143 Regina Nguyen, "Harriet Brooks" (submitted as coursework for PH241, Stanford University, 2018), http://large.stanford.edu/courses/2018/ph241/nguyen2.

144 Johana Godfrey, "Barnard Fraternity Ban of 1913," Johana Godfrey, Barnard Archives and Special Collections, September 30, 2010, https://barnardarchives.wordpress.com/2010/09/30/barnard-fraternity-ban-of-1913.

145 Editorial, *Barnard Bulletin*, November 23, 1910.

146 Ibid.

147 Letter to the editor, *Barnard Bulletin*, November 23, 1910.

148 Wellesley Alumnae Association card of Marguerite Stitt Church, 1941, Marguerite Stitt Church biographical file, WCA_7B_Stitt_Church_Marguerite_1914, Wellesley College Archives, Library and Technology Services.

149 "Coeducation at Columbia: 'Coed at Last': Columbia College and the Road to Coeducation," Columbia University Archives, accessed on April 19, 2021, https://library.columbia.edu/libraries/cuarchives/resources/coeducation/collegiatecourse.html.

150 Gloria Steinem, "Commencement Speech to the Class of 1988" (speech, Wellesley College, Wellesley, MA, May 27, 1988).

151 Paul Lauter and Florence Howe, "The Women's Movement: Impact on the Campus and Curriculum. Current Issues in Higher Education, 1978," presented at the Annual Meeting of the American Association for Higher Education (Chicago, IL, March 1978), 12, https://files.eric.ed.gov/fulltext/ED193996.pdf.

152 Charlotte Howard Conant, *Address Delivered in Memory of Henry Fowle Durant in Wellesley College Chapel, February Eighteenth MDCCCCVI* (Cambridge, MA: Riverside Press, 1906), 23.

153 Arlene Cohen, *Wellesley College*, The Campus History Series (Charleston, SC: Arcadia Publishing, 2006), 9.

154 Wellesley College, "The Most Powerful Women's Network in the World Joins the 'World's Largest Professional Network,'" news release, February 27, 2014, https://www.newswise.com/articles/the-most-powerful-women-s-network-in-the-world-joins-the-world-s-largest-professional-network.

155 Wellesley College, *1942 Record Number of the Wellesley College Bulletin* vol. 32, no. 1 (September 1942), *vii*, Wellesley College Digital Repository.

156 "History of the Department," Department of Psychology, Wellesley College, accessed April 19, 2021, https://www.wellesley.edu/psychology/history.

157 Cohen, *Wellesley College*, 16.

158 Florence Morse Kingsley, *The Life of Henry Fowle Durant: Founder of Wellesley College* (New York: The Century Company, 1924), 238–239.

159 Helen Lefkowitz Horowitz, *Alma Mater: Design and Experience in the Women's Colleges from Their Nineteenth-Century Beginnings to the*

1930s (New York: Alfred A. Knopf, 1984), 44.
160 Ibid., 44.
161 Wellesley Alumnae Association card of Marguerite Stitt Church, 1941, Marguerite Stitt Church biographical file, WCA_7B_Stitt_Church_Marguerite_1914, Wellesley College Archives, Library & Technology Services.
162 Cohen, *Wellesley College*, 9.
163 Marguerite Stitt Church, "I Remember," in *Wellesley After-Images: Reflections On Their College Years By Forty-Five Alumnae*, ed. Betsy Ancker-Johnson (Los Angeles: Wellesley College Club of Los Angeles, 1974), 17.
164 Ibid., 17.
165 Ibid., 19.
166 Wellesley College, *Wellesley College Bulletin: Annual Reports, President and Treasurer 1913–1914* (March 1915), 23, Wellesley College Digital Repository.
167 Course list of Marguerite Stitt, 1911–1914, Wellesley College Archives, Library and Technology Services; Wellesley College, *Wellesley College Bulletin: Calendar 1913–1914* (January 1914), 142, Wellesley College Digital Repository.
168 Ibid.
169 Course list of Marguerite Stitt, 1911–1914, Wellesley College Archives, Library and Technology Services; Wellesley College, *Wellesley College Bulletin: Calendar 1913–1914* (January 1914), 75, Wellesley College Digital Repository.
170 "Notices," Alumnae Department, *Wellesley College News* (Wellesley, MA), March 27, 1913, Wellesley College Digital Repository.
171 "Socialism Club," *Wellesley College News* (Wellesley, MA), February 6, 1913, Wellesley College Digital Repository; "Club for the Study of Socialism," *Wellesley College News* (Wellesley, MA), May 29, 1913, Wellesley College Digital Repository.
172 "The Debating Club Elects Officers and Discusses the Vassar Debate," *Wellesley College News* (Wellesley, MA), October 2, 1913, Wellesley College Digital Repository.
173 "The Debate," *Wellesley College News* (Wellesley, MA), April 6, 1914, Wellesley College Digital Repository.
174 "Mt. Holyoke Debating Team," *Wellesley College News* (Wellesley, MA), March 5, 1914, Wellesley College Digital Repository.
175 "Wellesley Wins Debate," *Boston Globe*, March 15 1914.
176 "Wellesley Debate Set for March 14th," *Boston Globe*, February 21 1914.
177 "The Debating Club Elects Officers and Discusses the Vassar Debate," *Wellesley College News* (Wellesley, MA), October 2, 1913, Wellesley College Digital Repository.
178 "The Debate," *Wellesley College News* (Wellesley, MA), April 6, 1914, Wellesley College Digital Repository.
179 Ibid.
180 Wellesley College, *Wellesley College Bulletin: Annual Reports, President and Treasurer 1913–1914* (March 1915), 36–37, Wellesley College Digital Repository; "350 Saved by Perfect Drill," *Boston Herald*, March 18, 1914.
181 "College Hall, Maker of Traditions," College Hall Fire, Box 1, 1VF, "General, letters, newspaper articles," Wellesley College Archives, Library and Technology Services.
182 "College Hall, Maker of Traditions," College Hall Fire, Box 1, 1VF, "General, letters, newspaper articles," Wellesley College Archives, Library and Technology Services; "First Edition Illustrations," Stephen Railton, University of Virginia, accessed April 19, 2021, http://utc.iath.virginia.edu/uncletom/illustra/52illf.html.
183 Horowitz, *Alma Mater*, 49.
184 "Walden University, Nashville, Tennessee, 1865–1926," Paul Batesel, last modified February 13, 2017, http://www.lostcolleges.com/walden-university.
185 "Disastrous Fire Destroys Chi Psi House and Results in Death of Four Undergraduates and Three Firemen," *Cornell Daily Sun*, December 8, 1906.
186 "Notes," *Wellesley College News* (Wellesley, MA), April 2, 1914, Wellesley College Digital Repository.
187 Ibid.
188 "Wellesley Fire Drill," *Evansville (IN) Press*, May 10, 1912.
189 "A Memory Book of College Hall," Barbara C. Bach Phipps, The Internet Archive, accessed April 19, 2021, https://ia800708.us.archive.org/32/items/PhotoAlbum_201402/Photo_Album_text.pdf; Virginia Moffat to Katherine Balderston, April 28, 1972, College Hall Fire, Box 1, 1VF, "General, letters, newspaper articles," Wellesley

College Archives, Library and Technology Services.

190 Lisa Scanlon Mogolov, "Up in Flames," *Wellesley Magazine*, Winter 2014, 20–23.

191 "The Burning of College Hall," *Wellesley College News* (Wellesley, MA), April 2, 2014, Wellesley College Archives, Library and Technology Services.

192 Tracy L'Engle Angas to Katherine Balderston, October 2, 1972, College Hall Fire, Box 1, 1VF, "General, letters, newspaper articles," Wellesley College Archives, Library and Technology Services.

193 "The Fire: An Interlude," Florence Converse, The Story of Wellesley, Project Gutenberg e-book #2362, produced by Stephanie L. Johnson, HTML version by Al Haines, last modified March 1, 2009, http://www.gutenberg.org/files/2362/2362-h/2362-h.htm#chap05

194 "A Memory Book of College Hall," Barbara C. Bach Phipps, The Internet Archive, accessed April 19, 2021, https://ia800708.us.archive.org/32/items/PhotoAlbum_201402/Photo_Album_text.pdf.

195 Ibid.

196 Ibid.

197 Ibid.

198 Undated correspondence from unknown author, "The fire alarm woke me Tuesday morning..." Box 1: 1VF, College Hall Fire, General, Letters, Newspaper Articles, Folder: Personal Accounts, Wellesley College Archives, Library and Technology Services.

199 "Occupants of College Hall: Those Who Escaped the Flames," *Boston Globe*, March 17, 1914.

200 An Alumna, "The Fire," *Wellesley College News* (Wellesley, MA), April 2, 1914, Wellesley College Digital Repository.

201 "Makeshifts," *Wellesley College News* (Wellesley, MA), April 6, 1914, Wellesley College Digital Repository.

202 Marguerite Stitt Church, "I Remember," in *Wellesley After-Images: Reflections On Their College Years By Forty-Five Alumnae*, ed. Betsy Ancker-Johnson (Los Angeles: Wellesley College Club of Los Angeles, 1974), 18.

203 "A Memory Book of College Hall," Barbara C. Bach Phipps, The Internet Archive, accessed April 19, 2021, https://ia800708.us.archive.org/32/items/PhotoAlbum_201402/Photo_Album_text.pdf.

204 Ancker-Johnson, *Wellesley After-Images*, 19.

205 Ibid., 20.

206 "The College Graduate and the Church," *Wellesley College News* (Wellesley, MA), June 4, 1914, Wellesley College Digital Repository.

207 Kate Parsons, "Of Misfits, Informally Observed," Alumnae Department, *Wellesley College News* (Wellesley, MA), June 11, 1914, Wellesley College Digital Repository.

208 Ibid.

209 Wellesley College, *Wellesley College Bulletin: Annual Reports, President and Treasurer 1914–1915* (March 1916) , 59, Wellesley College Digital Repository.

210 Year: 1912; Arrival: New York, New York, USA; Microfilm Serial: T715, 1897-1957; Line: 14; Page Number: 24, Ancestry.com. New York, Passenger and Crew Lists (including Castle Garden and Ellis Island), 1820-1957 [database on-line]. Provo, UT, USA: Ancestry.com Operations, Inc., 2010. [Original data: Passenger Lists of Vessels Arriving at New York, New York, 1820-1897. Microfilm Publication M237, 675 rolls. NAI: 6256867. Records of the U.S. Customs Service, Record Group 36. National Archives at Washington, D.C.]; Year: 1914; Arrival: New York, New York; Microfilm Serial: T715, 1897-1957; Microfilm Roll: Roll 2360; Line: 13; Page Number: 73. Ancestry.com. New York, Passenger and Crew Lists (including Castle Garden and Ellis Island), 1820-1957 [database on-line]. Provo, UT, USA: Ancestry.com Operations, Inc., 2010.

211 "Talked across Continent," *New England Shoe and Leather Industry*, July 1915, 11; "Boston to San Francisco," *American Shoemaking*, July 10, 1915, 71.

212 Adelaide Marguerite Stitt, "The Social Function of Certain Metropolitan Journals" (masters essay, Columbia University, 1917).

213 "The Alumnae Association Turns to Washington," *Wellesley Magazine*, vol. 24, 1939–1940, 490.

214 "Gender on the Home Front," National WWII Museum, accessed April 19, 2021, https://www.nationalww2museum.org/war/articles/gender-home-front.

215 "Just a Moment," *SCAA News*, April 1918, 4; "Ralph Church's Wife at His Side in 12

Campaigns," *Chicago Daily Tribune*, March 27, 1940.

216 "Just a Moment," *SCAA News*, April 1918, 4.

217 "History," Illinois Council of Child and Adolescent Psychiatry, accessed April 19, 2021, http://www.iccap.org/history_past_and_present.aspx.

218 "Rev. M. L. Robinson Weds," *New York Times*, February 6, 1914.

219 "Femininity vs. Feminism," *Wellesley College News* (Wellesley, MA), March 12, 1914.

220 Ibid.

221 Irene Steyskal, "Ralph Church's Wife at His Side in 12 Campaigns," *Chicago Tribune*, March 27, 1940.

222 Church, oral history.

223 Una Corley Groves, telephone interview by author Christine Wolf, April 12, 2018.

224 Norma Lee Browning, "She's Hardest-Working Congressman!" *Chicago Tribune*, July 22, 1951.

225 "Just a Moment," *SCAA News*, April 1918, 4.

226 "Church Wins NY Bride," *Chicago Examiner*, April 8, 1918.

227 "Not a Wedding Trip, Says Ralph Church," *Evanston (IL) News-Index*, November 24, 1916.

228 Ibid.

229 "Church Wins NY Bride," *Chicago Examiner*, April 8, 1918; "Mr. and Mrs. William James Stitt, of New York have announced..." *Washington Post*, April 11, 1918; "The engagement of Miss Marguerite Stitt..." *Chicago Tribune*, April 21, 1918; "Ralph Edwin Church, a young attorney of Chicago..." *Dispatch* (Moline, IL), April 10, 1918.

230 Una Corley Groves, interview by author Christine Wolf, May 16, 2018.

231 Elsie L. Stitt, 1930, United States Federal Census, Manhattan, New York, New York, Page: 19A, Enumeration District: 0488, FHL microfilm: 2341294, image available at https://www.ancestry.com; "Miss Stitt A Bride," *New York Times*, December 22, 1918; "Wellesley 1915 Winner of Gym Meet..." *Boston Globe*, April 25, 1915.

232 "Occupants of College Hall," *Boston Globe*, March 17, 1914.

233 "Miss Stitt A Bride," *New York Times*, December 22, 1918; "Ralph E. Church to Wed," *Chicago Tribune*, December 20 1918.

234 Louise Ryan, "Mrs. Church Leaving for Asia; Grants *The Life* an Exclusive Interview," *The Life* (Niles Township, IL), September 29, 1955.

235 Una Corley Groves, telephone interview by author Christine Wolf, April 15, 2018.

236 Groves, interview, May 16, 2018.

237 Irene Steyskal, "Ralph Church's Wife at His Side in 12 Campaigns," *Chicago Tribune*, March 27, 1940.

238 "Two More Dry Bills Up Before the Legislature," *Decatur (IL) Herald*, January 31, 1917.

239 Genevieve Flavin, "Ralph Church Keeps Career Family Affair," *Chicago Daily Tribune*, September 10, 1944.

240 Ralph E. and A. Marguerite Church, "United States Census, 1920," database with images, FamilySearch (https://familysearch.org : 15 December 2015), Illinois > Cook > Evanston Ward 3 > ED 75 > image 31 of 62; citing NARA microfilm publication T625 (Washington, DC: National Archives and Records Administration, n.d.).

241 "Brundage and Small Line Up For a Showdown," *Chicago Tribune*, July 6, 1921.

242 Yearbook of the Woman's Club of Evanston, 1922, records of the Woman's Club of Evanston, series 55/31, Northwestern University Archives.

243 "Mrs. Carrie Catt Here For National Suffrage Meeting," *Chicago Tribune*, February 9, 1920.

244 "19th Amendment," History.com editors, A&E Television Networks, last modified February 25, 2021, https://www.history.com/topics/womens-history/19th-amendment-1

245 Mark W. Robbins, "Awakening the 'Forgotten Folk': Middle Class Consumer Activism in Post-World War I America" (PhD dissertation, Brown University, 2009), 4, https://repository.library.brown.edu/studio/item/bdr:151.

246 Ibid., 315.

247 Mary Barr, *Friends Disappear: The Battle for Racial Equality in Evanston* (Chicago: University of Chicago Press, 2014), 44.

248 Jesse J. Holland, "Few Recall Killing of Blacks in 'Red Summer' Rampage," *Pantagraph* (Bloomington, IL) July 25, 2019; "Hoodlums the Cause," *Gazette* (Cedar Rapids, IA) July 29, 1919; "Why Race Should Support

Republican Party Ticket," *Chicago Defender*, October 18, 1924.

249 "The Auto: An Indispensable Part of Business," *Kinmundy (IL) Express*, February 24, 1921.

250 "Lawmakers May Vote by Machinery," *McHenry (IL) Plain Dealer*, March 10, 1921.

251 "Chance at Last for McBride to Abandon Small," *Chicago Tribune*, December 19, 1922; "Lawmakers Head for Chicago to Pick a Speaker," *Chicago Tribune*, December 26, 1922.

252 "General Assembly On Whole Was Quiet," *Carbondale (IL) Daily Free Press*, June 21, 1923.

253 "Charity Ball For Children's Home Wednesday Eve," *Chicago Tribune*, December 15, 1929.

254 Undated membership card titled "Family File of Members," First United Methodist Church, Evanston, IL.

255 "History," Stone Porch by the Lake, accessed June 10, 2017, http://www.stoneporchbb.com/history.html (site discontinued).

256 "Evanston M. E. near Decision on Moving Proposal," *Chicago Tribune*, June 2, 1929.

257 "300 Church St./1640 Sheridan Rd.," historic building files, Evanston History Center.

258 Margery B. Perkins, *Evanstoniana: An Informal History of Evanston and Its Architecture* (Chicago: Chicago Review Press, 1985), 88.

259 "Shines Forth as Social Diplomat: Tact as Hostess Proves Priceless to Husband," *Chicago Tribune*, June 10, 1920.

260 Wasniewski, *Women in Congress, 1917–2006*, 1.

261 Paid advertisement, "To the Republican Women Voters..." *Chicago Tribune*, September 14, 1920.

262 Wasniewski, *Women in Congress, 1917–2006*, 1.

263 "Society Personals," *Chicago Tribune*, September 25, 1927.

264 "'Cusser' Wanted for Bank Raids Shot by Police," *Chicago Tribune*, October 13, 1918.

265 "Senator R. E. Church Arrives Here," *Palm Beach (FL) Post*, February 24, 1927.

266 Marguerite Stitt Church, "None But The Brave" (address, Evanston Historical Society, Evanston, IL, February 12, 1967.

267 Ibid.

268 "William J. Stitt Dies on a Train," *New York Times*, March 31, 1930.

269 Estate of Stitt v. Commissioner 7 T.C.M. 920 (1948).

270 Ibid.

271 Ibid.

272 Ibid.

273 Irene Steyskal, "Ralph Church's Wife at His Side in 12 Campaigns," *Chicago Tribune*, March 27, 1940.

274 Ibid.

275 Paid political advertisement, *Evanston (IL) News-Index*, February 24, 1932, in Marguerite Church Collection, Evanston History Center.

276 Parke Brown, "Some Drys Defy Referendum In Replies To Polls," *Chicago Tribune*, October 2, 1930.

277 "Wets and Drys Announce Their Ballot Choices," *Chicago Tribune*, October 26, 1930.

278 Ibid.

279 "Crusaders Ask R. E. Church for Dry Law Stand," *Chicago Tribune*, August, 3, 1931.

280 "Church Silent On Prohibition," *Waukegan (IL) Sun*, September 9, 1931; "Modification of Prohibition Law Favored by Congressman Chindblom of 10th District," *Waukegan (IL) Times*, February 21, 1932.

281 Arthur Evans, "Wet-Dry Issue Holds Stage in Governor Fight," *Chicago Tribune*, March 6, 1932.

282 Irene Steyskal, "Ralph Church's Wife at His Side in 12 Campaigns," *Chicago Tribune*, March 27, 1940.

283 "United States Census, 1930," database with images, FamilySearch (https://familysearch.org : accessed 21 January 2019), Adelaide M. Church in household of Ralph E. Church, Evanston, Cook, Illinois, United States; citing enumeration district (ED) ED 2109, sheet 3A, line 9, family 22, NARA microfilm publication T626 (Washington DC: National Archives and Records Administration, 2002), roll 499; FHL microfilm 2,340,234.

284 "Evanston Sets $95,242 as Goal in Charity Drive: 627 Workers Will Seek Contributions," *Chicago Daily Tribune*, September 13, 1931.

285 "Out for a Stroll in Evanston," *Evanston (IL) News-Index*, September 22, 1932.

286 "A Candidate's Family," 1932, scrapbook in Collection No. 321-325F, box 4, "Church,

Marguerite Stitt 1919-1981," Evanston History Center.

287 "Mrs. Ralph Church is Guest at Glencoe Tea," *Glencoe (IL) News*, October 21, 1932.

288 "Ralph E. Church Out in Front for Congress," *Glencoe (IL) Times*, October 8, 1931.

289 "Candidate in 13th," *Glencoe (IL) News*, September 11, 1931.

290 Arthur Evans, "Simpson and Day Start Fight for Congress Seat," *Chicago Tribune*, January 24, 1932.

291 Ibid.

292 Paul R. Leach, "Church Decides against Running for Congress," *Chicago Daily News*, February 8, 1932.

293 Arthur Evans, "Church Running for Congress as Modificationist," *Chicago Tribune*, February 28, 1932.

294 "Simpson Wins over Church for Congress," *Chicago Tribune*, September 28, 1932.

295 "Simpson Wins Congress Seat by 1,222 Votes," *Chicago Tribune*, November 19, 1932.

296 Arthur Evans, "Congress Race Stirs Up Ghost of the Dry Era," *Chicago Tribune*, April 6, 1934.

297 "To Talk on Taxes," *Evanston (IL) Review*, February 11, 1932.

298 "Zonta International History," Zonta International, accessed April 20, 2021, https://www.zonta.org/Web/About_Us/Zonta%20_History/Web/About/ZI_History_Home.aspx.

299 Arthur Evans, "Ickes Injects His Views into Congress Race," *Chicago Tribune*, April 5, 1934.

300 Paid political advertisement, "Send Ralph Church To Congress..." *Wilmette (IL) Life*, March 29, 1934; "Simpson Sends Answer to Cable from R. Church," *North Chicago Tribune*, April 3, 1934.

301 Paid political advertisement, "Comparison of the Official Public Records..." *Evanston (IL) Review*, April 5, 1934.

302 "Simpson Opens Slashing Attack on Church in Reply to Telegram," *Evanston (IL) Review*, April 5, 1934; "Simpson Sends Answer to Cable from R. Church," *North Chicago Tribune*, April 3, 1934.

303 United States Congress, *Biographical Directory of the United States Congress, 1774–Present* (Washington, DC: United States Congress, 1998).

304 "Go to Capitol," *Evanston (IL) Review*, January 10, 1935; "Betrothal of Marjory Church Announced at Evanston Party," *Chicago Tribune*, October 1, 1951; Marguerite Stitt Church Wellesley Alumnae card of Marguerite Stitt Church, "Class of 1914," "Card File of Information on Individual Class Members," 6C/1914, box 2, Wellesley College Archives, Library and Technology Services.

305 "Congressional Hostess," *Evening Star* (Washington, DC), March 29, 1935.

306 Duncan Aikman, "As a Congress Wife Sees It," *New York Times*, May 10, 1936.

307 Neola Northam, "Mrs. Church Describes Life in Capital City," *Evanston (IL) News-Index*, November 26, 1935.

308 Ibid.

309 Ibid.

310 Ibid.

311 "Arranges President's Tea," *Evanston (IL) News-Index*, October 5, 1934.

312 "Feminine Leader is Attending Institute," *San Bernardino County Sun*, December 19, 1935.

313 Marguerite Church, "Feminine Force in a Changing World," in *Proceedings of the Institute of World Affairs Thirteenth Session*, eds. Rufus B. von KleinSmid and Herbert Wynford Hill (Los Angeles: University of Southern California, 1936).

314 *Proceedings of the Institute of World Affairs Thirteenth Session*, eds. Rufus B. von KleinSmid and Herbert Wynford Hill (Los Angeles: University of Southern California, 1936) , *vii*.

315 Marguerite Church, "Feminine Force in a Changing World," in *Proceedings of the Institute of World Affairs Thirteenth Session*, eds. Rufus B. von KleinSmid and Herbert Wynford Hill (Los Angeles: University of Southern California, 1936), 254.

316 Ibid.

317 Ibid.

318 Ibid.

319 Ibid.

320 Ibid.

321 Ibid., 261.

322 "Strong Fleet is Chief Theme for Navy Day," *Chicago Tribune*, October 29, 1935.

323 "List New Deal Efforts to Kill Industry, Thrift," *Chicago Tribune*, October 26, 1935.

324 Lloyd Wendt, *The Chicago Tribune: The Rise of a Great American Newspaper* (Chicago: Rand McNally & Co., 1979), 569.

325 Ralph E. Church to Col. Robert R. McCormick, 26 January, 1935, Robert R. McCormick Archives, Cantigny, IL.

326 "House Ready to Vote 21–3 More Billions Costs," *Chicago Tribune*, May 9, 1936.

327 Burton A. Boxerman, "Adolph Joachim Sabath in Congress: The Roosevelt and Truman Years," *Journal of the Illinois State Historical Society* 66, no. 4 (1973): 428–43.

328 "Tells House of Sabath Bond Inquiry," *Chicago Tribune*, March 26, 1937.

329 Willard Edwards, "House Responds to Protest of Sabath Probers," *Chicago Tribune*, March 31, 1937.

330 Willard Edwards, "House Responds to Protest of Sabath Probers," *Chicago Tribune*, March 31, 1937; "Tells House of Sabath Bond Inquiry: Church's Blast at Committee Causes Storm," *Chicago Tribune*, March 26, 1937.

331 "Tells House of Sabath Bond Inquiry: Church's Blast at Committee Causes Storm," *Chicago Tribune*, March 26, 1937.

332 Drew Pearson, "Washington Merry-Go-Round," *Honolulu Star-Bulletin*, October 15, 1938.

333 Harris & Ewing, "'Most Unpopular' Member of Congress," November 30, 1937, Library of Congress Prints and Photographs Division, Washington, DC.

334 House Echoes to Holiday Plea for Tax Relief," *Chicago Tribune*, November 26, 1937; "Ham Fish Thankful and Regretful, Too," *Evening Sun* (Baltimore), November 25, 1937.

335 Drew Pearson, "Washington Merry-Go-Round," *Evening Times* (Sayre, PA), April 15, 1937.

336 Katharine Brooks, "Brilliant Reception Closes Season at White House," *Evening Star* (Washington, DC), February 25, 1938

337 "Alumni Council 1942 Update," Box 3, 6C/1914, Class of 1914: Notebook of News—Class Secretary's Material, File: Notebook of News Of Members of 1914 (1932–1969): Necrologies, News of 1914 and Families (1932–58), Wellesley College Archives, Library and Technology Services.

338 Marguerite Stitt Church, "Wanted: A Will for Peace," *Zontian*, October 1939, 13.

339 Ibid.

340 Ibid.

341 "Mrs. Church to Speak on 'American Dream' at 1st Baptist Sunday," *Evanston Review*, September 13, 1951.

342 Ralph E. Church, "At Washington: China-Japan Situation," *Arlington Heights (IL) Herald*, September 17, 1937.

343 "Curtiss Field Bought for Use of Naval Flyers," *Chicago Tribune*, November 7, 1940.

344 William Edwards, "Rebuff Roosevelt on Guam," *Chicago Tribune*, February 25, 1939.

345 "HOLC's Politics Blamed In Loss of 100 Million," *Chicago Tribune*, August 3, 1939.

346 Ralph E. Church, "Church Finds Farm Bill is Most Complex," *Belvidere (IL) Daily Republican*, December 11, 1937.

347 "Fish Says France Expects War Soon," *New York Times*, August 13, 1939.

348 Arthur Deerin Call, "Interparliamentary Union Oslo Jubilee Conference," *World Affairs* 102, no. 4 (December, 1939), 221.

349 Ralph Church, "Congress Not Rubber Stamp," *Crystal Lake (IL) Herald*, August 10, 1939.

350 "Another is out for Senatorship," *Daily Republican-Register* (Mount Carmel, IL), December 9, 1939.

351 Percy Wood, "Ralph E. Church Enters G.O.P. Senatorial Race," *Chicago Tribune*, February 14, 1940.

352 George Tagge, "Careers of U.S. Senate Rivals are Far Apart," *Chicago Tribune*, October 31, 1940.

353 "Congressman Heeds Call in Wheel Chair," *Detroit Free Press*, September 22, 1939.

354 Irene Steyskal, "Ralph Church's Wife at His Side In 12 Campaigns," *Chicago Tribune*, March 2, 1940.

355 Parke Brown, "Victors Pile Up Huge Leads," *Chicago Tribune*, April 10, 1940.

356 "Republicans Assail New Deal at Rally," *Altoona (PA) Tribune*, November 2, 1940.

357 "Organize Help for Paddock in Congress Race," *Chicago Tribune*, September 25, 1941.

358 "Vigorous Prosecution of War Demanded by Candidate Church," *Evanston (IL) Review*, April 9, 1942.

359 Parke Brown, "Church Denies He Started Senate Draft Campaign," *Chicago Tribune*, February 17, 1942

360 "Ralph E. Church Files for G.O.P. Senator Race," *Chicago Tribune*, February 24, 1942.

361 Parke Brown, "Church Drops Out of Senate Primary Race," *Chicago Tribune*, March 1, 1942.
362 Harold Smith, "Paddock-Church Congress Fight Steps Up Tempo," *Chicago Tribune*, March 15, 1942.
363 Ibid.
364 Harold Smith, "George Paddock, Church Line Up for Hot Contest," *Chicago Tribune*, March 8, 1942.
365 Election advertisement, *Evanston (IL) Review*, April 9, 1942.
366 Harold Smith, "Paddock Gains New Backing in Congress Race," *Chicago Tribune*, March 22, 1942.
367 Harold Smith, "Church Victory Major Upset in Congress Races," *Chicago Tribune*, April 16, 1942.
368 "Congress Fight Starts Early in Tenth District," *Chicago Tribune*, May 24, 1942.
369 "Memorial: Ralph Edwin Church Jr. '42," Princeton Alumni Weekly, Trustees of Princeton University, accessed April 21, 2021, https://paw.princeton.edu/memorial/ralph-edwin-church-jr-'42.
370 Judith Cass, "Caryl Casselberry is Betrothed to Lt. Erskine Phelps Wilder; Announce Engagement of Janet Richardson," *Chicago Daily Tribune*, December 22, 1942.
371 Judith Cass, "Parties Also Arranged for Janet Richardson," *Chicago Tribune*, May 4, 1943.
372 Chicago Tribune Press Service, "Church Misses Son's Wedding to Save Record," *Chicago Tribune*, May 12, 1943.
373 Ibid.
374 Untitled clipping, February 1947, 6C/1914, "Notebook of Classnotes from Wellesley Alumnae Magazine (1940-1969)/(1969-1977)", Box 3, Wellesley College Archives, Library and Technology Services.
375 "Letter From Madame Chiang Kai Shek to Marguerite Church 7/30/1942," WorthPoint, accessed April 21, 2021, https://www.worthpoint.com/worthopedia/letter-madame-chiang-kai-shek-1782130553.
376 "Presenting Charming Mrs. Church, a Model of Cultured Intellect," *Washington Post*, February 13, 1949.
377 Ruth De Young, "Mrs. Roosevelt Table Partner of Mrs. Hughes," *Chicago Tribune*, April 23, 1937.
378 "The Congressional Club Museum and Foundation," The Congressional Club Museum and Foundation, accessed April 21, 2021, https://www.thecongressionalclub.com.
379 Jane Eads, "Mrs. Church Teaches Speech in Washington," *Waukegan (IL) News-Sun*, December 3, 1947.
380 Jane Eads, "Washington Daybook," *Morning Herald* (Gloversville, NY), April 10, 1947.
381 William Klemm photograph, *Washington Post*, February 10, 1949.
382 Genevieve Flavin, "Ralph Church Keeps Career Family Affair," *Chicago Tribune*, September 10, 1944.
383 "Pearl Harbor 'Truth' Hidden for Politics, House Told," *Pittsburgh Sun-Telegraph*, August 21, 1944.
384 Willard Edwards, "House Rejects Island Fort by 205 to 168 Vote," *Chicago Tribune*, February 24, 1939.
385 "Not on the Alert," *Journal Times* (Racine, WI), September 1, 1944.
386 90 Cong. Rec. A1671 (1944) (extension of remarks of Rep. Church).
387 Drew Pearson, "Washington Merry-Go-Round," *Madison (WI) Capital Times*, April 3, 1944.
388 Geo. W. Robnett, "Misrepresenting Northwestern," Voice of the People, *Chicago Tribune*, August 8, 1944.
389 R.M.V., "Mr. MacDougall's Rebuttal," Voice of the People, *Chicago Tribune*, August 23, 1944.
390 "Hillman Issues Challenge to Un-American Committee," *Cincinnati Enquirer*, August 29, 1944.
391 Edward Wilson, "Press Finish Fight in 10th District Race," *Chicago Tribune*, April 7, 1947.
392 Judith Cass, "Five Make Debut amid Holly of Yule Season," *Chicago Tribune*, December 22, 1946.
393 "Rep. Church Dies While Speaking to House Group," *Chicago Tribune*, March 22, 1950.
394 Ibid.
395 "Longworth House Office Building," History, Art & Archives, United States House of Representatives, accessed November 9, 2020, https://history.house.gov/Exhibitions-and-Publications/House-Office-Buildings/Longworth/Longworth-intro.
396 United Press, "Congressman Dies While Testifying: Ralph Church Dies on Stand," *Princeton (IN) Daily Clarion*, March 21, 1950.

397 Associated Press, "Rep. R. E Church Stricken, Dies in Testifying," *Mercury* (Pottstown, PA), March 22, 1950.
398 United Press, "Ralph Church Dies Today," *Daily Chronicle* (DeKalb, IL), March 21, 1950; Harold Smith, "Church's Death Poses Problem on Succession," *Chicago Tribune*, March 22, 1950.
399 Harold Smith, "Church's Death Poses Problem on Succession," *Chicago Tribune*, March 22, 1950.
400 Ibid.
401 Ibid.; "Rep. Church Dies While Speaking to House Group," *Chicago Tribune*, March 22, 1950.
402 Harold Smith, "Church's Death Poses Problem on Succession," *Chicago Tribune*, March 22, 1950.
403 96 Cong. Rec. 3,744 (1950) (statement of Sen. Saltonstall).
404 96 Cong. Rec. 3,744 (1950) (statement of Sen. Douglas).
405 96 Cong. Rec. 3,752 (1950) (statement of Rep. Short).
406 96 Cong. Rec. 3,745 (1950) (statement of Rep. McCormack).
407 96 Cong. Rec. 3,745 (1950) (statement of Rep. Allen).
408 96 Cong. Rec. 3,748 (1950) (statement of Rep. Rogers).
409 "Funeral," *St. Louis Star-Times*, March 22, 1950.
410 Una Corley Groves, telephone interview by author Christine Wolf, April 10, 2018.
411 Ibid.
412 Harold Smith, "Church's Death Poses Problem on Succession," *Chicago Tribune*, March 22, 1950.
413 "Names of Note in Today's News," *St. Louis Star and Times*, March 22, 1950.
414 "Evanston Joins National, State Leaders at Rites for Church," *Evanston (IL) Review*, March 3, 1950.
415 Harold Smith, "G.O.P. Jockeys for Successor to Rep. Church," *Chicago Tribune*, April 2, 1950.
416 Ibid.
417 Ibid.
418 "Spending Slash Urged by Widow of Rep. Church," *Chicago Daily Tribune*, May 17, 1950.
419 Ibid.
420 Ibid.
421 "Mrs. Church Issues Statement; Popular Demand for Her Grows," *Evanston (IL) Review*, April 6, 1950.
422 "Predict Choice of Mrs. Church for House Race," *Chicago Daily Tribune*, June 9, 1950.
423 Joan Beck, "Politics Just Comes Naturally for Mrs. Church," *Chicago Tribune*, October 13, 1950.
424 Ibid.
425 Ibid.
426 Antoinnette Donnelly, "First Week's Program and 10 Commandments of Fatties Anonymous," *Chicago Tribune*, October 13, 1950.
427 "Republican Women To Hear Mrs. R. E. Church At Spring Luncheon-Fashion Show," *Arlington Heights (IL) Herald*, May 5, 1950.
428 Vera Folkman, "Mrs. Church Urges Republican Women to Work for 100% Vote in November," *Arlington Heights (IL) Herald*, May 19, 1950.
429 "The Fence Post," *Arlington Heights (IL) Herald*, May 19, 1950.
430 "Grateful, Calm Mrs. Church is Foe of Truman," *Chicago Tribune*, June 10, 1950.
431 "G.O.P. Choice," *Chicago Sunday Tribune*, June 11, 1950.
432 "Harmonious Rage Envelops Dear Ladies of Staid Congressional Club," *Austin (TX) American-Statesman*, June 21, 1950.
433 Ibid.
434 "Frances Harper and Black Women in the WCTU; Truth Telling: Frances Willard and Ida B. Wells," Frances Willard House Museum, accessed July 8, 2020, https://scalar.usc.edu/works/willard-and-wells/black-women-and-the-wctu.
435 Frances Harper, "Work Among the Colored People of the North," *Union Signal* (Evanston, IL), May 28, 1885.
436 "Frances Harper and Black Women in the WCTU; Truth Telling: Frances Willard and Ida B. Wells," Frances Willard House Museum, accessed July 8, 2020, https://scalar.usc.edu/works/willard-and-wells/black-women-and-the-wctu; Ida Husted Harper, ed., *History of Woman Suffrage*, (New York: J. J. Little & Ives, 1922), 5:751.
437 Kerry Luft, "Marguerite Stitt Church, Ex-Congresswoman," *Chicago Tribune*, May 27, 1990.

438 Joan Beck, "Politics Just Comes Naturally for Mrs. Church," *Chicago Daily Tribune*, October 13, 1950.
439 Ruth Montgomery, "DC Wash," *Daily News* (New York), January 20, 1951.
440 Associated Press, "Rep. Ralph Church Left $25,000 Estate to Wife," *Decatur (IL) Herald*, April 7, 1950.
441 "Developing a Segregated Town, 1900–1960," Larry Gavin, Evanston RoundTable, last modified December 5, 2019, https://evanstonroundtable.com/2019/12/05/developing-a-segregated-town-1900-1960.
442 Ibid.
443 Wasniewski, *Women in Congress, 1917–2006*, 998.
444 Irwin Gertzog, *Congressional Women: Their Recruitment, Integration, and Behavior*, 2nd ed. (Westport, CT: Praeger, 1995), 17–36; Irwin Gertzog, "Changing Patterns of Female Recruitment to the US House of Representatives," *Legislative Studies Quarterly* 4, no. 3 (August 1979): 429–445.
445 Gertzog, *Congressional Women*, 34; Wasniewski, *Women in Congress, 1917–2006*, 996–999.
446 Wasniewski, *Women in Congress, 1917–2006*, 5; Gertzog, *Congressional Women*, 17–36; Gertzog, "Changing Patterns of Female Recruitment to the US House of Representatives," 429–445.
447 Wasniewski, *Women in Congress, 1917–2006*, 6.
448 Wasniewski, *Women in Congress, 1917–2006*, 367.
449 Church, oral history.
450 136 Cong. Rec. 14,002–14,004 (1990) (statement of Rep. Porter).
451 Church, oral history.
452 Groves, interview, May 16, 2018.
453 "Mrs. Church Set to Carry Fight to Washington," *Chicago Tribune*, November 9, 1950.
454 Ibid.
455 "Acheson Ouster Urgent, Feeling of Mrs. Church," *Chicago Tribune*, December 14, 1950.
456 "Republican Women of the 13th District Form Permanent Campaign Organization," *Arlington Heights (IL) Herald*, December 22, 1950.
457 International News Service, "New Women in Congress; One Is Real Career Girl and Other Is Typical Wife," *Cincinnati Enquirer*, November 12, 1950.
458 Ibid.
459 "Mrs. Church to Attend Methodist Anniversary," *Times* (Munster, IN), November 16, 1950.
460 Arnel Tirado (operations and compliance manager, Methodist Home for Nursing and Rehabilitation), telephone interview with author Christine Wolf, October 29, 2018.
461 "Women Candidates for Congress Find It Rough Going," *Morning Call* (Allentown, PA), November 9, 1950.
462 E. R. Noderer, "US Deceived on Events in Korea: Dirksen," *Chicago Tribune*, November 6, 1950.
463 Ibid.
464 Groves, interview, May 16, 2018.
465 "Bells, Sirens, Whistles Add to Din as General Lands," *Palatine (IL) Enterprise*, April 20, 1951.
466 Political advertisement, *Daily Herald* (Arlington Heights, IL), October 31, 1952.
467 John Fisher, "Europe Aided by 350 Million," *Chicago Tribune*, August 18, 1951.
468 Ibid.
469 Ibid.
470 Ibid.
471 136 Cong. Rec. 14,003 (1990) (statement of Rep. Porter).
472 Groves, interview, May 16, 2018.
473 Una Corley Groves to author Christine Wolf, May 26, 2018.
474 Church, oral history.
475 Groves to author Wolf.
476 Ibid.
477 Groves, interview, May 16, 2018.
478 Ibid.
479 Groves, interview, April 10, 2018.
480 Una Corley Groves, telephone interview with author Christine Wolf, May 7, 2018.
481 Groves, interview, May 16, 2018.
482 Ibid.
483 "Aide to Former Congressman with McClory," *McHenry (IL) Plaindealer*, July 15, 1970.
484 Steven Anderson, e-mail message to author Christine Wolf, March 28, 2019.
485 Esther V. W. Tufty, "New Congresswomen Know Their Politics," *Olean (NY) Times Herald*, December 8, 1950.
486 Ibid.

487 Norma Lee Browning, "She's the Hardest Working Congressman," *Chicago Tribune*, July 22, 1951.

488 John Barrow, "Powder-Puff Fight Shapes Up; Women Candidates to Clash in Race for Congress in Illinois," *Lubbock (TX) Avalanche-Journal*, February 26, 1956.

489 Wasniewski, *Women in Congress, 1917–2006*, 140.

490 Chase Going Woodhouse, interview by Betty G. Seaver and Morton J. Tenzer, September 29, 1977–June 13, 1979, Former Members of Congress, Inc. oral history interviews, 1962–1985 (bulk 1969–1980), Manuscript Reading Room, Library of Congress, Washington, DC.

491 Wasniewski, *Women in Congress, 1917–2006*, 149.

492 Ibid., 4.

493 Matthew A. Wasniewski, interview with the authors, O'Neill House Office Building, Washington, DC., November 27, 2017.

494 Church, oral history.

495 Ibid.

496 "Women Draft Urged by Texas Jurist at Capital Meeting," *Wisconsin State Journal* (Madison, WI), January 14, 1951.

497 Wasniewski, *Women in Congress, 1917–2006*, 278–283; Church, oral history.

498 Edna Flannery Kelly, interview by Charles T. Morrissey, May 10–11, 1976, Former Members of Congress, Inc. oral history interviews, 1962–2985 (bulk 1969–1980), Manuscript Reading Room, Library of Congress, Washington, DC.

499 Ruth Montgomery, "DC Wash," *New York Daily News*, January 20, 1951.

500 Church, oral history.

501 Ibid.

502 "The Evanston Revue," *Evanston (IL) Review*, November 3, 1960.

503 Groves, interview, May 16, 2018.

504 Groves, interview, April 10, 2018.

505 "Former Springfield Woman, Helen Nelsch, Found Dead," *Jacksonville (IL) Daily Journal*, July 29, 1951.

506 John Fisher, "GOP Standard Kept High by Mrs. Church," *Chicago Tribune*, September 2, 1951.

507 Joan Beck, "Two Women Vie for Congressional Seat," *Chicago Tribune*, October 31, 1956.

508 Curtis MacDougall campaign document, "The Record of Ralph Church," 1944, Marguerite Stitt Church Collection, Evanston History Center.

509 Dick Lee, "Truman Policy Perils Nation," *New York Daily News*, January 27, 1952; George Tagge," Taft: 'It's Truman's War,'" *Chicago Tribune*, November 3, 1951.

510 "19 Illinois Members of Congress Assist Capital's Taft Club," *Chicago Tribune*, March 2, 1952; Ruth Moss, "Inside Story of the Taft Family," *Chicago Tribune*, July 10, 1952.

511 Guy Gentry, "Let Nation Lift Own Yoke First," *Chicago Tribune*, July 9, 1952.

512 Wellesley Alumnae Association card of Marguerite Stitt Church, 1941, Marguerite Stitt Church biographical file, WCA_7B_Stitt_Church_Marguerite_1914, Wellesley Alumnae Association.

513 Eleanor Page, "Meet the Women Leaders at the Convention," *Chicago Tribune*, July 7, 1952.

514 Gladys Priddy, "Women Return from Capital 'Ready To Fight,'" *Chicago Tribune*, May 31, 1951.

515 Vincent J. Burke, "Women Take Growing Interest in Congressional Contests," *Corpus Christi (TX) Caller-Times*, April 21, 1952.

516 Ibid.

517 Ibid.

518 Harold Smith, "Feeling Runs High in House Battle in 9th," *Chicago Tribune*, October 26, 1952.

519 Kelly, oral history.

520 Bascom N. Timmons, "This Lady Played on Both Teams," *(Nashville) Tennessean*, March 20, 1956.

521 Nancy McKeon, "Women in the House Get a Restroom," *Washington Post*, July 28, 2011.

522 Lee Graham, "How You Can Be Liked," *St. Louis Post-Dispatch*, March 14, 1954.

523 "League Defended on House Floor by Mrs. Church," *Evanston (IL) Review*, August 20, 1959.

524 Church, oral history.

525 Ibid.

526 Ibid.

527 Ibid.

528 Ibid.

529 Ibid.

530 "Urges US Ban On Shipment Of Fireworks" *Chicago Tribune*, June 21, 1951.

531 99 Cong. Rec. 9,288 (1953) (statement of Rep. Church).
532 United Press, "Beloit Boy Loses Both Hands in Home-Made Fireworks Blast," *Journal Times* (Racine, WI), July 6, 1953.
533 99 Cong. Rec. 9,288 (1953) (statement of Rep. Church).
534 99 Cong. Rec. 9,290 (1953) (statement of Rep. Lanham).
535 99 Cong. Rec. 9,292 (1953) (statement of Rep. Vorys).
536 W. N. S., "Bootlegging Fireworks Is Now a Federal Case," *Courier-Journal* (Louisville, KY), July 4, 1954.
537 Church, oral history.
538 "5 Solons Deny Europe Dragging Fee on Defense," *Boston Globe*, April 21, 1953.
539 "Mrs. Church Tells Junior League U.S. Is Losing 'Cold War,'" *Chicago Tribune*, October 15, 1952.
540 Rita Fitzpatrick, "GOP Progress In Capital Told by Rep. Church," *Chicago Tribune*, April 4, 1953.
541 Church, oral history.
542 Joan Beck, "Two Women Vie For Congressional Seat—Newcomer Opposes Veteran Mrs. Church," *Chicago Tribune*, October 31, 1956.
543 Church, oral history.
544 Joan Beck, "Two Women Vie For Congressional Seat—Newcomer Opposes Veteran Mrs. Church," *Chicago Tribune*, October 31, 1956.
545 "Rambling Roundup," *Chicago Defender*, October 20, 1956.
546 "Tidbits and Tattlings," *Chicago Defender*, August 10, 1957.
547 "Rambling Roundup," *Chicago Defender*, October 20, 1956.
548 "Hold Line on 'Rights' Is Bullock's Advice," *Chicago Defender*, September 7, 1957.
549 Ibid.
550 Unattributed column, February 25, 1954, File 7B_Stitt_Church_Marguerite_1914, Wellesley College Archives, Library and Technology Services.
551 Church, oral history.
552 Ibid.
553 Ibid.
554 Ibid.
555 Harrison A. Williams, "A Congressman Defends 'Junkets,'" *New York Times*, September 11, 1955.
556 Church, oral history.
557 Jane Eads, "Must Know World, Says Mrs. Church," *Journal Times* (Racine, WI), February 13, 1954.
558 Jane Eads, "What's Doing in the USA," *Lancaster (Ohio) Eagle-Gazette*, February 4, 1954.
559 Associated Press, "Member of Congress Says She's No Lady," *Clarion-Ledger* (Jackson, MS), March 15, 1954.
560 Church, oral history.
561 Ibid.
562 Ibid.
563 Undated biography, File 7B_Stitt_Stitt_Church_Marguerite_1914, Wellesley College Archives, Library and Technology Services.
564 "Mrs. Church Abroad," *Chicago Daily Tribune*, December 18, 1959.
565 Church, oral history.
566 Ibid.
567 Ibid.
568 United Press, "Woman, Two Men Seized; 25 to 30 Shots Rake Floor," *St. Louis Post-Dispatch*, March 1, 1954.
569 Associated Press, "5 Congressmen Shot, Wounded by Spectators," *Palladium-Item* (Richmond, IN), March 1, 1954.
570 136 Cong. Rec. 14,003 (1990) (statement of Rep. Porter).
571 "Mrs. Church Notes Lessons in Gun Attack on Congress," *Evanston (IL) Review*, March 4, 1954.
572 "Congressman Church Was Last 'Man' Down," *Daily Herald* (Arlington Heights, IL), March 4, 1954.
573 Clayton Knowles, "Five Congressmen Shot in House by 3 Puerto Rican Nationalists; Bullets Spray from Gallery," *New York Times*, March 2, 1954.
574 John Fisher, "5 Congressmen Shot Down," *Chicago Tribune*, March 2, 1954.
575 Groves, interview, May 16, 2018.]
576 "Mrs. Church Notes Lessons in Gun Attack on Congress," *Evanston (IL) Review*, March 4, 1954.
577 Ibid.
578 Ibid.
579 Ibid.
580 "Rep M. S. Church Speaks Tonight at Northwestern," *Roselle (IL) Register*, July 29, 1954.
581 "Rep. Church Sees 'World In Flux,'" *Summer Northwestern* (Evanston, IL), July 30, 1954.

582 Norma Lee Browning, "She's the Hardest Working Congressman," *Chicago Tribune*, July 22, 1951.
583 "Ike's Foreign Aid Bill Survives House Votes," *Wisconsin State Journal* (Madison, WI), May 14, 1958.
584 "Debate Is Begun on Foreign Aid," *Billings (MT) Gazette*, June, 29, 1955.
585 "Foreign Aid under Fire," *Daily Courier* (Connellsville, PA), June 28, 1955.
586 Lorraine M. Lees, *Keeping Tito Afloat: The United States, Yugoslavia, and the Cold War* (University Park: Penn State University Press, 1997), 188–190.
587 "50,000 Words To Explain $70,000,000,000," *Chicago Tribune*, March 14, 1958.
588 Philip Warden, "Truman Plugs Ike's Foreign Aid Spending," *Chicago Daily Tribune*, May 6, 1959.
589 Ibid.
590 Ibid.
591 "Rep. Church Warns GOP Ladies of Welfare State," *Daily Herald* (Arlington Heights, IL), September 11, 1958.
592 Ibid.
593 George Dixon, "Washington Scene: Finland's Lady Barbers," *San Francisco Examiner*, January 25, 1955.
594 Ibid.
595 "Moral Force," *Corpus Christi (TX) Caller-Times*, January 15, 1957.
596 Ibid.
597 Ibid.
598 Joan Beck, "Two Women Vie for Congressional Seat—Newcomer Opposes Veteran Mrs. Church," *Chicago Tribune*, October 31, 1956.
599 "Female Side of 84th Congress is 'Sweet 16,'" *Chicago Daily Tribune*, December 30, 1955.
600 Ibid.
601 Ibid.
602 Rose McKee, "17 Women Will Serve in New Congress to Set New Record; 11 Are Reelected," *Corsicana (TX) Daily Sun*, November 11, 1954.
603 "2122 Massachusetts Ave NW, Washington, DC 20008," Redfin, accessed June 26, 2021, https://www.redfin.com/DC/Washington/2122-Massachusetts-Ave-NW-20008/home/9050673.
604 Groves, interview, April 10, 2018.
605 Groves, interview, May 16, 2018.
606 John Barrow, "Powder-Puff Fight Shapes Up; Women Candidates to Clash in Race for Congress in Illinois," *Lubbock (TX) Avalanche-Journal*, February 26, 1956.
607 Joan Beck, "Two Women Vie for Congressional Seat—Newcomer Opposes Veteran Mrs. Church," *Chicago Tribune*, October 31, 1956.
608 "Powder Puff Derby Shapes Up between Two Illinois Women," *Springfield (MO) News-Leader*, March 2, 1956.
609 136 Cong. Rec. 14,002 (1990) (statement of Rep. Porter).
610 Joan Beck, "Two Women Vie for Congressional Seat—Newcomer Opposes Veteran Mrs. Church," *Chicago Tribune*, October 31, 1956.
611 Ibid.; "Powder Puff Derby Shapes Up between Two Illinois Women," *Springfield (MO) News-Leader*, March 2, 1956.
612 Esther V. W. Tufty, "'Ladies' Day' At Polls," *Lancaster (OH) Eagle-Gazette*, October 4, 1956.
613 Sylvia Cassell, "Chicagoans Attend Inauguration Program," *Chicago Daily Tribune*, January 21, 1957.
614 Cynthia Harrison, *On Account of Sex: The Politics of Women's Issues, 1945-1968* (Berkeley: University of California Press, 1988), 144.
615 Ibid.
616 Marie McNair, "Mrs. Church Dons New Role," *Washington Post*, January 21, 1951.
617 "Capital Letter," *Record-Argus* (Greenville, PA), August 6, 1957.
618 Ibid.
619 Ibid.
620 Ibid.
621 Ibid.
622 Timothy A. Church, e-mail message to author Christine Wolf, July 28, 2020.
623 Ibid.
624 Ibid.
625 Ibid.
626 E. R. Noderer, "US Deceived On Events In Korea: Dirksen," *Chicago Tribune*, November 6, 1950.
627 Rita Fitzpatrick, "Defense Waste Is Denounced by Rep. Church," *Chicago Tribune*, November 10, 1951.
628 "Chinese Gunners Downing Planes at Dien Bien Phu, Secretary Says," *St. Louis Post-Dispatch*, April 5, 1954.

629 "I Will Not Vote for Bloodshed—Rep. Church," *Chicago Tribune*, April 20, 1954.
630 Virginia Laughlin, "Suburban Mothers In Plea For Peace," *Arlington Heights (IL) Herald*, November 9, 1961.
631 Ibid.
632 Ibid.
633 Ibid.
634 Philip Dodd, "Jury Trials Ruled Out In Rights Cases," *Chicago Tribune*, June 15, 1957.
635 Ibid.
636 Ibid.
637 Associated Press, "Chinese Marine Battles Deportation To Formosa," *Los Angeles Times*, July 8, 1954.
638 New York Times News Service, "Man's Life in Jeopardy; Congress Also Sits as Judge," *Courier-Journal (Louisville, KY)*, April 8, 1958.
639 Percy Wood, "Mrs. Church Has Say," *Chicago Tribune*, October 26, 1958.
640 "Signs Order For Deporting Hsuan," *Chicago Tribune*, June 22, 1961.
641 Robert Goldsborough, "Whatever Happened?" *Chicago Tribune*, January 1, 1967.
642 "Rips Security School Shown At Glenview," *Chicago Tribune*, September 11, 1960.
643 "Mrs. Church Praises Suburb GOP Strength," *Arlington Heights (IL) Herald*, October 20, 1960.
644 Ibid.
645 Ibid.
646 "Claim Smear Not Done by Birchers," *Freeport (IL) Journal-Standard*, May 25, 1961.
647 UPI, "Cleric Reveals Racist Letters," *Chicago Defender*, August 16, 1960.
648 Ibid.
649 136 Cong. Rec. 14,003 (1990) (statement of Rep. Porter).
650 Jack Gottlieb, *Working with Bernstein: A Memoir* (New York: Amadeus Press, 2010), 73.
651 Philip Warden, "Rusk Aid Plea Stirs Barrage from Critics," *Chicago Tribune*, June 8, 1961.
652 McClure Newspaper Syndicate, "Worth the Battle: Woman Solon Tries Vainly to Block 'Junk Mail' Bill," March 15, 1960, File WCA_7B_Stitt_Church_Marguerite_1914, Wellesley College Archives, Library and Technology Services.
653 "GOP Event Attracts 3," *Bridgewater (NJ) Courier-News*, March 10, 1961.
654 "GOP Sees Win In '64," *La Grande (OR) Observer*, March 6, 1961.
655 Groves, interview, May 16, 2018.
656 "Boost White House Police—For Watching Macaroni?" *Des Moines Register*, May 11, 1962.
657 Ibid.
658 "This Is Time for Action," *Arlington Heights (IL) Herald*, June 15, 1961.
659 "Election Puts Party on Toes: Mrs. Church," *Evanston (IL) Review*, April 6, 1961.
660 Ibid.
661 Ghita Cary, "Chicago's 10 Best-Dressed" *Chicago Daily Sun-Times*, January 30, 1959.
662 George Dixon, "Pretty Soft Drink Dispensers Desert Tasks for Martinis," *Pensacola (FL) News Journal*, August 2, 1960.
663 Joseph Hearst, "Adlai's Plea For UN Stirs Bitter Words," *Chicago Tribune*, June 28, 1962.
664 Ibid.
665 Philip Warden, "Write In New Curbs in Bill for UN Loan," *Chicago Tribune*, August 9, 1962.
666 Kathleen McLaughlin, "More Women Find 'Place' in UN," *New York Times*, September 26, 1961.
667 Stuart R. Paddock, "Editor's Column," *Arlington Heights (IL) Herald*, September 7, 1961.
668 107 Cong. Rec. 17,770 (1961) (Statement of Rep. Church).
669 "Mrs. Church Tells UN Experiences," *Arlington Heights (IL) Herald*, June 20, 1963.
670 Ibid.
671 107 Cong. Rec. 19,503 (1961) (Statement of Rep. Church).
672 Marguerite Stitt Church, "Wanted: A Will for Peace," *Zontian*, October 1939, 13.
673 John James, "United States Cold War Policy, the Peace Corps and Its Volunteers in Colombia in the 1960s" (master's thesis, University of Central Florida, 2008), 17, http://purl.fcla.edu/fcla/etd/CFE0002114.
674 Ibid.
675 Ibid., 20.
676 *The Peace Corps: Hearings Before the Committee on Foreign Affairs, House of Representatives*, 87th Cong. 25 (1961) (statement of Rep. Church).
677 "Founding Documents of the Peace Corps," National Archives, accessed July 13, 2020, https://www.archives.gov/education/

lessons/peace-corps; "Nixon Supports Peace Corps," *Tuscon (AZ) Daily Citizen*, March 14, 1972.

678 Peter Edson, "Peace Corps Outlined to Young Enterprisers" *Evening Sun* (Hanover, PA), July 30, 1962.

679 "Speech at the National Conference of Returned Peace Corps Volunteers and Staff," Sargent Shriver Peace Institute, accessed June 27, 2021, http://www.sargentshriver.org/speech-article/speech-at-the-national-conference-of-returned-peace-corps-volunteers-and-staff.

680 Catherine May Bedell, interview by Fern S. Ingersoll, March 1, 1979 and April 20, 1979, Former Members of Congress, Inc. oral history interviews, 1962–2985 (bulk 1969–1980), Manuscript Reading Room, Library of Congress, Washington, DC.

681 Ibid.

682 Una Corley Groves, interview by author Christine Wolf, May 17, 2018.

683 107 Cong. Rec. 19,503 (1961) (statement of Rep. Gross).

684 107 Cong. Rec. 19,503 (1961) (statement of Rep. Church).

685 Joseph Hearst, "Peace Corps, 40 Million Fund Approv'ed by House," *Chicago Tribune*, September 15, 1961.

686 Groves, interview, May 16, 2018.

687 Church, oral history.

688 "Rep. Church Named to UN Delegation," *Evanston (IL) Review*, August 31, 1961.

689 Ibid.

690 "Rep. Church Reports Power of New Nations Is 'Most Impressive,'" *Evanston (IL) Review*, undated, Marguerite Stitt Church biographical file, folder 1 of 3, Evanston History Center, Evanston, IL.

691 Ibid.

692 Church, oral history.

693 Ibid.

694 Ibid.

695 Lois Wille, "Mrs. Church's Cherished Possession, A Wishing Tree Is Retired," *Chicago Daily News*, January 3, 1962.

696 Church, oral history.

697 "GOP Woman Surprises," *New York Times*, December 8, 1961.

698 108 Cong. Rec. 22,423 (1962) (statement of Rep. Schwengel).

698 "Retail Merchants Honor Mrs. Church in Washington, DC," *Evanston (IL) Review*, May 17, 1962.

699 "United Republican Fund to Honor Mrs. Church," *Evanston (IL) Review*, September 27, 1962.

700 Robert Dunham, "Asia Policy Too Soft, Mrs. Church Warns," *Evanston (IL) Review*, April 26, 1962.

701 Bruce Ladd, "Marguerite Stitt Church Not to Run Again," *Arlington Heights (IL) Herald*, December 14, 1961.

702 George Tagge, "Rep. Church Says She Will Not Run Again," *Chicago Tribune*, December 8, 1961.

703 Lois Wille, "Mrs. Church's Cherished Possession, A Wishing Tree Is Retired," *Chicago Daily News*, January 3, 1962.

704 "Rep. Church Poses Vital Questions for NU Grads," *Chicago Sunday Tribune*, June 17, 1961.

705 Ibid.

706 Ibid.

707 James McCartney, "House and Senate 'Lame Ducks' Off for Exotic Spots," *Corpus Christi (TX) Caller-Times*, November 21, 1962.

708 Frank Mankiewicz, Joel Swerdlow, *So As I Was Saying... My Somewhat Eventful Life* (New York: Thomas Dunne Books, 2016), 129.

709 Associated Press, "Injured Legislators Return," *Montgomery (AL) Advertiser*, December 8, 1962.

710 "Marguerite Church Recovering in Bethesda Hospital," *Evanston (IL) Review*, December 7, 1962.

711 Associated Press, "Injured Legislators Return," *Montgomery (AL) Advertiser*, December 8, 1962.

712 "Farewell Salute Set to Honor Rep. Church," *Chicago Tribune*, January 3, 1963.

713 "600 Welcome Mrs. Church Home," *Evanston (IL) Review*, January 10, 1963.

714 "Testimonial Dinner Held for Marguerite Church," *Dispatch* (Moline, IL). January 9, 1963.

715 "District Honors Retiring Congresswoman," *Evanston (IL) Review*, January 10 1963.

716 "Politics Won't Sway Him, Economic Chief Asserts," *New York Times*, July 15, 1953; "No Politics in His Advice, Chief Economic Aide Says," *Wall Street Journal*, July 15, 1953.

717 "600 Welcome Mrs. Church Home," *Evanston (IL) Review*, January 10, 1963.

718 "Laud Mrs. Church as a 'Lady With Guts,'" *Chicago Daily Tribune*, January 9, 1963.
719 "600 Welcome Mrs. Church Home," *Evanston (IL) Review*, January 10, 1963.
720 Ibid.
721 Ibid.
722 Church, oral history.
723 Donald H. Rumsfeld, interview by author Christine Wolf, May 11–12, 2021.
724 136 Cong. Rec. 14,003 (1990) (statement of Rep. Porter).
725 Joyce Rumsfeld, interview by author Christine Wolf, May 11–12, 2021.
726 "Mrs. Church Tells UN Experiences," *Arlington Heights (IL) Herald*, June 20, 1963.
727 "GOP Leaders Uphold Stand on Goldwater," *Chicago Tribune*, November 28, 1963.
728 Bob Setlik, "Four Names Mentioned For GOP Post—Brown Favored to Succeed Church," *Arlington Heights (IL) Herald*, September 3, 1964.
729 Groves, interview, April 17, 2018.
730 Eleanor Page, "When the Carolers Came to Dinner," *Chicago Tribune*, December 24, 1969.
731 Marguerite Stitt Church, "None but the Brave" (address, Evanston Historical Society, Evanston, IL, February 12, 1967).
732 Lorraine Bannon, "GOP Club Grows Older and Bigger," *Evanston (IL) Review*, June 3, 1971.
733 "Snowballing of Car Leads to Tragedy," *Chicago Tribune*, March 16, 1972.
734 "400 Attend Funeral Service of Young James Wood," *Evanston (IL) Review*, March 23, 1972.
735 "Report of Contacts/Change of Address," contacts with Marguerite Stitt Church 1962-1974, archives of First United Methodist Church, Evanston, IL.
736 D. Daniel Baldino, telephone interview with author Christine Wolf, April 20, 2021.
737 "President Ford Committee—Lists of Officials and Staff, Nov. 1975," Box 18, Richard B. Cheney Files, Gerald R. Ford Presidential Library.
738 136 Cong. Rec. 14,003 (1990) (statement of Rep. Porter).
739 Barbara Sullivan, "At 91, Ex-Rep. Church Keeps Her Following," *Chicago Tribune*, October 25, 1983.
740 "Political Shorts," unknown publication, File 7B_Stitt_Church_Marguerite_1914, Wellesley College Archives, Library and Technology Services.
741 Barbara Sullivan, "At 91, Ex-Rep. Church Keeps Her Following," *Chicago Tribune*, October 25, 1983.
742 William H. Rentschler, "They Came… Loved… Lauded," *News/Voice*, October 27, 1983, Wellesley College Alumni Biographical File, Stitt Church, Marguerite, 1914, 7/B, Wellesley College Archives, Library and Technology Services.
743 Ibid.
744 Ibid.
745 Ibid.
746 Pat Campbell Shaw, "Mrs. Church Praises 'Her' District," *Evanston (IL) Review*, October 27, 1983.
747 "In Celebration of the Life of Marguerite Stitt Church," June 1, 1990, archives of First United Methodist Church, Evanston, IL.
748 108 Cong. Rec. 22,423 (1962) (statement of Rep. Schwengel).
749 Donald R. Kennon, "Marguerite Stitt Church, 1892–1990," *The Capitol Dome*, August 1990, 2; Jeffrey Hearn, "The US Capitol Historical Society Reaches Fifty, Part I: Fred Schwengel and the Founding of the United States Capitol Historical Society," *The Capitol Dome*, Winter 2013, 16–19.
750 Donald R. Kennon, "Marguerite Stitt Church, 1892–1990," *The Capitol Dome*, August 1990, 2.
751 William H. Rentschler, "They Came… Loved… Lauded," *News/Voice*, October 27, 1983, Wellesley College Alumni Biographical File, Stitt Church, Marguerite, 1914, 7/B, Wellesley College Archives, Library and Technology Services.
752 Church, oral history.

ACKNOWLEDGEMENTS

Early in this project, one of our sources in Washington, D.C. asked, "So what brings the two of you to write about two dead congressmen?"

Like most people, we'd never heard of Ralph E. Church or Marguerite Stitt Church, but the more we learned, the more we wanted to know. And, throughout the process of researching and writing this book, we came to know how compelling these people were — as individuals and as an American political power couple. For example, despite their distinctly different pedigrees, their passion for public service was nearly identical.

We've been honored to stand in the room where Ralph Church took his last breath, and to learn how Marguerite, with dignity and integrity, carried her late husband's torch throughout the country and the world. We've been fascinated by how this couple, both in life and in death, inspired others to serve in their communities and beyond. And, while bringing their lives to the page, we've felt an enormous weight of responsibility, knowing this is the first biography about the lives of (not one, but) two former members of Congress.

To be sure, ours has been a unique approach, with two authors writing about two deceased legislators. From the beginning, we've been struck by the cinematic nature of the couple's history, including disparate backgrounds, groundbreaking political accomplishments, an indefatigable partnership, global travel and influence, and multiple personal and professional tragedies.

We recognize that this book barely scratches the surface of the lives of these two individuals. For example, we know very little of the couple's early romance, of their day-to-day interactions, or how they truly felt about one another. We also found very little information on Marguerite's visibility in the press when Ralph was in office. Was this by design, or simply a sign of the times? When turning in this manuscript, we were left with so many more questions than answers. For example, what would the couple think of their formerly conservative district, now that it's proudly liberal? How would they approach Evanston's challenges regarding affordable housing, which has, without doubt, influenced the Black population's decline from 22.5% in 2000 to 16.5% in 2020?

While we've tried our best to document aspects that inspire further research and attention, we acknowledge the limitations and unintentional oversights that sometimes plague a first biography. To be sure, deeper dives are warranted about race, about Evanston, and about the Churches' interactions beyond those documented in the press. We acknowledge that our efforts here are merely a start.

We hope this book serves as the first of many steps toward a deeper understanding and appreciation for this remarkable couple, for the community in which they served, and for the broader societal lessons to be learned.

While the following list is hardly exhaustive, we wish to thank the following individuals and organizations for their their generous time, assistance and interest in this project, and to honor and acknowledge their invaluable support, including Dr. Matthew Wasniewski, Farar Elliott, Erin Hromada, and the staff at the Office of the Historian, U.S. House of Representatives; Rep. Jan Schakowsky (D-IL) and her staff, including Leslie Combs, Kim Muzeroll, and Andrew Goczkowski; David McMillen and Adam Berenbak of The Center for Legislative Archives at The National Archives and Records Administration; Janet C. Olson, Kevin Leonard, and Anne E. Zald at Northwestern University; Eden Juron Pearlman, Suzanne Farrand, and Grace Lehner of the Evanston History Center; Dino Robinson of Shorefront Legacy Center; Peter M. Weichlein of the Association of Former Members of Congress; Cheryl Gunselman at the Washington State University Libraries; Mur Wolf, Auriel Haack, Sara Ludovissy, Rebecca Goldman, Marci Hahn-

Fabris, Margaret Keane, Krithika Sivaramakrishnan, and Melissa Bruehl, and Kimberly Maccini of Wellesley College; Arlene Balkansky, Edith Sandler, Margaret Kieckhefer, Chamisa Redmond, Dr. Sahr Conway-Lanz, Bruce Kirby, Dr. Ryan Reft, Harrison Behl, Rosemary Hanes, and The Researcher and Reference Services Division/KD at the Library of Congress; The Staff at the Offices of History, Art & Archives, U.S. House of Representatives; Kevin Ramsey at Trinity School; Crystal Toscano of The Patricia D. Klingenstein Library at The New-York Historical Society; Chelsea Hill of the Center for American Women and Politics, Eagleton Institute of Politics at Rutgers University; David L. Kohn and Cheryl Ziegler at the Union League Club of Chicago; Patrick J. Souders of the Office of Sen. Richard J. Durbin (D-IL); Dr. Adam Berenbak of the Center for Legislative Archives; Marybeth M. Kemm, Shannon O'Neill, and Martha Tenney at Barnard College/Columbia University; Hal Grossman at Hunter College Library; Eric Graf of the Library of Congress National Audio Visual Conservation Center, Melody Farley of the Women's Club of Evanston; Ashley Swinford, Katie Armstrong, Roger J. Meyers and Patricia A. Ballesteros at the University of Arizona Libraries; Ruth Keyso at Lake Forest Academy; Gay Riseborough of the Evanston Women's Sculpture Project; Lori Osborne and the Evanston Women's History Project; David Joens and Catheryne Popovitch of the Illinois State Archives; Gillian Lusins, Brittany Rubino and Scott Norman of NBC Universal Media, LLC; Liza Romanow of the Madeleine Albright Foundation; Steve Jajkowski, Museum of Broadcast Communications Archives; Arnel Tirado and Maria Elena Perez at the Methodist Home for Nursing & Rehabilitation; Peace Corps alumni Sally Brown, Bill Thomas, Les Jacobson, Patrick Harrigan and John Sweeney; Wayne Kempton of the Episcopal Diocese of New York; Patty Pope of the Danville Public Library; Sara Cast at the Catlin Historical Society; Ellen Keith at the Chicago History Museum Research Center; William Offhaus of the University Archives at the University at Buffalo; Maryrose Grossman of the John F. Kennedy Presidential Library and Museum; Megan Klintworth and Meghan Harmon of the Abraham Lincoln Presidential Library and Museum; John Hughes of the Washington State Archives; Lynn Johnson, National Board Girl Scouts of the USA; Joanna Rios of the Columbia University Archives; Beth Harvey at The Congressional Club; Audrey Niffenegger and Artist's Book House; and the late Former Secretary of Defense Donald H. Rumsfeld, Joyce Rumsfeld, Marcy Rumsfeld Vaca, and Sarah Tonucci of The Rumsfeld Foundation.

We also extend our deepest thanks to Dr. A. Timothy Church, Rhonda Craven, James Nowlan, the Honorable John Edward Porter of Illinois, Cokie Roberts, Carmen Korleski, Paul Janicki, D. Daniel Baldino, Danny Baldino, Mary Barr, Halle Edwards, Steve Fiffer, Sharon Fiffer, Eli J. Finkel, Laura Biddle-Clarke, Megan Lippert, Judine O'Shea, Debbie Jarvis Meitl, and the late Robin Tucker and the late Una Corley Groves.

An enormous debt of gratitude goes to the following individuals who contributed to and supported our efforts throughout the writing of this book: Angela Vennemann; Megan Lippert; Robert K. Elder; Bill Nelsch; Alex Cronheim; Brandi Jackson; Vaughn Jones; Steven Anderson; Howard Simpson; Taylor G. Moore; Patricia and Robert Leahy; Virginia Lazarus; Kathleen & Robert Cieslak; John Gallo; Dawn Overend; John Otterbacher; Vanna Paoli and Eric Ronne.

We also owe tremendous thanks to Colonel (IL) Jennifer N. Pritzker, IL ARNG (Retired), Mary Falcon, and Michelle Nakfoor of TAWANI Enterprises, Inc.

And finally, we offer our endless gratitude to Sonya Sindberg of Master Wings Publishing for her wisdom, encouragement, and enthusiasm.

As a result of the dedication from these individuals to this project, the world may now better understand the legacies left by Ralph E. Church and Marguerite Stitt Church.

Jay Pridmore and Christine Wolf
November, 2022

INDEX